Advance Praise for
You Are the Boss of You

"*You Are the Boss of You* is SUCH an empowering read for anyone who's looking to level up and wants to live life on their own terms. Shauna's book will help you realize who you are, what you want, and how to get it. She tackles all the details. I highly recommend this uplifting book! It is the path to recognizing your power and creating the life you want."

~LAURYN BOSSTICK, Creator of The Skinny Confidential

"This book outlines a brilliant and meaningful path to breaking out of emotional cages and stepping into the power of who you truly are. Practical, smart, and completely relatable, *You Are the Boss of You* is a miraculous offering to anyone wanting to live their fullest and most authentic life."

~JILLIAN MICHAELS, Wellness Expert and
New York Times Bestselling Author

"Shauna's wisdom fills these pages. She shares these lessons and tools so we can ALL connect with our true nature."

~HENRY WINKLER, Actor, Author, Producer, and Director

"Written with humor, grace, and vulnerability, *You Are the Boss of You* is a stunning gift to anyone wanting to grow and heal."

~VARUN SONI, PH.D., International thought leader, Dean of
Religious and Spiritual Life at University of Southern California

"A genius book for anyone wanting to thrive and not just survive. *You Are the Boss of You* targets the most significant pillars of emotional health and promises relief from the perspective of a boss who truly walks her talk."

~CLIFF MICHAELS, *New York Times*
Bestselling Author of *The 4 Essentials*

YOU are the BOSS of YOU

CULTIVATE THE MINDSET AND TOOLS TO LIVE LIFE ON YOUR TERMS

SHAUNA BRITTENHAM REITER

A REGALO PRESS BOOK
ISBN: 979-8-88845-577-7
ISBN (eBook): 979-8-88845-578-4

You Are the Boss of You:
Cultivate the Mindset and Tools to Live Life on Your Terms
© 2025 by Shauna Brittenham Reiter

Cover Photo by Catherine Asanov
Cover Design by Nikki Canale

Publishing Team:
Founder and Publisher – Gretchen Young
Editor – Adriana Senior
Editorial Assistant – Caitlyn Limbaugh
Managing Editor – Aleigha Koss
Production Manager – Alana Mills
Production Editor – Rachel Hoge
Associate Production Manager – Kate Harris

As part of the mission of Regalo Press, a donation is being made to Nest Global, as chosen by the author. Find out more about this organization at https://nestglobal.org/.

Regalo Press
New York • Nashville
regalopress.com

Published in the United States of America
1 2 3 4 5 6 7 8 9 10

For anyone who believes they were born to feel free

CONTENTS

INTRODUCTION

Bonus workbook available at www.helloshauna.com

There is a current pandemic far more insidious than any virus. A quarter of the way into the twenty-first century, the US surgeon general warned of a growing mental health crisis among youth that began even before the pandemic of 2020–2022 and has only accelerated since.[1] Sleeplessness, depression, and anxiety are on the rise as our uncertainty about our inner and outer worlds intensifies. People are desperate both to feel and not feel, to be heard, and in some cases, to vanish entirely. Within the mind can exist perplexing complexities and dichotomies that lead to confusion about one's purpose and intrinsic value. Many of the people closest to me are finding themselves spinning from one medication to the next, one dysfunctional relationship to the next, and even one *identity* to the next. Struggles with mental health can affect anyone and may be the most pervasive crisis of our time. And yet most of us are still afraid to talk about them.

For some people, the heart of the conversation is deeply rooted trauma. For others, it is a profound level of sensitivity that makes our ever-evolving, overstimulating world nearly impossible to metabolize. And there are people like me, whose history of trauma, acute perceptivity, and desire to feel worthy of love create the perfect storm of longing. The commonality among all of us who suffer is that every one of us wants to be accepted. We want to feel safe and rooted in an identity and a community that are unshakable. And we want to believe—*need* to believe—that we are not alone.

When a forty-day fast landed me in a psychiatric ward at age nineteen, I was unable to write my own name. The culmination of years of striving to be perfect, coupled with an abusive past I was not yet ready to accept, rendered me dissociated, often regressing in age, and descending into a debilitating paranoia while trying to define who I was. Some days, I thought I was six. Other days, I believed I was nine. While under the impression that I was these ages, I reenacted scenes from my past that my conscious mind had dampened into oblivion. After receiving a diagnosis of delayed post-traumatic stress disorder (PTSD) associated with childhood sexual abuse, I was transferred to a mental health clinic in Kansas, which I fled after less than a month.

Although my adolescence was in part defined by ulcers, Crohn's disease, insomnia, disordered eating, and obsessive-compulsive disorder (OCD), the world labeled me a talented overachiever. I began college at fifteen, and my singing voice and lyrical way of communicating created a persona of elegance that carried me with ease from opportunity to opportunity and relationship to relationship. But behind the scenes, my physical and emotional struggles quietly intensified. They culminated with my stay at the psychiatric hospital, an experience that provided me with a profoundly unique perspective on the way our country approaches mental health, and the startling disconnect between what patients truly require to heal and what the system provides.

After the birth of my daughter when I was thirty-five, a new wave of flashbacks and nightmares surfaced that I could no longer deny. Having spent decades pursuing alternative healing of various kinds, I was forced once and for all to abandon any superficial coping mechanisms that remained to plunge with a new kind of faith into the awareness of all that I had repressed. In doing so, the cycle of intergenerational violence against women and children that I had inherited was broken, and I was able to cultivate not only the business and family I had always dreamed of but the inner life as well. Though my path from there was long and arduous, it gifted me with tools not only to soothe myself but also to seize and create magnificent opportunities.

Words cannot express my gratitude to the psychologists, psychiatrists, scientists, and doctors who have dedicated their entire lives to supporting the emotional and mental health of complete strangers like me. I have learned from them, relied on them, and celebrated their knowledge and compassion. But those of us who have clawed our way through sleepless nights and been swallowed whole by unshakable fears procure hope from the stories of others who have risen from the ashes. We want to relate to those who help us break free from our emotional cages. At times, we require solutions and answers based on real-life experience. The desire to connect with others who have made art from their confusion and pain has become a primary goal for those of us who experience anxiety, depression, and disconnection from ourselves and others, and who yearn to heal from trauma.

Ever since I was diagnosed with Crohn's disease at age fourteen, I have been learning how to heal emotionally, physically, psychologically, and spiritually. My unrelenting commitment to knitting my psyche back together, in conjunction with a passion for nutrition, has set me on a therapeutic path of deeply understanding the interconnectedness of body and mind. Over the course of my life, I have spent hundreds of hours in therapy of many kinds, worked with naturopathic and allopathic healers, practiced meditation, and excavated my own soul for the answers it already possessed. I became a certified Reiki therapist and founded the wellness company Alaya Naturals to provide a source of therapeutic nourishment for others. *You Are the Boss of You* is the culmination of all that I have learned, and my greatest offering to those who desire to heal.

If you desperately need emotional relief, are exhausted by old patterns and beliefs from which you cannot seem to detach, and feel as if you know there's more for you to experience in the world but are not sure how, this book is for you. If you are eager to burst out of contrived boxes and redefine your identity, want to process your feelings in ways that are empowering, and are ready to claim your bold and exquisite future, keep reading. From A to Z, I will break down the building blocks necessary for you to gain relief, reconnect with joy, question old assumptions, and create a game plan for your life that is more satisfying and inspired than you ever imagined possible.

Your problems are everyone's problems. In other words, how you feel affects how the people around you feel. It affects how your friends and coworkers feel. If you have children, it affects how they feel. It even affects how *their* children will feel. By committing to the exploration of your most authentic feelings, you begin to say yes to all of who you are. Once you believe in the magic that is inside you, it will begin to pour out in unimaginable ways. You will become brave enough to pursue your deepest passions. Your artistry will flourish. You will not be afraid to speak your mind or advocate for yourself and for the life you consciously design moment by moment. You will feel inspired and grounded regardless of what is going on around you. You will choose intimacy with people who respect, encourage, and soothe you. And perhaps most importantly, you will respect, encourage, and soothe yourself.

Dimming your light, presence, and voice as a result of external influences is a kind of apology. My intention is to help equip you to be your own parent and best friend, to nurture yourself through life's unpredictable terrain, and to boldly navigate your dreams and desires. By shining a light on all that is and is not working in your life, you will offer healing not only to your own heart but to every generation that follows. By claiming your version of the truth, you will energize humanity and honor your deepest knowledge. My hope for this book is that it helps you experience the magic of who you already are and who you are choosing to become without apology.

While the sequencing of *You Are the Boss of You* reflects the chronology of my own evolution, you can enjoy its chapters in any order, based on what your heart craves in real time. My guidance draws from the many therapeutic techniques that have benefited me over the years, including but not limited to cognitive behavioral therapy (CBT), Emotional Freedom Techniques (EFT), Rapid Transformational Therapy (RTT), and neurofeedback. In addition to exploring fundamental concepts such as identity and elements of healing here, I have designed exercises to put this guidance into practice, which you can find in the companion workbook at www. helloshauna.com. If you choose not to use the workbook, you can still continue to follow along as we release limiting thought patterns and consciously transform all that no longer feels true for us. If you are experiencing thoughts of self-harm and are in the United States, please put this book down and dial 988 to reach the 988 Suicide & Crisis Lifeline, or dial 911. If you are outside of the US, please refer to the following link to locate a crisis lifeline in your area: https:// support.google.com/websearch/answer/11181469?

In chapter 1, "Defining Boundaries," we explore why boundaries are essential, how to trust your intuition, and how to familiarize yourself with your *yes*, *no*, and *maybe*. I teach you how to stop apologizing for what you need, and why we sometimes say yes when we mean no. I also unpack the connections between boundaries and self-blame, and how to separate boundaries from projected meaning and identity. I walk you through why shame is counterproductive to building boundaries, how to untangle perceptions of abandonment with boundaries, and how to soften or dismantle boundaries if necessary. We deep-dive into boundaries in relation to self, how to distinguish between boundaries and control, why boundaries are and should be fluid, and how to disentangle yourself from enmeshed identities.

In chapter 2, "Soothing Yourself," I guide you in understanding why so many of us have a difficult time nurturing ourselves, and I equip you with practical strategies for cultivating inner calm—especially in relation to anxiety. We explore the concept of shadow parents, and as you develop a deep awareness of the parental qualities you find comforting, I help you access the parts of yourself that are competent at meeting those specific needs. Drawing from external influences, I show you how to integrate into your own being the parental attributes you crave, and how to empower yourself to self-soothe.

In chapter 3, "Softening Perfectionism," I break down why perfection isn't a real thing, and why the pursuit of it is counterproductive. We examine the link between perfectionism and hypervigilance, and determine why neither is useful in systematically avoiding triggers. I then provide therapeutic recommendations to support you more deeply in letting go of limiting beliefs.

Chapter 4, "Redefining Your Self-Concept," establishes the many influences that have contributed to your perceived identity and addresses barriers to authenticity. I dissect core value versus created value, who you are versus how you feel, and core identity versus fluid identity. I challenge the common assumption that external events have the power to define us, and I support you in creating space to truthfully acknowledge what you want more of in your life. I then differentiate between comparison and inspiration, and outline a framework for creating a bold vision for your future.

In chapter 5, "Honoring Sleep," I share how insomnia and sleep disturbances are outrageously common and have a profound impact on mental health. I list some of the most prevalent reasons why people can't sleep and offer practical and simple solutions. As someone who was addicted to sleeping pills for eleven years, I explain why it isn't useful to identify as an insomniac, and I walk you through my personal, medication-free sleep routine. I conclude with a highly regarded therapeutic recommendation to help ease sleeplessness.

In chapter 6, "Healing Trauma," we explore both the official definition and my own personal definition of trauma. I make the case that trauma cannot be measured, and I break down the many reasons why I believe people avoid confronting their trauma. Due to trauma's propensity for triggering uncomfortable emotions and sometimes causing repressed memories to surface, I provide several therapeutic recommendations for coping with trauma. Severe trauma often requires professional support to avoid a state of disassociation or overwhelming feelings that may impede one's ability to function practically. My hope is that by the end of this chapter, you will be open to the possibility of exploring your past in a safe and gentle way.

In chapter 7, "Feeling It All," we explore why we characterize some feelings as unacceptable or feel that they are inaccessible. I touch on the unique roles of epigenetics and anxiety in relation to emotions before exploring the beauty of befriending all of our feelings. I highlight the danger of repression, along with the necessity of giving ourselves permission to authentically feel. I also unveil some of the clever strategies people employ to avoid their feelings, and I offer actionable guidance to support awareness and healing.

Chapter 8, "Creating Your Rhythm," addresses establishing an organic way of moving through the world that values flexibility and adaptation. I introduce the concept that all work is creative work, and I walk you through how to tune in to your physical and emotional cues in order to reset. At the end of this chapter, you will be armed with the tools you require to slow down, reset, and establish a rhythm that is truly in alignment with the needs of your body and mind.

In chapter 9, "Advocating for Yourself," I urge you to be your own advocate. Together we analyze the many reasons why people struggle to advocate for themselves, then shift our focus to effective and consistent self-advocacy. I use case studies to provide more detailed examples of self-advocacy.

In chapter 10, "Building Your Future," I encourage you to use all that you have learned foundationally to recognize and manifest your dreams. I share with you my signature method of identifying the "soul of your dreams," which will profoundly impact how you view your goals and desires. We then delve into the necessity of creating space to dream, the imperative of allowing dreams to evolve, and the significance of seizing the moment. I also outline my signature process, The Five Steps to Creating Dynamic and Inspired Possibilities, and discuss the importance of asking for help. I close with a brilliant manifestation metaphor created by a friend and mentor.

There are massive gaps in the mental health system that leave the majority of those who suffer without any sustainable tools for coping and thriving. While I am an avid advocate for therapy and recommend it throughout this book, many of us are searching for more accessible, affordable, and direct forms of support. We not only require this, we deserve it. *You Are the Boss of You* will provide you with a beautiful foundation for healing and growth.

In addition to having had the privilege of experimenting with so many therapeutic methods, I have spent countless hours creating my own theories and techniques. I have asked myself myriad questions to help ease the burden of my own anxiety and perceived helplessness in the face of overwhelming emotions. Everything I am offering to you and suggesting for you, I have first offered to myself. Each and every idea I present was born out of my own desperation and commitment to heal. I have engaged in every single therapy that I recommend.

This book is the product of a lifetime of effort to gain access to the emotional freedom that I now experience. Once riddled with anxiety, paranoia, hypervigilance, and inexplicable sadness, I now walk in peace. I laugh with ease. I create with grace. You too are meant to live an inspired and deeply satisfying life. You were born to be emotionally free. Right now, I am taking your hand and walking with you as you explore whatever is holding you back. I am encouraging you to be truthful, to be raw, and most important, to be who you were made to be. We are on this journey together. I've got you.

CHAPTER 1

DEFINING BOUNDARIES

We create boundaries all day long without even realizing it. When you lock your front door, you create a boundary. When you choose not to pick up the phone because you're in the middle of a conversation, you create a boundary. When you pause a work project to eat a meal or stretch your legs, you create a boundary. But the majority of people I know, including myself, have struggled with boundaries at some point in their lives.

Boundaries can be physical, mental, emotional, or psychological. Often, these categories overlap. If someone hits you, the abuse violates all four boundaries. If someone calls you a hurtful name, that person also is crossing multiple boundaries. Ultimately, you are responsible for creating the boundaries that determine whether you accept abuse of any kind in your life. When other people cross one or more of your boundaries, it is your job to create a boundary in response to their lack of one.

Every single relationship of every kind requires boundaries. We tend to see boundaries as a negative or severe choice, mostly because many of us wait too long to create them. When solid boundaries don't exist within a relationship, the eventual necessity of establishing entirely new ground rules can result in tension and confusion. The healthiest relationships include and honor healthy, clear boundaries that facilitate ease and support mutual respect. Boundaries may—and often should—evolve over time, which is why communication is an essential part of the equation. If you have internally created a boundary that you don't clearly communicate, the other party or parties cannot be expected to help you maintain it. While it may feel awkward to express your boundary, in doing so, you are actually benefiting your relationship in the long run by creating a foundation of honesty and setting the stage for sustainability.

Note: While I am going to focus on nonphysical boundaries in this chapter, I urge you to immediately seek protection and refuge if you are in a physically abusive relationship. Please go to the police, check into a shelter, or stay with a friend or family member if you are experiencing sexual or physical abuse of any kind.

THE BEGINNING

Clinical psychologist and professor Beatrice Beebe at Columbia University Medical School has done profound work illuminating the nature of face-to-face interaction between mothers and their infants, and investigating interaction patterns that predict secure or insecure attachment at one year. Similar to the concept of "good enough" mothering proposed by pediatrician and psychoanalyst Donald Winnicott, Beebe and her colleagues found that an "optimal mid-range" degree of coordination is associated with secure (compared to insecure) attachment.[2] What this means is that the facial, vocal, visual, and touch coordination that occurs between a mother and an infant is best when it is not too "high" and not too "low," leaving room for improvisation and flexibility. Beebe suggests that "too high" coordination may reflect vigilance, and "too low" coordination may indicate a lack of attunement.

If the primary caregiver of a child is typically anxious, over-whelmed, depressed, stressed, or distracted, they may lack the tools and internal resources necessary to interact in a comfortable mid-range, where the infant feels attended to and emotionally connected without being smothered. Caregivers who are chronically stressed in this way are often not able to offer the infant comfort when the infant is distressed. Providing such comfort is a key caregiver pattern that predicts secure attachment and provides a sense of safety. Infants of an emotionally unavailable caregiver may grow up and inadvertently seek out relationships in which they are ignored and neglected, or they may crave validation from a person who withholds connection.

Essentially, we seek out what is familiar. A shame cycle can recur in the presence of partners or friends who promote feelings of being unworthy or unlovable. I've even heard it suggested that some people aim to replicate elements of their past in order to transmute a formerly disappointing or devastating dynamic. If you are subconsciously driven to reframe uncomfortable or upsetting narratives and secure resolution, being consciously aware of your patterns may empower you to change course and stop putting yourself in compromising positions.

Another potential outgrowth of not experiencing secure attachment as a child is the chronic fear of abandonment. Adults who carry the threat of abandonment in their hearts will mostly likely do one of two things: placate their partner and abandon their own needs, or never allow themselves to be fully loved. If you believe that once you allow people into your heart, they will most likely hurt you, fail to meet your needs, or deny you the opportunity to feel seen, heard, understood, loved, and validated, why would you let anyone in? Expecting the worst in a relationship could easily drive any one of us to put up emotional walls and create overly rigid boundaries. The ultimate enforcement of a boundary, of course, is walking away from a relationship in order to avoid feelings of loneliness and insecurity within the relationship itself.

Alternatively, some people seek out relationships in which they receive the kind of mothering or fathering they did not receive as a child. This can lead to an imbalanced, skewed dynamic because they are relying exclusively on another person to make them feel safe and seen. People who have habituated themselves to saving others as their version of comfort or safety may appreciate or accept this imbalance, but the relationship is severely limited, because by nature it is at least partially defined by roles that are not inclusive. Ideally, every relationship would allow all parties involved to experience and express all that they are. The more you categorize yourself (even without words) as a savior or a victim—or anything else, for that matter—the more that role gets reinforced and shapes your behaviors and personality.

In my experience, the roles that we establish in relationships are based on a mix of the attachment styles of our caregivers when we were children, the person we believe ourselves to be at our core, the image of ourselves we consciously want to project into the world, the role we desire to play in the relationship, how we believe our partner perceives us, the ways our partner engages with us (both behaviorally and in dialogue), and how we react to that person's communication (which either reinforces preestablished roles or alters and adjusts them). What's tricky is that the roles we establish in partnerships (for ourselves and others) are often heavily influenced by the quality and degree of guidance and nurturing we did or did not receive when we were too young to consciously form an identity, or to question our self-concept relative to how we were being parented. Because of this, it may take a lot of conscious unlearning to strip away influences from the past and create a new identity based on a clear understanding of our core nature and who we desire to be.

The feedback loop in relationships is unavoidable, so the more you show people who you really are, how you expect to be treated, and the ways in which you wish to operate in the world, the more they will modify their expectations and perceptions of you accordingly, thereby reinforcing your authentic self-concept, not the one that you unconsciously inherited or that was projected onto you. By clinging too tightly to outdated categories and roles in relationships, we don't just cut off access to parts of ourselves, we cut off access to all that others have to offer. We also limit our potential to comfort ourselves in the midst of confusion or distress, and may even end up severing the commitment of others as part of self-soothing. Instead of aligning with labels and assumptions, such as the victim, the hero, the strong one, or the sensitive one, at any moment, we can choose to simply be. If we recognize a pattern of healing others to avoid healing ourselves, saving others to avoid saving ourselves, or relying on the strength and confidence of others to avoid cultivating self-trust, we can shift those patterns by learning to self-soothe. If we are in a position to comfort ourselves, there is no need to be the savior or the one saved, because we are free to be the one thing we are meant to be: human.

When it comes to creating boundaries, most of us have an easier time setting limits or reframing expectations with certain people than with others. You may have no problem ignoring the irrational demands of your mother, but find yourself scrambling to appease your father. You may, without hesitation, deny help to one friend, while dropping everything you're doing for another friend whose attention, admiration, or affection you desire. You may find yourself resisting the demands of all of your family members, with the exception of one sibling whose needs have always had a way of trumping yours. Relationships are complicated, and more often than not, most of us have one person or a handful of people we find ourselves consistently saying yes to at the expense of our own comfort and priorities.

The cost of sacrificing our own wishes and needs to please those with whom we feel the most vulnerable and insecure may at first seem minimal, but the effects are cumulative. When, over and over again, we find ourselves saying yes when we really want to say no, we give ourselves the message that the person we are saying yes to is more important than we are and more worthy of self-care, respect, and love. There certainly can be times when sacrificing our own preferences to show up for others is necessary or valid, but when we habitually ignore our own desires to appease others and ensure their comfort, we gradually erode the integrity of how we care for ourselves.

Self-care doesn't simply involve showering, exercising, and eating nourishing food. It necessitates that we hear and respond to our inner guide, the part of us that intuitively knows how we want to spend our time, where we want to go, and who we want to be in the presence of. And it starts with believing that, regardless of how others may respond, we deserve to create boundaries that form the framework for a joyful, peaceful life.

TRUST YOUR INTUITION

Step one in creating boundaries is to trust your intuition, or what some may refer to as your internal guidance. This guidance may be embedded in your DNA from prehistoric times in order to keep you safe, or it may be an extension of your soul. It may be your brain's response to external stimuli, or an energetic connection to what is true. Regardless of its source, when we doubt or talk ourselves out of what we are truly sensing, it is very hard to act on the signals and impulses of our bodies. If we believe that our bodies are constantly providing clues as to what feels right and what doesn't, we are more likely to pay attention and, hopefully, to act accordingly.

Creating boundaries starts with listening to and believing the messages of your body. If you receive an invitation to attend a dinner party and a feeling of dread overtakes your body, that gathering may not be for you. If you are asked to create a work presentation and are filled with a bright sense of possibility, it's possible that this presentation may move the needle in your career.

You may never know how or why your body gives you a *yes* or *no* when it comes to agreeing to an event, interaction, or opportunity, and you do not have to know. One of the mistakes I made repeatedly in my young life was feeling that I needed to understand why I was saying no to something in order to justify my decision. You do not need to know on a rational basis why something feels right or wrong; intuition often cannot be explained, justified, or proven with concrete evidence. In fact, trying to make sense of our intuition may only obscure it. From a state of pure physical experience rather than intellect, we are able to receive the messages of our bodies with greater clarity. We are also equipped to learn the language of our bodies: what *yes*, *no*, and *maybe* feel like.

GETTING TO KNOW YOUR *YES, NO,* AND *MAYBE*

Our bodies speak to us all the time, especially when we have decisions to make. The instinctual feeling in your body that springs up in response to a question, a request, an invitation, an idea, or a possibility is part of that communication. Over the years, I've come to learn how I experience *yes, no,* and *maybe* on a physical basis. For me, *yes* often feels like a tingly butterfly sensation in my chest, an experience of elation or ease, and a sense of expansiveness or openness. When something or someone feels really right, it's almost as though my heart wants to jump out of my body and fly toward that experience or person. *No* in my body tends to feel like restriction, almost as if my body were narrowing and getting tighter simultaneously. My *no* is sometimes accompanied by a feeling of dread, pervasive and unrelenting hesitation, anxiety, and/or overthinking. My body shrinks, retracts, and recoils in a more protective way, and I spend more time in my head (the analytical space) than in my body. The overthinking tends to kick in when I'm not sure why something feels like a *no,* and I assume that I have to justify or support my resistance with an explanation. *Maybe* feels a bit more neutral for me. It lacks the physical sensations of tightness and clenched muscles that accompany fear, and it involves a sense of curiosity. When my body experiences a *maybe,* I know that I need more information. Obtaining that information may require research, or simply a pause and a stretch of time before I make a decision or commitment.

We can even distinguish between the physical experience of our bodies when we *want* to say yes versus feeling that we *should* say yes, which is an assumption of the mind. A perceived obligation can obscure or diminish our natural capacity to feel our way physically and intuitively into understanding what is true for us. When we try to convince ourselves that we *should* feel a certain way, it's often because of the cultural, societal, familial, romantic, or professional expectations that have paved a trajectory we feel pressured to align with. Part of creating a healthy boundary is separating from expectations and simply reacting to what is happening in the now according to how our bodies feel. This doesn't mean we should never question the impulses of our bodies or make conscious decisions to refrain from impulsive behavior. But it does mean that we should give ourselves permission to first acknowledge and process physical sensations before welcoming the commentary of our mind.

Many people have a hard time distinguishing between the feeling of their *no* and an experience of fear that is not necessarily attached to a warning. Fear may be part of how the body communicates that something or someone is a *no*. Other times, it may be the embodiment of our ancestors' experiences, as those experiences live on in our bodies, or it may be a product of self-doubt or an expression of insecurities relating to the future. It also could be symptomatic of generalized anxiety, hesitation regarding change, concerns about the unknown, or unresolved trauma. I have spent many years trying to establish what a pure *no* feels like in my body, and when I'm not sure if my reaction to something or someone is colored by the residue of trauma or deeper fears unrelated to intuition, I ask fear to step aside, so that I can feel what my body truly needs to feel.

Fear is an essential stress response when it comes to avoiding truly dangerous situations—a dark alley where a criminal may be lurking, an unsafe person who rings our doorbell or follows us home, and the like. But by and large, people experience fear on a much broader and more chronic basis than they need to. Instead of keeping us safe, consistent and habituated fear actually confuses our nervous system and makes it difficult to determine when there is a real threat. Many of us have a hard time discerning our true *no* because we have woven fear into even benign moments. Having experienced trauma of any kind makes us far more likely to remain hypervigilant to threats, even after a threat has passed.

In addition to asking unhelpful fear to step aside, pausing and breathing can help reset your nervous system and invite clarity. A pause could be ten seconds, ten days, or a year. I often measure my instinctual reaction to a proposition, an idea, an opportunity, or a person against how I feel several minutes or even days later, to see how fear may have played a role in my gut reaction. The mind creates fear, whereas instincts recognize danger. When we instinctually recognize a threat, healthy stress or the instinct to protect ourselves or others will follow.

*Turn to "Understanding Your Yes, No, and Maybe"
in the workbook.*

STOP EXPLAINING YOURSELF AND APOLOGIZING

Many of us have come to believe that we always owe people an explanation for why *no* is the appropriate response for us. I believe that this false sense of obligation can actually prevent us from saying no when we want to say no, especially when we're not clear on why something feels uncomfortable or not right. Often, there isn't an objective *yes* or *no* at play, simply a preference generated by numerous factors. These factors may include mystical influences relating to manifestation and what some may call destiny, and they often include practical factors related to what we've eaten that day, the mood we're in, our energy level, our hormone levels, what we did the day before, and so on. If someone invites me to a party, my body's *yes* or *no* to that invitation may be based on all of these factors and more—or it may be based solely on my wanting to stay home and watch *The Bachelorette*.

Regardless of what is influencing your *yes*, *no*, or *maybe* at any given time, you are very rarely—if ever—obligated to explain yourself. When my sister was studying law, she told me that in a courtroom, the defendant should say as little as possible. Often, we unnecessarily believe that we have to defend our decisions and reactions to events and people, or justify why we're making a certain choice. Additionally, we tend to lead with an apology of some kind, which sends the message to both us and the other party that something is inherently wrong with or unkind about our decision. I'm going to compare and contrast some examples of the things people might say when they feel obligated to defend their choices versus what might get communicated when they don't.

> "I'm *so* sorry... I really want to come to your party, but my brother's in town, and I feel really over-whelmed, and I had food poisoning last night and am kind of exhausted."
> **Compare that to:** "Sadly, I won't be able to make it your party, but I can't wait to hear all about it!"

> "I feel really bad because I want to go on a date with your brother, but I just had three bad dates in a row and am not sure I'm up for it. Plus, I need to wax and am feeling kind of depressed about a work thing."
> **Compare that to:** "Thank you so much for suggest-ing that I meet your brother! Now isn't the right time, but may I circle back around when I feel ready?"

> "Ack! I'm sorry, but I don't think I can go to the museum right now, because I have massive autoim-mune issues and the flu is rampant—but if I didn't have these issues, I would totally go! Plus, my dad has cancer, and I see him every week."
> **Compare that to:** "I can't join you at the museum, but I would love to connect at the park when you're available for an outdoor visit. Thanks for the invite!"

In addition to cutting out unnecessary apologies, empower yourself by taking responsibility for your choices. Notice that in the examples above, I never deferred to the opinion of others to make my choice for me. Sometimes, we ask others what they think we should do in order to avoid ownership over decisions that we fear may hurt or offend them. For example, "I'm feeling really crappy today, but was looking forward to dinner with you. What do you think we should do?" State your needs plainly and honestly, and others will feel free to do the same.

Turn to "You Are Not the Defendant" in the workbook.

DO NOT WAIT UNTIL YOU FEEL READY

One of the biggest mistakes I've made over and over again in my life is waiting until I *feel* ready to create my boundaries before I take the plunge. Rationally, I know that a boundary needs to be in place, but my intellect becomes convoluted by fears. These fears often contain predictions of rejection—including, but not limited to, judgment and gossip—along with predictions of punishment and abandonment. Because the feelings accompanying these predictions often are overwhelming and hurtful, I postpone creating my boundary until I feel more at ease with the idea. This is problematic, however, because the discomfort that accompanies risk-taking never guarantees that we will feel emotionally ready to take the plunge. If we are waiting to feel brave instead of acting bravely, we may suffer for months or even years while working to eliminate fear.

Being brave when creating boundaries isn't being fearless; it's knowing what needs to be done and doing it, despite having potentially agonizing feelings. When we allow our anxiety to dictate our decisions and guide our life choices, we may end up on a dissatisfying or potentially dangerous path for far longer than we need to be. You may or may not ever *feel* ready to create any boundaries. Still, it may be essential to commit to a game plan that preserves your integrity and honors your internal experience, even when your confidence is wavering.

WHY WE SAY YES WHEN WE MEAN NO

In some ways, it is easier to say yes than to say no—at least in the short term. Saying no may disappoint a family member, work colleague, or friend. It may incite fear in us that we are missing an opportunity or closing a door. It may induce a false sense of shame or guilt that we are letting someone down. Creating a boundary may generate anxiety that a relationship will be negatively impacted, or we may even fear losing someone or something we believe to be significantly valuable. Thoughts such as *If I keep doing things for this person, they will need me and like me and want me around* may not even be conscious. In extreme cases where children were raised by a dangerous caregiver, those people may, as adults, put themselves in harm's way or remain in compromised situations because their sense of who or what to trust is perverted, skewed, or confused. Adults also may fail to create a boundary if, when they were children, a fundamental emotional, physical, or sexual boundary was crossed, so they haven't learned what healthy boundaries are or how to create them. Sometimes we say yes because at some point in our lives, it did not feel safe to say no.

Regardless of why we say yes to others when we mean no, it is essential that we always say yes to ourselves. This is perhaps the truest definition of self-care. And part of saying yes to ourselves may mean saying no to somebody else. Perhaps a friend wants to take a walk when what we really need is to stay home and rest. Maybe our boss is giving us more than our fair share of work. We may find ourselves frequently committing to things that, even when meaningful, deprive us of much-needed downtime. Our time, energy, and mental resources are not endless, and our primary obligation is to ourselves.

BOUNDARIES AND SELF-BLAME

Resistance to creating boundaries often mirrors a propensity for self-blame. Often, people who habitually and unconsciously blame themselves for negative situations or experiences were raised in households where caregivers failed to take responsibility for their own mistakes. If you were raised in a home where adults alleviated their burden by casting blame onto others, you may have wrongly assumed their guilt. If, as a child, you never witnessed your primary caregivers reflecting on their actions and words and making amends for their mistakes, you might have blamed yourself for their wrong-doings. Children who feel responsible for the behaviors, attitudes, and reactions of their parents may become adults who are not able to differentiate between their preferences and ideologies and the needs, demands, and beliefs of those around them.

In an ideal world, every adult would look within when con-fronting a problem and seek to understand their contribution. But as we've all experienced at some point or another, insecurities and ego often prevent that from happening. So, if the people around you (especially people in positions of authority, or who you feel possess all the power) never admit to wrongdoing, you may be tempted to turn against yourself. When fear and blame are attached to decision-mak-ing, it is nearly impossible to create boundaries that support account-ability and ownership over our choices.

SEPARATING BOUNDARIES FROM PROJECTED MEANING

It's natural to resist creating a boundary because you're afraid of hurting someone's feelings. At different points in my life, when I questioned my worth, I assumed that something was wrong with me or that I wasn't truly valued when someone I cared about created a boundary. If you have experienced boundaries being personalized in this way, you may actively work to avoid the potential divisiveness and discomfort that can occur when someone inaccurately interprets a boundary. Instead of allowing other people to project *their* experi-ences onto *your* boundary, you may go so far as to not set one at all. This is a self-destructive way of trying to maintain peace in a rela-tionship. If you think a boundary might trigger someone, you may avoid establishing it in order to prevent a negative reaction to it and any additional emotional fallout that might follow. Unfortunately, avoidance only secures a false sense of control that is rooted in fear, not truth.

Here are some things I've said in conjunction with creating a boundary:

"My alone time doesn't mean I don't love you or cherish being in your presence. This is a need that has nothing to do with you. My nervous system just requires a solo reset."

"I really appreciate the invitation, but today I'm going to rest, because that's what my body is telling me I need."

"I'd love to come visit you, but sadly, travel isn't in the cards right now. I look forward to a time when it is."

If you are on the receiving end of a boundary, do your best not to judge, overanalyze, or assign meaning to it. The reason for it will become apparent if a person consistently draws a hard line with you and doesn't create fluidity or space in their life for a meaningful relationship. However, they might postpone a lunch because they have a sour stomach or just bombed a work presentation. You cannot fully know all of the textures and dimensions of another person's life, and you aren't privy to the many variables that impact their decision-making.

If friends relay to you that you call them too much, or they stop picking up the phone when you call, use their boundary as a catalyst for growth. Invite self-love, unconditional self-acceptance, and resilience to color how you receive feedback, as hard as that may be. We are all growing and learning, and what is desired by one friend might feel claustrophobic or overstimulating to another. We teach all individuals in our lives how to treat us through the behaviors and situations we accept and don't accept, and they do the same, consciously or not. Instead of judging yourself or wallowing in the shame attached to a perceived rejection, take a deep breath and remind yourself that the healthiest relationships not only require but also invite feedback, so that longevity and mutual respect are possible. As empowerment specialist and life coach Andrea Quinn so brilliantly articulates, if an individual chooses not to include you in their life, they are simply not your person!

SEPARATING BOUNDARIES FROM IDENTITY

It's easy to label yourself a "bad" person for creating a boundary, or to accuse yourself of being selfish. But prioritizing yourself is part of being kind to yourself. In my own experience, my fear that *other* people may think I'm selfish, inconsiderate, or unthoughtful drives me to label myself as these things. Labeling ourselves in harsh ways is a form of self-pressure meant to drive us to act in favor of others.

In reality, we have no idea what people are thinking of us at any given moment. Usually, we make assumptions about who other people believe us to be based on our own insecurities, fears, and negative past experiences. But assumptions are not reality. If someone calls you self-absorbed or narcissistic for saying no to them, is this the kind of person you truly want to be connected with? Should a bully, manipulative coworker, or family member define your boundaries and identity? At all costs, do not bully yourself to avoid being bullied by others.

SHAME IS AN ANTIDOTE TO BOUNDARIES

My dear friend Grace is caught in a shame cycle that is all too familiar to me. For twenty-five years, she has worked with a woman whose friendship she has relied on heavily. The relationship was buoyant and light for the first decade or so, and Grace celebrated seeing her friend and feeling seen. But over time, the dynamic morphed: her friend consistently forgot her birthday, took advantage of her professionally, and was frequently unthoughtful in the way she communicated with her. For many years, I've listened to Grace recount stories that reflect hurt and irritation rather than a sense of safety and satisfaction. And yet the less considerate her friend is, the more attached Grace becomes to saving the friendship.

In my experience, when people with deep insecurities feel shame, they are more likely to return again and again to a dysfunctional or disappointing relationship for validation. Ultimately, they hope to receive confirmation that they are worthy, desirable, and lovable. And since actions tend to be the outgrowth of beliefs, their sense of emotional safety and assessment of self-worth are based on how other people treat them. The qualities Grace felt when she *first* met her friend (alive, inspired, witty, warm) are qualities that she still values in herself and wants to identify with. But since her friend isn't reflecting these qualities back to Grace, she continues to hope that if she does or says the right thing, she eventually will be rewarded. The reward in Grace's case is attention, validation, praise, invitations to gatherings, and so on, which she interprets as proof that she is worthy of love.

The shame of not being seen and valued drives Grace to stay committed to an unhealthy friendship; she is hoping to receive different feedback and secure a more positive perception of herself—one that confirms her identity as a person worthy of attention and love. Instead of concluding that her friend is not treating her according to her value, she is concluding that she is not valuable and that the way to regain confidence in her worth is to find a way to be treated differently. Subsequently, Grace bends over backward to appease and show up for her friend in the hope that her friend will do the same for her. When this doesn't occur, Grace is left once again feeling worthless, and the shame cycle continues. Subconscious thoughts associated with this type of shame cycle may include:

If I am perfect and say all the right things, she will never leave me as a friend.

If I just love him enough, he will love me back.

If I do everything for them, they will realize they need me and will never abandon me.

If I am the ideal friend, she will pay attention to me.

If I continue to show up as my best self, eventually he will show up as his best self.

If I truly were lovable, they would treat me differently.

If I receive the adoration of this person, I will feel at peace.

Notice the many contingencies attached to love and approval. Rationally, if a person is mistreating us or is not able to provide what we require, the appropriate response would be to walk away or make significant changes that reinforce reasonable standards, as we define them. But if we question our own lovability and desirability, instead of creating a boundary and taking space, we may remain in a toxic relationship and attempt to prove why we are worth somebody's time and love, and why we are special enough to receive their attention. In other words, the shame that arises when somebody ignores us, takes advantage of us, or fails to see us prompts us to want to "fix" the relationship, as opposed to deeming it unworthy of our time and energy.

In my freshman year of college, I learned one tidbit in Psychology 101 that has remained with me through the years: if we are listening to a song that gets turned off abruptly before it ends, we are far more likely to dwell on that song over any other melody we hear that same day. The reason for this is that most of us want closure and a tidy resolution. Our desire to hear the ending of a song is not unlike our desire for the ending of a relationship: we do not want it to be turned off before we've experienced our version of a clean ending. Even if it isn't our favorite song, and even if the song we are playing invites heartache and grief, we often choose to listen all the way through. Either way, we want the song to be turned off on our terms.

BOUNDARIES AND ABANDONMENT

When a person turns off emotionally or physically in a relationship, the individual on the receiving end may be left with a sense of incompletion that drives them to want to replay or at least finish the song. This is especially true if the recipient of the aloof or dismissive behavior assumes they are at fault. Many of us have, at one point or another, assumed that we are not enough, or that we are too much, or that something is fundamentally wrong with us because we can't secure the feedback we desire.

The experience of abandonment isn't limited to when a partner or loved one walks away. It can occur again and again within the context of an intact relationship. If a person feels ignored, unloved, unseen, or uncelebrated by the person they are in a relationship with, they may experience a sense of neglect or abandonment daily. Ideally, if we feel cut off in some capacity from the person we're in partnership with, instead of taking it personally, we would become curious investigators. We would not assume that we lack something but rather seek to understand what has shifted and why. This may involve sharing our experience of the relationship with our loved one and asking for clarification regarding their experience.

The feeling of being unloved or neglected may be particularly challenging for people whose caregivers were inaccessible or cold to them in their childhood. When we were young and theoretically learning to self-regulate, we were dependent on our caregivers to make us feel safe and connected. Attachment theory, formulated by psychologist John Bowlby, suggests that a young child must form a deep and trustworthy bond with at least one primary caregiver in order to develop socially and emotionally in a healthy way. He refers to "secure attachment," in which children feel safe and soothed by their caregiver, as the ideal form of attachment. Securely attached children expect their caregiver to respond lovingly to their needs and emotions, which eliminates feelings of guilt or the assumption that they are a burden.[3]

A child whose primary caregiver is physically not present—or who is present in the flesh but absent emotionally—may get triggered later as an adult by a friend, lover, family member, or coworker who ignores them or communicates by word or deed that they're not a priority. When children are ignored or mistreated, they assume that something is wrong with *them* and seek to remedy the situation by pleasing their caregiver and providing whatever it is they believe their caregiver needs. This cycle continues into adulthood: instead of walking away from people who are behaving poorly, or creating a boundary with them, the scared child part of us pipes up and takes responsibility for our mistreatment. Instead of gracefully accepting the boundaries and limitations of others, we assign blame to ourselves and assume that we've done something wrong.

If you are having trouble ending a dysfunctional or dissatisfying relationship, take the power back by asking yourself if *your* needs are being met. Challenge any assumption that you lack something by questioning the other party's capacity to give. Speak to the child part of you that feels scared of being abandoned, neglected, or forgotten, and gently reassure that part that nothing is wrong with you. How others behave is *not* a reflection of your fundamental worth, and you can—and should—create a boundary with people who take you for granted or communicate in ways that are disrespectful. You are unique and lovable, regardless of the feedback you receive.

When I was in my twenties, the scared child part of me frequently sabotaged my relationships by refusing to believe that people truly loved me. As a consequence of this, I felt constantly abandoned even in the presence of loving, committed partners. If you find yourself feeling neglected or emotionally distraught in relationships where your significant other is doing their best to show up fully, compassionately ask yourself if you may be having a hard time receiving their love. Others can move mountains to "make" you feel loved, but if deep down inside, you feel unlovable, you may struggle to connect with the experience of being enough until you heal the imprint of rejection from early childhood.

BOUNDARIES AND FOOD

When I was fourteen, I struggled with disordered eating. For about a year, I severely restricted calories to the point of starving myself. After that, I ate an appropriate quantity of food but was obsessed with its visual aesthetic. I also spent an inordinate amount of time thinking about food, planning my next meal, and visualizing what it would look like. Even the shape of the bowl I was eating from or the size of my fork could impact my experience of food and influence my mood.

Recently, I was listening to a podcast interview with author and activist Glennon Doyle, who was describing her struggles with bulimia and bingeing. As I reflected on Doyle's words, it occurred to me that the complexity of how some individuals relate to food may be largely influenced by the perception that they do not have permission to create boundaries. If we don't trust our ability to create and maintain healthy and consistent boundaries with other humans, we may seek to create them with inanimate objects that won't talk back, physically harm us, or react emotionally to our boundary. We can, in essence, assert some level of control, risk-free. This may be especially true for empaths, whose boundaries are frequently crossed simply by them being human and in the same room as other individuals, whose feelings and experiences they absorb.

While we tend to think about setting boundaries as an assertive physical act or verbal declaration, sensitive people, who are like sponges soaking up the energy, emotions, and reactions of those around them, have to work even harder and more consciously to create conscious boundaries. Otherwise, the experiences of others become their own by proxy. If you are a ten-year-old girl in a family rife with turmoil, and anger permeates most communication, you may have a huge perceived inability to create boundaries. If you are

»•«

PRACTICE: Saying No

For the next week, practice saying no. If a partner asks you to stay up and watch a movie, and you really need to snooze, choose sleep. If a friend calls, and you'd rather take a bubble bath than chat, don't pick up. If an associate invites you to a sporting event, but you're dreaming of Thai food and a movie, stay in. If you're in the habit of making exotic meals for your family, but don't feel like cooking, make macaroni and cheese from a box. There is plenty of time to say yes, but just for a moment, experience saying no. As a friend once wisely said, by closing one door, you are freed to open another door. The beauty of being able to create boundaries is that when you do say yes, you are more likely to mean it. When you agree to an opportunity or exchange, you will be fully present. When you give, you will do so from a place of abundance.

Since it can be challenging to create boundaries, you may want to choose a friend or loved one with whom you feel safe. Explain that you are practicing saying no and would love to have this person's support in allowing you to be completely and unapologetically honest for an entire week. If this is your romantic partner, your roommate, or someone you work with, you will have ample opportunities to practice saying no, or "not now," or "maybe later, but thank you!"

»•«

a child whose mother has been wounded by a divorce or whose father doesn't have a verbal filter, you are, once again, in a position of feeling helpless and unable to create boundaries.

The path of the sensitive empath is rarely to cry out with objections or loudly call attention to convoluted family dynamics; instead, the person turns the chaos inward. The internalization of pain, rage, and sadness has the potential to lead to perfectionism, controlling tendencies, superstitious and/or OCD behaviors, and the micromanaging of food, appearance, performance, and so on. If you do not feel empowered to rage against that which harms you, the perception of helplessness may cause you to rage against yourself.

SOFTENING AND DISMANTLING BOUNDARIES

While many of us struggle with creating boundaries, others struggle with softening them. It's even possible for a person to fail to create boundaries with some people in one category of their life, while maintaining overly rigid boundaries with others in that same category or another category. For instance, you may have extremely clear boundaries when it comes to your work life but not when it comes to your love life. You may have no difficulty whatsoever saying no to one friend but cave in every time another friend demands your time and attention. In my own life, I struggled for years to create boundaries with female family members whom I felt emotionally reliant on and was afraid of disappointing, while never hesitating to create boundaries with girlfriends.

When we feel secure, we are able to create boundaries selectively as needed. We can assess a situation, take inventory of our internal world, and make decisions that reflect our real-time needs and desires. Of course, our roles as professionals or caretakers may demand things of us that don't always feel good or match our moods or preferences. But all in all, a person who knows their worth is able to sense what feels good and what doesn't, even when obligations are involved. They are able to tap into their true motivations, and more often than not, make decisions that reflect their truth rather than the expectations of others.

For people who have habituated to systematically protecting themselves from real or perceived physical, emotional, mental, or psychological threats, it can be more challenging to know what and who to let in and when. It's natural to generalize after we've experienced pain and want to block any potential harm from occurring in the future. Sadly, when we universally say no to everything and anyone who may possibly hurt us, we are saying no to potential experiences and people that may bring us joy, a deep sense of comfort, or sincere love.

As I see it, the difference between people who have been hurt and are willing to open their heart again and those who clench their heart and refuse to allow anyone in is self-trust. Since none of us can truly predict the outcomes of our relationships or lives, we are all in a position of having to believe that we possess the internal resources to get us through hard times. Hard times may include experiencing a deep sense of rejection, pain, or betrayal. They may include feeling misunderstood or unknown. They may even include feeling unloved by the person we desire to love us the most. If we trust that we possess the internal resources necessary to get us through hard times, we are free to explore relationships and experiences that have unknown outcomes. In order to feel safe letting down our guard and softening our boundaries, we must trust not in the other person, but in ourselves. Below is a list of some of the primary internal resources that support our willingness to dismantle boundaries and allow others in.

The ability to create boundaries and say no. This may seem counterintuitive at first, but if we don't trust our ability to create boundaries, softening boundaries most likely will feel very unsafe. If we dismantle certain boundaries and allow ourselves to show up selectively for relationships or opportunities, we must feel capable of shifting course if new information, understandings, or priorities inspire us to redirect our energy, time, and internal resources.

The willingness to exit toxic relationships, situations, and environments. It is incredibly common for people to linger far too long in relationships, jobs, living situations, and entire identities that do more harm than good. If you are a person who gets comfortable existing in mediocre situations or tends to fear that there's nothing better out there for you, you may remain in jobs or partnerships that do not support your ultimate growth. I've noticed that this tendency is especially prevalent among individuals who have grown up in families where initial understandings of how to love and be loved were skewed by abuse. If you have normalized being mistreated, condescended to, neglected, ignored, misunderstood, or hurt, you may not only put up with these experiences but associate them with intimacy and/or love.

The ability to be present at any given moment. Many of us live in the future or in the past more than in the current moment. If you can allow yourself to alternate between experiencing and evaluating a real-time relationship or opportunity, you can avoid the tendency to project former trauma or anticipate an imagined ending. It's common to project to some degree, even unconsciously, but the more we bring our conscious awareness to the fact that we are doing it, the easier it becomes to drop old stories and practice objectivity.

Resiliency. The majority of successful entrepreneurs and artists I know have experienced some form of real or perceived rejection and disappointment before achieving some form of success. While hearing "no" from someone you are hoping to hear "yes" from can be heart-wrenching, it need not be so. Our hearts don't break when we experience pain; they simply feel more deeply than we ever imagined possible. Deeply feeling pain is part of being human, and in my opinion, it is preferable to feeling nothing at all.

A sense of safety and a practice of self-love. We cannot expect to cultivate intimacy if fundamentally we don't trust ourselves or others and are constantly on the lookout for potential danger. Self-love is equally essential but confusing, because many of us unconsciously assign to others the job of making us feel loved. But for better or for worse, we cannot fully rely on others to love us. We can hope for it and desire it, but ultimately it is our responsibility to love ourselves so deeply and without condition that our identity, happiness, and sense of safety are not contingent on the love of others. Of course, this is a work in progress for every one of us, and unequivocal self-love is certainly not a requirement to love others or receive love.

Because we associate love with approval, worthiness, and a sense of belonging and safety, it is ingrained in the fundamental fabric of our beings to seek love from others. But without the foundation of self-love, we may find ourselves cracking when others don't love us the way we want to be loved, when their version or manifestation of love differs from ours, or when they choose consciously or unconsciously to withdraw their love. If at the root of our being, we believe that we are lovable and can reassure ourselves of this regardless of the circumstances in which we find ourselves, or how the people around us treat us, we are more likely to allow deserving individuals into our hearts.

The ability to self-soothe. I did not learn how to self-soothe until I had children. In the process of comforting them, using very clear, direct, and loving language, I created a road map for self-soothing. Using very simple words to define and support their feelings, I began to do the same for myself. "You seem very sad right now," I would tell them. "I will sit with you while you have this feeling. I'm not going anywhere. It's okay to be sad. I love you even when you're sad." In telling my son and daughter that I loved them even when they were sad or angry or stomping their feet, I realized that I wasn't fully loving myself when I was having those same experiences. Instead of nourishing my heart in the midst of confusion and pain, I was judging myself for having complex feelings. "Grow up," I would tell myself. "Get over it. You're fine." But I wasn't fine, and rattling around inside of me was a little girl who wasn't grown up at all; she was scared and felt incredibly alone. As I nurture my children, I practice nurturing my inner child with kindness and compassion, promising in a gentle voice not to abandon her when she feels something she wishes she weren't feeling.

BOUNDARIES IN RELATION TO SELF

In addition to managing the boundaries we create in relation to others, it's helpful to examine the boundaries we create for ourselves. Many of us wrongly believe that it's not okay to experience emotions that surface without warning or are inconvenient and uncomfortable. We create stipulations and boundaries for our feelings that dictate not only what we are allowed to feel but to what extent. Often these assumptions form when as children, we watch our caregivers for verbal and nonverbal cues as to what is acceptable, healthy, and "good." When you were a child, if a parent scolded you for crying or suggested in some way that you were weak when you expressed vulnerability, you may have internalized the notion that crying is for babies only. If your grandmother never allowed you to feel disappointed because, in her eyes, she had survived much worse, you may have come to believe that a state of constant gratitude is necessary.

If, at a very early age, you cut yourself off from your feelings in order to feel safe, keep the people around you happy, or prevent them from criticizing or harming you, it may be harder for you to access those feelings as an adult. You may, without even realizing it, still not approve of them. You may even think it's okay for everyone except you to experience sadness. Or you may believe it's okay for other people to be angry, but it's unsafe for you to express rage. Sometimes we categorize feelings as good or bad without even realizing we're doing it. Of course you do not need to act on everything you feel. But kindness means permitting yourself access to all that exists within you. If we judge our feelings and classify which ones are acceptable to feel and which ones aren't, we cut ourselves off from crucial understandings. All of our feelings teach us something about who we are, what we want, what we don't want, and what requires comfort or transformation. So, try to embrace all of your feelings as equally valid. This is surely what you would encourage a child or a beloved friend or family member to do.

Turn to "Taking Ownership of Your Fears and Desires" in the workbook.

DISRUPTING ASSUMPTIONS OF ALL-OR-NOTHING/BLACK-AND-WHITE THINKING

Let's practice disrupting black-and-white thinking by breaking down some of the thoughts we may associate with the decisions we make, starting with a made-up example of my sister repeatedly dropping her kids off at my house unannounced. My primary resistance to saying no in this case may be based on the following thoughts: *I am a bad sister. I am selfish. My sister doesn't have anyone else looking out for her since her husband left her. I am responsible for her. She won't survive without my help and support. She will hate me if I'm not available for her the moment she needs me. She will never speak to me again. She will be disappointed with me if I don't show up for her when and how she wants me to.*

Making assumptions often leads to decisions that are rooted in fear. I am going to address the above statements briefly to give you a sense of how to begin to question declarations that might feel definitive and empirical in your mind, but which in reality are subjective and cannot be proven. In order to challenge our underlying belief systems, we must first remove judgment. We cannot effectively create boundaries if we attach judgment of any kind to who we fundamentally are as we work to create and redefine our value systems. We often inherit value systems from parents, caregivers, and mentors that differ from the ones we would authentically, organically, and honestly create apart from their influence. So, just for a moment, can you suspend judgment and create the space to successfully manage your expectations, redefine your roles, and revise your value systems if necessary? Now let's take a closer look at the thoughts I described above.

I am a bad sister. Implied in this statement is the following belief: *A good sister does everything her sibling wants and desires, even when there is a personal or professional cost.* If we drop the assumed requirements of what we perceive a good sister to be, we are left with one statement only: *I am a sister.* The inferred value from the statement *I am a bad sister* is that it is important to be a good sister. But our concept of what it means to be a good sister may be convoluted or warped by conditioning and outdated beliefs, such as: *Good sisters sacrifice without questioning the impact on themselves; good sisters protect each other at all costs; good sisters put other siblings first without exception.*

Every belief has an origin story. In the above example, maybe a set of siblings survived a home with an alcoholic parent. Banding together and having each other's backs may have been the equivalent of surviving emotionally or physically. But part of becoming an adult is questioning and revising our belief systems to match the current profile of our lives, including what we require and what we desire. Removing judgment creates the freedom to redefine what we need and clarify what and who adds to or subtracts from our lives. Once we establish those things, it is far easier to define a boundary. When I am not a good sister or a bad sister, but simply a sister, I can examine my choices, feelings, requirements, and expectations from a place of objectivity. Siblings bonded together in childhood by trauma may continue to function as allies once they become adults, but it is very important to differentiate between obligation and choice. We can be committed to someone we love without binding ourselves to old patterns.

I am selfish. Implied in this statement is the following belief: *When I say no to my sister, I am a person who thinks exclusively about myself.* In this case, I would suggest a contextual reframing and demand greater specificity. If I say no to my sister one time, am I always, in every circumstance, saying no to my sister? Not at all; I am saying no to a request or demand that doesn't work for me in the moment. There is no need to generalize. There is no reason to assume that saying no to one thing means saying no to everything. Part of creating healthy boundaries means examining each specific and unique situation as it arises and making real-time decisions that feel appropriate and wise.

My sister doesn't have anyone else looking out for her since her husband left. I am responsible for her; she won't survive without my help and support. Very often, we have trouble creating a boundary because we assume that we are responsible for something or someone we are not actually responsible for. The children of caregivers who are unable or unwilling to meet their emotional and/or physical needs often compensate for this negligence by assuming the role of the parent and taking on an enormous amount of responsibility. This role reversal creates a tremendous amount of confusion for the children, who in some cases grow up believing that they are responsible not just for themselves, but everyone around them.

As difficult and saddening as it may be to watch people around you suffer, you are not responsible for fixing what isn't working in their lives. You may lovingly and willingly be a part of the healing of others, but you are not their healing. You may contribute to the scaffolding of their lives, but they cannot rely on you exclusively for help. You may make yourself available to ease their burden, but you have a right to weigh the investment of energy and time associated with what someone is asking of you against its potential emotional and physical impact on your life. It is also appropriate to consider how what someone is asking of you affects your relationship with other family members or friends, your job, your passions and dreams, or simply your need for space and downtime.

Many of us have hobbies or other things we enjoy doing without an agenda in addition to the obligations that require our attention and talent. When we continue to invest in all that we value and cherish, two things happen. The first is that we model for those around us what it looks and feels like to pursue a thrilling life. The second is that we allow the people in our lives, especially those we love, to trust themselves to create a support system that is comprehensive and sustainable.

If I allow my sister to ring my doorbell unannounced multiple times a week despite it feeling disruptive to me, she may or may not be incentivized to look elsewhere for help. She may not even realize the impact that spontaneous babysitting has on my work or love life.

Sometimes people who cross boundaries are not even aware that they are crossing them. It's helpful to let them know how their choices are impacting you and what changes you expect in order to create harmony and balance in your relationship. Ultimately, we cannot sustain relationships that don't feel reciprocal and balanced. So, in the long run, it is in everyone's best interest for you to be honest, straightforward, and vulnerable about what is and isn't working for you.

She will hate me if I'm not available for her the moment she needs me. She will never speak to me again. She will be disappointed with me if I don't show up for her when and how she wants me to. These kinds of thoughts are designed to keep us from making changes and prevent us from creating boundaries. If we are more comfortable maintaining the status quo even when it's negatively impacting us, we may tell ourselves all kinds of terrible and frightening things to keep ourselves from rocking the boat. In the short run, the known may feel less scary than the unknown, even when it's dysfunctional, but the harmful effects of existing in a relationship that doesn't honor your needs will eventually surface. If you continue to agree to relationship dynamics that exclude the protection and honoring of self, you may ultimately end up suffering physically and/or emotionally.

Now let's entertain the idea that if you create a strong boundary with people, they may end up being upset with you. This is truly a possibility. There are people, especially those who aren't equipped to self-soothe or care for themselves, who become so reliant on others that when the person they are leaning on creates a boundary, they get upset. At times, they may even act out.

In my experience, people who present as disproportionately or irrationally angry are usually, at their core, experiencing a different emotion. They may be feeling helplessness or sadness. They may have grown so accustomed to the role another person has traditionally played in their life, they fear that everything will fall apart if a role shifts. They may even fear that *they* might fall apart. They may resent that the modification or withdrawal of one source of support will require that they form a support system that involves other players and variables. It may feel inconvenient or exhausting for them to take the action necessary to ensure that their needs are met. They are most likely comfortable and content with how things have always been, and with what it looks and feels like for others to overextend themselves on their behalf. Or perhaps they wrongly attach meaning to boundaries and accuse those who define them of loving or supporting them less.

In a thoughtful relationship, here's how a healthy exchange about boundaries might play out. Let's pursue the sister example and experiment with the kinds of statements that might help create a boundary.

"Sister, I want so badly to support and help you right now. I know you've been through hell, and you rely on me. It scares me to think I might let you down. I worry that you're going to be upset with me if I modify our current arrangement. I value your friendship so deeply, and it gives me anxiety to think that our connection may change if I express my needs."

Notice that I named the fear. I let the other person know what I am feeling. I also let her know what I am afraid of losing.

"But when you drop by unannounced, I am often in the middle of a Zoom meeting or have made other plans that I have to cancel at the last minute. I'd really prefer it if you would call me ahead of time to ask me if I'm available to watch your children. Maybe we can create a schedule, so I can plan accordingly. If you need help finding other friends and babysitters who can pitch in, I'm happy to help you make some calls. You know I'll always be here for you in the case of a true emergency, but I'm hoping we can work together to create a rhythm that is sustainable for me."

Ideally, the response to this statement would be something along the lines of "It's hard for me to hear this, but I appreciate your honesty, and I want to act in ways that make you feel respected and considered. Let's work together to make this happen." But here's the thing about creating boundaries: you cannot control how others respond to them. Regardless of your delivery, others will have their own experiences that have nothing at all to do with you. When you create a boundary, some people may end up feeling neglected, abandoned, unloved, dismissed, uncared for, or offended. That's not your problem. Very often, people confuse boundaries with a lack of love and care. When they hear the word "no," or when a paradigm that works for them doesn't work for you, old memories or disappointments may surface and get projected onto current events. That's okay. Let others have their experience. Allow them to be angry, disappointed, depressed, or have whatever other feelings, without trying to control, influence, or manipulate their reaction. Part of creating and respecting boundaries is allowing other people to feel their feelings and have their experiences without trying to change those feelings and experiences. That is perhaps the most crucial boundary of all.

It's tempting to try to control other people's feelings and reactions, because it makes us feel safe. But true safety comes from allowing everybody around us to swirl in their own internal dialogues, assumptions, verbal accusations, and emotions, because we know that we are able to self-soothe, which provides a sense of security. If we can take a deep breath and calm ourselves while the people around us feel their feelings, everyone will be safe.

The worst-case scenario is when a person we feel connected to cuts us off because we aren't doing what they want us to do, being who they want us to be, or agreeing to play exclusively by their rules. If this happens, we must ask ourselves if we aren't better off without someone this punitive in our lives. If someone isn't genuinely concerned with our well-being as we—not they—define it, do they really deserve to take up space in our lives? In the long run, might we evolve more if we release partnerships in which we cannot honestly and without punishment create our boundaries? By freely expressing our needs and desires, we learn who genuinely has our back and will support our growth. It may feel scary to say goodbye to people and relationships we've grown accustomed to, but familiarity shouldn't define attachment. Sometimes, in order to make room for new people in our lives who truly inspire us to flourish, we have to let go of the people who don't.

Once you've spoken your truth and created a boundary, the best-case scenario is that others adapt and adjust to respect it. They may be disappointed that the dynamic is shifting, but once those initial feelings pass, hopefully a deeper sense of mutual trust, respect, and support will emerge. When you are comfortable creating boundaries, you liberate others to create boundaries as well. Just as kindness and joy inspire, so do self-respect and self-care. When you create parameters and stipulations that promote your well-being, the people around you may take note and begin to prioritize their own needs. The most magical relationships occur when both parties feel free to create healthy boundaries, and when those boundaries are not only respected but celebrated. When transparency and honesty are present, no one has to guess about what is and isn't working. Clear communication and the freedom to experience a broad spectrum of feelings set the stage for a vibrant, life-giving connection that honors the other and the self.

Every time I respect myself by listening and responding to my intuition, the trust I have in myself increases. This may include saying a larger no to habits, people, and patterns in my life that consistently detract from my sense of well-being. Whatever and whoever is taking up space in your life has an impact. Nothing and no one is neutral. It is essential to make space for the people, events, and experiences that will invite in beauty and tranquility and support your evolution.

BOUNDARIES VERSUS CONTROL

Creating healthy boundaries doesn't always involve saying no. It may mean choosing something that isn't your preference, but that serves your family or community. This is a conscious choice, not something that you feel is being done *to* you or is out of your control. True control is understanding why you are saying yes or no and believing that at any moment, you have the right to change your mind.

Many of us have grown accustomed to feeling safe by trying to manipulate the world around us: obsessing over details and nuances related to material things, logistics, scheduling, food, our work life, how people respond to us, what we look like, and so on. But establishing boundaries is different from asserting control in order to feel safe. Boundaries are rooted in healthy self-respect; control is rooted in fear. Controlling certain aspects of your life by avoiding potential triggers can lead to the creation of extreme and very rigid boundaries. For example, because of my history of insomnia, I generally don't go out at night past a certain time. While in general I am deeply committed to this boundary, my fear of bending my own rule occasionally leads to a level of inflexibility that is more damaging than it is helpful.

BOUNDARIES SHIFT AS WE EVOLVE

Just as we are not static, boundaries change as we evolve. As circumstances and opportunities shift, so do boundaries. There are times in my life when I don't answer my phone for days on end because I'm focused on a project. Other times, I will chat for hours with the same friend about practically nothing, for days on end. I feel safe enough in my relationships to let my loved ones know when I am and am not available, and I trust that they will not take it personally.

At any point, we have the right to modify our boundaries according to what's going on in our lives, minds, and hearts. If a friend you usually see on Saturday nights is suddenly involved with the partner of their dreams, they may no longer be available to hang every weekend. You may at one point have said yes to every thrilling work project, but you now feel that sleep is equally important and choose on occasion to say no. That's not only okay, it's appropriate.

We are not machines, so our lives cannot and should not operate in an automated fashion. We can and should adapt to what is happening in the now and communicate our current needs and desires in a kind but firm way. The consequences of not creating boundaries have a wide impact, ranging from you feeling generally disgruntled to not sleeping or feeling physically unwell. You may even find yourself quitting jobs or stepping away from relationships that have the potential to be wonderful because your unwillingness to create boundaries along the way leads to being emotionally, mentally, and/or physically overwhelmed. Practice prioritizing what feels essential and significant to you, and try not to let pressure from others interfere. You know in your body and heart what feels right.

DISENTANGLING IDENTITY

Many of us are in or have been involved in relationships where boundaries are crossed so frequently and insidiously that it's hard to know what is what and whose is whose. In reality, we are all far more connected than we realize, and our thoughts, beliefs, energy, and actions have a ripple effect on everyone around us. But our connection to others energetically does not negate the need for personal boundaries. If anything, it should reinforce them, since the truer we are to ourselves and the more self-trust we cultivate, the more those around us benefit.

When I recognize that I am in a relationship where I am crossing boundaries, or where my boundaries are being crossed, the first thing I do is forgive myself and the other party—regardless of who has done what. Forgiveness doesn't mean surrender and doesn't negate the need for action; it just removes judgment from the equation and allows us to make decisions from a place of love. When we release our propensity to judge and the urge to categorize actions as right or wrong, we lean into the compassion and understanding that anchor our boundaries.

A foundational part of establishing clear boundaries in relationships is letting go of judgment, including the desire to label ourselves and others. When we stop putting people—especially ourselves—in

YOU ARE THE BOSS OF YOU

boxes, we are free to establish authentic rhythms, experience our truest emotions, identify our true needs and wants, and become aware of the signs and signals of our bodies. We also are free to distinguish between what is supporting our well-being and what is not, including the extent to which boundaries have been successfully established in our relationships.

Because many of us have grown accustomed to prioritizing other people's feelings at the expense of our own, it can be very freeing to practice detangling what truly belongs to us from what belongs to those around us. In some cases, we have internalized the requirements, personalities, and emotional experiences of people who are not even physically present in our lives. If you lived with a depressed mother who passed away ten years ago, you may still be living internally with the sadness you experienced day after day when you were under her roof. If you were physically hurt by a caregiver, you may still be in survival mode, adrenaline spiking without any present threat or danger lurking. If a parent or teacher communicated to you in some way that you weren't capable of achieving your dreams, you may still be replaying old narratives that suggest you're worthless, limited, or inadequate.

It is natural to carry the past into our present lives, but it is not necessary. At any point, we can free ourselves from the beliefs that inspire the thoughts that catalyze the actions that reinforce the perception of limitation. We all possess the power to distance ourselves from the burden and pain of what came before this present moment. It is unrealistic to assume that overnight, we can disengage entirely from the beliefs and memories that live in us subconsciously, but instantaneous freedom is deciding that none of them need to define us. It is determining that who we are is completely separate from what we feel. We are in control of how we interpret, redefine, and assign value to every aspect of our lives. In the blink of an eye, we can return to others the feelings, beliefs, and behaviors that were never ours to keep.

Turn to "Differentiating Yourself from Others"
in the workbook.

REMOVING JUDGMENT TO CREATE HEALTHY BOUNDARIES

Judgment seems to be at the heart of almost everyone's struggle with boundaries. We hinder the creation of boundaries by making unkind declarations about how these boundaries define who we are as individuals. We also negate our instinct to create boundaries by anticipating the potential judgment of others. The solution is clear: remove fear of judgment from the equation when a boundary is required. Here's how this works: every time a judgment pops up in your mind, or someone makes a statement that you interpret as a judgment, ask yourself, "Would this judgment be admissible in a court of law?" Another way of asking this question is, "Is this judgment provable, unquestionable, and empirically undeniable?"

When we make value judgments, we often do so with a degree of passion that convinces us that what we are thinking or believing is true in an absolute sense. But the reality is that what is true for one

> »•«
>
> ### Tip: Focus your attention on your success
>
> If you feel that you are having trouble creating healthy boundaries, start to bring your attention to the situations or circumstances in which you *are* successfully drawing a hard line. You may feel that you are never able to say no or prioritize yourself, but even closing the bathroom door is creating a boundary! Celebrate the small wins and reward yourself in meaningful ways every time you say yes to yourself by closing the door on something or someone that doesn't feel right. Your reward could be a cup of hot chocolate, a walk, a ten-minute nap, self-affirming words, or whatever tickles your soul. Recognize and applaud each boundary you create in a way that feels joyful and lifts your spirit.
>
> »•«

person may not be true for someone else. Very few things are absolute. It is true that I have hazel eyes. It is true that my legal name is Shauna. It is true that I have two children. But it can never be true in an absolute sense that I am a bad sister or a perfect friend or the best lover. Most of what we or others judge falls into the category of subjective, and perception is never provable, unquestionable, or empirically undeniable. That being said, at any point, you can question the nature of your and anyone else's judgment, and dismiss it in favor of acceptance and compassion. Because most of life exists in a gray zone, you can consciously choose the narrative that leads to an experience of peace and satisfaction.

— CHAPTER SUMMARY —

Boundaries are one of the most essential ways to maintain self-trust and create sustainable, healthy relationships with others. By knowing when and how to strengthen or soften our boundaries, we create space to learn and grow. We also practice giving and receiving love in abundance, because we are respecting each other's requirements, desires, and limits. When we allow our choices and actions to reflect our internal world, we equip ourselves to navigate relationships with bravery, resilience, and self-respect. Honor your truest self by using the beautiful tool of boundaries to create a richer, more expansive, and more authentic life.

CHAPTER 2

SOOTHING YOURSELF

When my son, Max, was six, and my daughter, Maya, and her friends were four, they spent a summer afternoon gleefully splashing around in a neighbor's pool. Max was playing the part of a dinosaur monster, and Maya and her friends squealed with the thrilling terror of trying to escape his full-bodied roar. But there was one child who whimpered and paddled to the edge of the pool, where her mother knelt down and whispered something in her ear. A beat later, the child turned to face Max and said, "I know myself." Then she swiveled around to lock eyes with her mother, who whispered again into her ear. "I get nightmares when I'm afraid in the daytime," the child said to Max. She looked again at her mother, who whispered a final time. Then the child said, "Can you please not be a dinosaur monster anymore?"

Tears welled in my eyes as I absorbed the scene. The child had felt afraid and sought refuge in her mother, who provided her with the language to advocate for herself and speak what was in her heart. In a perfect world, all caregivers would pay close enough attention to their children to notice when they feel out of control, anxious, unsettled, or fearful. Ideally, when a child is struggling, a caregiver does the following:

- Pauses their own activity
- Validates the child's experience by allowing them to feel whatever it is they are truly feeling, without trying to manipulate, control, or change the feeling

- Provides some form of comfort: encouraging words, a warm embrace, a nod of understanding, or in some cases, a potential solution

Positive affirmation assures children that they are okay and safe, even in the midst of uncomfortable and stressful experiences. Validation comes when caregivers don't react in an overly emotional way to children's feelings, and don't walk away from the children, punish them, or narrate the scene in ways that make them feel shamed, immature, or wrong for having their feelings, whatever they may be.

Unfortunately, as children, many of us did not receive positive affirmation in the midst of our emotional struggles, and our experiences were not fully validated. If a caregiver demonstrates feeling inconvenienced, scared, irritated, or overwhelmed in reaction to their child's experience, the child may squash their feelings in an attempt to maintain stability, peace, and order. Additionally, if a caregiver assumes responsibility for their child's feelings instead of simply being a witness to the human experience, they are inadvertently and unintentionally shutting the child down. The children may then internalize this pattern and evolve into adults who behave similarly. When carried into adulthood, this propensity to try to curb or mitigate the pain of others may negatively impact romantic partnerships, friendships, dynamics between coworkers, and really all relationships. If you are in love with someone who is sobbing, and you feel responsible for your partner's grief, how can you respond with pure compassion? If your sibling is angry, and you feel it's your job to eradicate their rage, how can you show up with grace?

The ability to create healthy boundaries distinguishes people who are able to compassionately observe and appropriately respond to the feelings of others from those who aren't. If I love you, but do not feel emotionally responsible for you, I can calmly show up for you in the midst of your distress. My not having a solution doesn't threaten my relevance or contribution to your relief. On the other hand, if I assume false ownership of your resolution, the feeling of helplessness associated with not being able to ease your discomfort may make me feel like I've done a bad job of loving you. The trick to effectively practicing empathy is that it never steals a person's right to experience all of their humanity. Instead, it sits patiently and without an agenda in the face of someone's grief, pain, loneliness, or rage, and it offers its presence without conditions or expectations. Showing up doesn't mean having all the answers or even necessarily easing the burden of another person's struggle; it means not walking away when the person reveals to you the darkest parts of their human experience.

A caregiver who lacks emotional boundaries may be tempted to ignore or stomp out the complex feelings of their child in an effort to salvage their own identity as a loving, competent, valuable human. Alternatively, if they are able to acknowledge that their child's inner world doesn't necessarily reflect their efforts as a caregiver, they are free to be objective and provide comfort without expecting a swift resolution. Children are almost constantly reacting to multiple sources of stimuli and attempting to process a vast and often overstimulating world. How a caregiver shows up and what they do or do not provide are just a few of many variables that impact a child's emotional life. Ultimately, these may become the most influential variables and affect the child most detrimentally if the pressure to support stability and growth overwhelms the caregiver. Yes, it is a huge responsibility to parent a small person. But what is expected of caregivers is not to perfect or curate their child's world to the exclusion of hard feelings; it is to provide the comfort of presence and the allowance of an imperfect experience. It is to offer the scaffolding that teaches a child to self-soothe. Children never truly expect a parent to fix their feelings, because feelings don't require fixing; they require acknowledgement and loving support. And simply by not running away, becoming terrified or exasperated, or expressing to children that their feelings are inappropriate or untimely, caregivers do their job.

When a child is left to cry alone or is ignored when they feel hurt, they may become an adult who leaves their lover to cry alone or ignores the frustration of a coworker. A grown individual who did not receive proper nurturing or feel understood as a child may stomp off, pouting, when there's a difference of opinion. They may not ask for help in the midst of feeling emotionally overwhelmed because they don't believe that they deserve it or that it's even possible. The inability of a caregiver to tolerate differences, tension, and discomfort in the presence of children perpetuates a cycle of individuals who flounder in the midst of confusing emotions. If what is being modeled to a child is that it's not alright to have certain feelings, or that there are stipulations or potential consequences associated with those feelings, one of two things generally happens: either the child disassociates and stops feeling their feelings, or the feelings heighten and become chronic, because they're never accepted, expressed, and processed.

It is not uncommon for children to be mocked, snickered at, punished, yelled at, ignored, glared at, abandoned, or beaten as a consequence of acting in a way that a caregiver disapproves of. Disapproval may be the result of a caregiver feeling publicly humiliated or generally overwhelmed by not instinctively knowing how to relieve their child's pain. It may stem from a lack of internal resources to self-soothe in the midst of their own discomfort, from the perception of being burdened, or from unconsciously repeating the modeling of their own caregivers. Whatever the reasons, if a child's behavior is met with disapproval, they do not assume it is because their caregiver is not equipped or willing to handle their imperfections. Children are entirely dependent on their caregivers for survival, so it is advantageous for them to believe that their caregivers are perfect and can do no wrong. Because of this, children do not blame their caregivers for unkind, incomplete, or unconscious reactions; they blame themselves.

So, how do adults who were not properly attended to as children calm themselves down? How do we find the courage within ourselves to believe that it is safe to experience the totality of our feelings when we've been trained to believe it's not? How can we create a deep foundation of self-love and reassure ourselves, when as children, in our most vulnerable and needy moments, we were shamed for being human? It is only natural that adults who were not nourished emotionally in their childhood most likely lack the internal resources to secure peace and inner calm, especially in the midst of change, confusion, struggle, or the unknown. But here's the good news: there's no better person to parent you than you. As an adult, you now have full control and can take complete responsibility for how you parent yourself, and you can do so in a way that is as loving, kind, and patient as you wish your caregivers had been with you.

SHADOW PARENTS: CREATING YOUR IDEAL CAREGIVERS

By now, you may have become aware that some of the parenting you received was misguided or missing crucial elements, or perhaps you experienced extended periods of time during which guidance or emotional support was absent altogether. But it's never too late to rewire your brain and bring deep comfort and relief to your heart by learning to parent yourself. You do not have to be the mother or father of a child or pet to learn to parent yourself. All that's required is an openness to learning to love yourself and accept your imperfections. You are imperfect, and thus you will parent yourself imperfectly, just as your caregivers did. That's okay. Parenting yourself isn't about making up for every instance when you felt abandoned or neglected, or atoning for all the wrongdoings of the people who raised you. It's about cultivating an awareness of how you really feel without the requirement for change or an internal commentary meant to align you with a "better" version of reality.

Additionally, you can craft what I refer to as a "shadow mother" and "shadow father" (or, if you prefer, a "shadow parent"). In essence, you can consciously create the mother and father figures you wish you had received nurturing from as a young person and invite the essence of these figures to inhabit or shadow you. The image associated with your shadow parent can be whatever you want it to be. It can have an entire body or be just a face. It can manifest as a ball of light, an animal, colors, or whatever else makes it the most tangible and accessible to you. If there is a person who has served a nurturing role in your life (a teacher, family member, mentor, or the like), you may choose for this person to be your shadow parent as opposed to creating one from scratch. Alternatively, you can combine characteristics from many people who have supported and loved you in significant ways into one representation of your shadow parent. Your shadow parent also may exist entirely within you as your core wisdom or as an older, wiser version of yourself. It also may exist within you as a younger version of yourself who has not yet been tainted by culture, societal or parental feedback, or a sense of shame.

When my ability to self-soothe or speak kindly to myself is compromised by my being in a state of judgment or fear, I visualize and deeply connect with one of my shadow mothers. (Yes, I have several!) One of my shadow mothers is an entirely fictitious woman who is about a hundred years old and speaks with a delicious Southern drawl. Another shadow mother is an older, wiser rendition of myself. I also often draw upon the memory of my beloved Jamaican nanny, who was all at once fierce, compassionate, brave, and warm. In meditating on the empowered energy of these women and recruiting their love, I feel more concretely supported. As I imagine them speaking to me, uplifting me, encouraging me, and nurturing me, I integrate their vibrations and ease into my own being. Their confidence becomes my confidence. I can rest in their arms. Ultimately, I absorb their spirit and integrity and strengthen my own maternal inner voice by reflecting on theirs.

*Turn to "Creating Your Shadow Mother and/
or Shadow Father" in the workbook.*

Consider drawing inspiration from movie or television characters, characters from books you've read, lyrics of songs you've listened
to, or even celebrities or folks on social media you feel a connection
with. Inspiration can come from anywhere. The common thread is
the qualities that this person or amalgamation of people provides in
supporting your concept of mother, father, or parent. Once you internalize these qualities, you can provide yourself with the same level
of nurturing and support that your shadow parents provide for you.
You will be empowered to talk to yourself, reframe circumstances,
embrace your feelings, and encourage yourself the way they would.

The key thing to keep in mind is that you already are your ideal
parent; your shadow parent is simply the truest, most unencumbered part of yourself that knows and has always known how to be
of comfort. In creating your shadow parent(s), you essentially are
coming home to the internal wisdom of your own all-knowing soul.
Everything that you imagine your shadow mother being, you already
are. Everything you dream of your shadow father providing, you
have the power to provide for yourself. The work is integrating what
you innately know with how you experience yourself and the world.

Your essence—who you are at your core, apart from all external
influences and experiences—is unshakable, unchanging, beautiful,
and complete. Our goal is not to become a better version of ourselves; it is to peel away the parts of ourselves that have learned to
be fearful and full of shame, so that we can experience our essence
unencumbered. If we trust in our ability to self-soothe, we are more
likely to give ourselves permission to feel. If we are a kind mother to
ourselves, we do not judge all that it means to be human. If we do
not conflate the experience of pain, sadness, or rage with failure, we
use our human experience to grow and evolve.

LEARNING TO SELF-SOOTHE FOR ANXIETY

The sources of anxiety are many, from a general feeling of being overwhelmed to an imagination that weaves unsettling narratives about future unknowns. The nervous system exists in the body to create a sense of balance as we navigate both thoughts and external stimuli. It is the brilliant messenger that helps us interpret information from the outside world and that translates our internal world into action. The sympathetic nervous system is the part that helps us respond to danger and possible threats, while the parasympathetic nervous system seeks homeostasis and supports healing. When the sympathetic nervous system is in overdrive, we may become flustered, anxious, or fatigued, which could lead to things such as hypervigilance and burnout.

Movement is a wonderful way to release yourself from the tension of your mind and activate your parasympathetic nervous system. Talking with a friend, journaling, meditating, and breathing deeply also may bring some relief. Another strategy that eases my anxiety is to imagine the resolution of an issue that I can't stop ruminating over. If I am preparing to record a song in the studio, I imagine myself singing in a state of total ease and inspiration, completely joyful and empowered. If I am entering an unknown situation, such as my daughter's first day of school, I meditate on the *feeling* I want to embody when walking into the classroom and witnessing my child joyfully engaging before I leave her. If I am anticipating a hard conversation with a family member or friend, I visualize them nodding their head in understanding and acknowledging my perspective, even if it differs from theirs. If I am concerned about investing money in a new project, I visualize my bank statement and add a bunch of zeros to my checking account balance.

Wellness coach Ashley James takes it a step further. She describes imagining a timeline that begins with where you are and ends fifteen minutes after the successful completion of the event you are anticipating. So, if the trajectory of your immediate life could be painted as a straight line, the far left is where you are in this moment, somewhere in the middle is the event you are anticipating, and to the right of that is fifteen minutes after the successful completion of the event you're having anxiety about. The exercise is not about imagining the event you are anticipating being a success, but rather dwelling on where you are and what you will be doing fifteen minutes after the event has unfolded exactly the way you wanted it to—or better. Are you having a glass of wine with friends? Are you unwinding and watching TV? Are you out having dinner? Are you in a bubble bath or celebrating with someone who adores you? If we can mentally position ourselves not only to expect our desired outcome but to practice internalizing the projected relief and joy that follow, our body relaxes into a state of security.

Because I struggled with insomnia for the first few decades of my life, I've come up with many creative ways to induce sleep when my anxiety spikes at bedtime. One of these strategies involves becoming something or someone else in my imagination, to separate myself from the fears of being human. For

>>•<<

Tip: Imaginary Conversation

Talk to the people who bring you comfort and joy, even if they are not actually in your presence. They may be alive, or perhaps they have passed on. They could be a celebrity, or someone you admire but have never met before. You could speak to Ruth Bader Ginsburg or Rosa Parks or your great-great-grandmother or your favorite poet. Our imaginations are wild and limitless, so there's no need to limit them.

We spend so much time narrating life in our minds that we may as well play with the idea that we can dialogue with people who are not in the room. Children do this all the time with dolls and stuffed animals and imaginary friends. Why shouldn't we engage with our perception of the brilliant souls and minds who bring positivity and light to our way of thinking? These conversations can take place internally or out loud—whatever feels comfortable for you.

>>•<<

instance, on a night when my mind is buzzing, I might imagine myself as the bark of a tree, still and serene, without any demands but to exist. I might imagine that I am the ocean, or a dolphin, or a baby who sleeps completely unaware of the responsibilities and considerations of adulthood. By sinking deep into the experience of how I would *feel* as water, I stop (even for a few moments) experiencing the anxiety of being human.

Turn to "Relieving Stress through Observation" in the workbook.

»•« Practice: Stress Meditation

Imagine that your whole body is a watercolor painting that lives in a wide-open field. Every part of you exists on the canvas in its own clean and distinct way. Now imagine a beautiful warm rain trickling down the painting that is your body. The painful parts of you merge with the parts that are at ease, so that every part of you becomes neutral. The delighted parts of you leak into the parts of you that hold sadness, so that your body is a swirl of colors and experiences.

Lend the parts of your being that are okay simply as they are, simply because they exist, to the parts that feel scared or compromised. It may be that your knee or big toe is the only part of your body that feels truly relaxed. Allow the ease and effortlessness of that part to offer comfort and healing to the parts that feel broken or need to let go. Your body is an ecosystem that can distribute and recycle its own love and healing.

»•«

VOICE MEMOS FOR UNCOMFORTABLE FEELINGS

My son, Max, recently had a difficult time extracting himself from some dark thoughts that were creating pain. He was deeply invested in a project that wasn't on track with how he envisioned it going, and the moment he seemed to have fully processed his grief, a fresh wave of it washed over him. I was busy with my daughter but could hear my husband talking to Max in the background. When nothing he said seemed to move the needle, my husband ran off and reappeared holding his phone up to Max's mouth. A few minutes later, Max was calm.

"What did you say to him?" I asked.

"I asked him to record a voice memo for himself, and when he listened to it, he calmed down," my husband said.

My seven-year-old's voice memo went like this: "Max, I know that you're really upset right now, but everything is going to be okay. Mommy is going to buy more tape, and you will have another chance to make a dinosaur collage."

Hearing my son's sweet voice speaking words of comfort to himself gave me chills. The wise, secure part of him that knew he was okay was able to soothe the scared part that felt out of control. This voice memo gave me another idea. Later that week, Max had soccer tryouts, which I knew would create some tension, since something important to him was at stake.

"Max," I said, "let's record a voice memo that you will play for yourself after soccer tryouts are over."

He loved this idea. My son's message to himself was this: "Max, you did great! You did your best, and that's all that matters. Now you get to go eat ice cream with Daddy!"

I played Max's message to him anytime he expressed nervousness surrounding the tryouts. Then he imagined himself choosing his favorite flavors at the ice cream shop, and how he would feel knowing that he had done his best and was being rewarded not for the results of the tryouts, but for his efforts. As adults, we can offer ourselves the same gentle intervention anytime we require it. If your mother speaks to you in a tone that makes you feel patronized, maybe you will record a voice memo to yourself that says something along the lines of: "Deep breath. This is about her, not me. I know who I am. Her need for control doesn't have to ruin my day." Then play it after a phone conversation with your mother. You can record preemptive voice memos, as well as voice memos to play in the midst of uncomfortable feelings. You also can ask a parent, friend, or loved one to send voice memos for you to store for times of anxiety, grief, or sadness. Hearing an actual voice rather than or in addition to an imagined one holds the potential to bring immense comfort in moments when our minds are spinning, or when we feel that we are drowning emotionally.

Every part of us is safe exactly as it is. Nothing needs to change in order for us to feel secure. But often we feel that something is wrong with us when we lack a sense of ease or experience anxiety. In reality, anxiety simply points to fear, and fear points to an imagination that isn't playing kindly. Stress is a positive in the case of a true emergency, when action is required to escape a dangerous situation or create useful momentum of some kind. But in our everyday lives, it is often not stress itself that depletes us, but the fear that accompanies it. We can practice alleviating our fears by imagining our future successes, soothing ourselves with comforting internal narratives, grounding ourselves in the present moment, having imaginary conversations with people we trust, and listening to recordings that offer hope during confusing and difficult moments.

Turn to "Self-Touch" in the workbook.

SELF-SOOTHING AND IDENTITY

It is not uncommon for people to judge themselves in their deepest moments of vulnerability when they feel the most scared. It is in these moments that we all require the most love, compassion, and support, but our tendency may be to self-punish when we feel out of control. The reason for our self-punishment is that sometimes we unknowingly conflate what we do and how we feel with who we are (please refer to chapter 1, "Defining Boundaries"), and our focus on negativity skews the potential to form a positive sense of self.

There was a time when I found myself barking commands at my children, mostly pertaining to things they should not have been doing. I had been dedicating so much attention to the "should nots" that it dawned on me that I needed to balance my warnings and requests with positive statements about my children's identities. Here are two examples of how I've attempted to reassure my children of their self-worth in the context of needing to concretely guide them:

"You are lovable, but it's not okay to jump on my bed right now. I see you really need to burn some energy, so let's go outside and jump in a safer place."

"You are full of beautiful ideas, but now is not the time to color because we're getting ready to head to school. Let's make a plan to color this afternoon."

Imagine if, as adults, we were to slow down and offer ourselves compassion instead of jumping straight to the correction. The imperative to self-soothe might naturally diminish if we did not have so much anxiety surrounding behaviors and choices that require redirection. As humans, we will constantly need to course-correct and adjust our attitudes, patterns, beliefs, and plans. This is not necessarily because something is wrong, but rather because we—and our lives—are evolving. It is completely legitimate for us as adults to speak to ourselves as we would to our children. Here's what this might sound like:

> "You are lovable, and you probably just hurt your sister's feelings. Take a deep breath and apologize."

> "You are talented, but this audition did not go your way. That's really disappointing, but this is not your last audition."

> "You are smart, but you did not get the promotion you were hoping for. Something better is coming."

Self-soothing is not just a series of words we speak to ourselves; it's the belief that we are fundamentally enough and okay as we are, and that anything we do and feel exists apart from our fundamental core value.

— CHAPTER SUMMARY —

One of the most profound and nonnegotiable abilities we may ever cultivate is the power to self-soothe. While ideally this training would have occurred in our childhood, as adults, we can learn how to calm and reassure ourselves regardless of what is going on around or inside of us. The worlds outside and within are often chaotic and unpredictable, and learning to ease our anxiety and comfort ourselves is an invaluable skill. In essence, by learning to soothe ourselves, we become the parent we may have never had.

CHAPTER 3

SOFTENING PERFECTIONISM

The concept of ego has been defined in slightly different ways over time. According to the legendary Austrian neurologist Sigmund Freud, the founder of psychoanalysis, the ego is the part of the personality that embodies people's conscious self-perception and what they wish to project outwardly.[4] The Merriam-Webster online dictionary echoes Freud's concept of ego, defining it as "one of three divisions of the psyche in psychoanalytic theory that serves as the conscious mediator between the person and reality, especially by functioning both in the perception of and adaptation to reality." An alternative definition of ego it offers is "the self especially as contrasted by another self or the world."[5]

I tend to think of my ego as the part of me that believes that I can and should control things. My ego gets bloated when I don't trust myself to get it wrong—when the fear of potential humiliation, isolation, or abandonment prevents me from being vulnerable, admitting to not having all the answers, or accepting my imperfections as valuable. Perfectionism is a tool my ego employs to prevent the external perception that I am unlovable, undesirable, and unacceptable. Since the consequence of being these things is potential humiliation, isolation, and abandonment, I may work very hard to secure my status as lovable, desirable, and acceptable. On a rational basis, my fear that others may perceive me in dark or unflattering ways is a reflection of my own insecurities and self-judgment.

Perfectionism and self-blame are deeply intertwined. We may seek to perfect ourselves to avoid the shame of potentially disappointing those we love or authority figures we have grown to rely on.

By equating perfection with blamelessness, we avoid doing and being what we consider to be wrong. But if we are unable to embody our concept of perfection, we may shame ourselves in advance of accusations so that others don't have the opportunity to find fault with us. Children especially may be inclined to blame themselves in order to maintain the notion that their caregivers are reliable and that the world is safe. As a way of alleviating the guilt of those they depend on, children hijack their accountability, which gives them a sense of control. Unfortunately, the pattern of self-blame and the resolve to be flawless in order to create a sense of security may extend into adulthood and make inner peace and self-acceptance less accessible.

Imagine that you are a child with an unstable caregiver who is constantly bursting into tears, shouting at you, or blaming you or others. Your instinct likely would be to do better and be better to prevent your caregiver from being triggered. Children use perfectionism as a tool to do two things:

- Keep their caregiver stable by creating ideal conditions
- Absorb all responsibility for external chaos and unpredictability in order to maintain or regain a sense of control

In essence, a role reversal takes place, whereby children parent their caregivers with consistency and stability while being careful to avoid potential triggers. If Mommy gets upset when I spill my milk, I may work extra hard to keep things clean. If Daddy hits me when I don't perform well in school, I will be highly motivated to get perfect grades.

In addition to noting and responding to negative reinforcement, both children and adults constantly note the moments when they are positively affirmed and rewarded for good behavior. If children make breakfast every morning for a hungover parent, and this elicits a smile, that smile is a reward. If Daddy takes a child out for ice cream only when an A is achieved on an exam, the child associates academic excellence with attention from Daddy. I believe that many of our perfectionistic behaviors can be traced back to this childhood thought: *Mommy and Daddy, love me and see me.* We cannot underestimate the primal desire to be loved and seen in order to secure not only our identity but our lives.

I've been addicted to many things over the course of my life, the most exhausting of which was perfectionism. There's something about pursuing perfection that at first glance could be perceived as arrogant or presumptuous. But the strategy of the addict is to continue to raise the bar so that perfection is unachievable and will always render the addict useless and ashamed. Since I'm an expert at the shame game, I would argue that aiming for perfection is the best and fastest way to acquire loads and loads of shame, which only ups the ante and deceives us into believing that we should try even harder to be perfect.

The pursuit of perfection may be rooted in the belief that no one will neglect us, abandon us, or fail to love us if we are perfect. It may point to a fear of being seen for who we truly are, warts and all. It may be a habituated early childhood response to an unreliable or unstable caretaker whom we were adamant not to sadden or anger. Perfectionism also is a way to avoid potential triggers that make us feel out of control. For example, if I write a perfect report for my job, my boss won't yell at me. When he does, my adrenaline spikes, I feel anxious, and the story I tell myself is that I'm worthless. While our intention in pursuing perfection of any kind is to feel safe and protected from potentially harmful feelings and experiences, it is a fear-based and controlling coping strategy that will inevitably burn us.

There are many problems with pursuing perfection, but as a starting point, the whole notion of being perfect is flawed. In order for us to maintain that something is perfect, there must be an empirically perfect reference point or source of comparison. But perfection is arbitrary, and society's concept of it shifts from day to day and era to era. On top of that, it's completely culturally subjective, and even individuals existing in the same society at the same time might have contrasting views on what they consider to be the perfect-looking person, the perfect career, the perfect relationship, the perfect outfit, and on and on. There is no objectivity surrounding perceptions of perfection, so striving for it is a futile exercise.

WHY PURSUING PERFECTION DOESN'T WORK

It isn't a real thing. As I said, perfection is elusive, and its definition changes from culture to culture and neighborhood to neighborhood. Moreover, *your own* concept of perfection is likely to change, making it a moving target that most likely will disappoint you when you fail to achieve it.

It's exhausting. Chasing perfection is maddening, because the whole nature of being human involves complexity and irreconcilable dichotomies: dark and light, up and down, and everything in between. Being human is sloppy and a learning experience for every one of us. When we measure ourselves against robotic standards, we invite the potential for harsh self-criticism and a sense of inferiority.

It keeps us from being our authentic selves. When we betray the totality of who we truly are, choosing instead to accept, celebrate, and reward only a small fraction of our core identity, we betray ourselves. And when we betray ourselves, we lose trust in ourselves. This incurs an even deeper, more troubling sense of shame than the shame of failing to meet our arbitrary standards of perfection. If our sense of worth is contingent on prescribed or artificial behaviors, emotions, appearances, and standards, we are reaching outside of ourselves to secure peace. True peace is the outgrowth of acknowledging and living through what we are really feeling and experiencing, versus consciously determining what we *should* be feeling and experiencing. Chasing authenticity and emotional freedom is far more likely to provide relief than achieving an arbitrary and impermanent definition of perfection.

It inhibits others from expressing themselves authentically and freely. If you don't allow yourself to embrace all of who you truly are, others may not feel comfortable expressing all of who they truly are in your presence. This may not only lead to potentially shallow relationships with yourself and others but may eliminate the joy and relief of shared vulnerability. Perfection isn't relatable, and for those who are comfortable with their raw, unpolished humanity, it isn't even desirable. In actuality, it's suffocating, stifling, and limiting.

It's boring! When I was twenty-two, I was head over heels for a man who was much older and seemed to have it all together. I convinced myself that if what I presented was the perfect woman, he would desire me and ask me to marry him. When I told my grandmother that I feared I wasn't perfect enough for him, she clapped her hands and said, "Thank goodness you're not perfect! Being perfect would be *so boring!*" She was right. Mechanical, automated living fueled by overthinking doesn't interest people who are ignited by passion and love.

It's imprisoning. If we are bound for too long by rigid structures and expectations, we may eventually crack. No creature is meant to exist in an artificial paradigm; we all crave what feels natural and real. The outcome of sustained imprisonment is anxiety, depression, irritability, anger, disease, or even violence.

It doesn't create space for growth. Experimenting and making mistakes are how we learn and evolve, and without the freedom to be beautifully imperfect, we stifle ourselves and lean into what is comfortable and predictable versus what is new and invigorating.

It's stressful! Inherent in the notion of perfection is the idea that there is a right way to be, behave, perform, look, and so on, which creates an all-or-nothing attitude that eventually renders us wrong.

It creates a false sense of control. In striving for perfection, we are hoping to prevent judgment or rejection and solidify a sense of safety. But because, as we've established, perfection isn't a real thing, and every person's definition of it varies over time, we end up as chameleons and change ourselves in response to our company, mood, or current fears.

It diminishes our capacity to cultivate resilience. If our underlying intention is to secure love, attention, or approval from others, we are setting ourselves up for the very thing we are clamoring to ward off: the wound of rejection. Someone at some point will judge us, ignore us, or disapprove of us, and the best way to get comfortable with that reality is to practice resilience and love for ourselves that is not dependent on any external thing or person. Unconditional love for ourselves—love that is not contingent on performance of any kind and has zero stipulations—may be the greatest antidote to perfectionism. Self-love and self-acceptance are a beautiful foundation for cultivating resilience and provide access to vulnerability, authenticity, and emotional freedom.

It is extremely isolating. When we create a set of rules to live by that do not reflect our true nature, we are less likely to enter new relationships and situations that might force us out of our comfort zone or render us incapable of clinging to preconstructed checklists. As a consequence, we might find ourselves physically and/or emotionally alone more often than we'd like to be. I believe that most people long to be seen and accepted for who they truly are. If you bury your true self beneath the cloak of what you think others want to see, you risk experiencing chronic loneliness.

It binds us to the wrong people. If we are associating with people based on a false sense of identity, value, and security, there is a good chance that our friends and other relations are not the people we would choose—or who would choose us—if we were authentically expressing ourselves. By choosing authenticity, we run the risk of saying goodbye to people in our lives whose interest in us is based on the manifestations of our perfectionism. This may at first make us fearful of loss or the possibility of ending up alone. But in reality, we are paving the way for relationships based on honesty and mutual trust.

In addition to the pursuit of perfection in my youth, my desire for security ultimately expressed as OCD. OCD involves very rigid requirements of how things should look, an obsession with nuance, and in my case, a preoccupation with how I was perceived by others. I was almost constantly fixated on details, the aesthetic of my environment, conversations, meals, and even potential future events with an excruciating level of specificity. The placement of objects around me, the dimensions of my sandwich, and the words I spoke all carried equal weight, and I had no practical discernment regarding where I should channel my energy. It was an exhausting and stressful existence.

All of my desires to control were a way of grasping at stability, but sadly, they only led to extreme anxiety. Deep down inside, we know that controlling our environment cannot guarantee that we will feel what we want to feel and avoid what we don't want to feel. We understand on the most profound level that perfectionism is a sloppy Band-Aid that disintegrates the moment our humanity leaks through. Our attempts to manage fear by attempting to control ourselves, our environment, and how those we depend on or care for perceive us only heighten our anxiety. To let go of perfectionism, we must consciously trust that our physical and emotional survival doesn't depend on what anyone else thinks of us. We are made to give and receive love, and also to feel safe. We should not have to manipulate ourselves or others to ensure these experiences.

Perfectionism points to deeply rooted fears and speaks to an underlying lack of commitment to the authentic self. When we don't give ourselves permission to be who we truly are, parts of us die, and this breeds depression. I am the saddest when I am not feeling all of my feelings. Perfectionists tend to be judgmental, especially of themselves, so please be gentle with your heart as you peel back any perfectionistic tendencies. You will not relieve yourself of perfectionism by continuing to judge yourself. The way out of judgement is accepting and loving all that you are. While you may not love all the habits you've developed over time, you can thank them for the purpose they once served in your life.

If you believed that being a perfect child was the way to avoid exposure to violence of any kind (emotional, mental, physical, or psychological), then you were a brave warrior for doing what you needed to do and being who you needed to be to survive uncomfortable or possibly even terrifying situations. Even people who are raised in stable home environments with loving and attentive parents can develop perfectionistic habits based on the positive reinforcement they receive. Regardless of the circumstances and conditions of your upbringing, most human beings want similar things: unconditional love, unqualified acceptance, opportunities to be seen, a consistent sense of safety, and a true sense of belonging.

When my friends obsess over their appearance or compulsively achieve without regard for how it's affecting their body, mind, and soul, I immediately wonder about the ways in which they're judging or disapproving of themselves. In my experience, the only way for someone to unpack perfectionism is to grapple with the underlying belief of not being enough, or that their value is contingent on certain things. A helpful starting point is to slow down and notice your patterns. If you can identify specific perfectionist behaviors, take note of what kind of event or exchange immediately precedes that behavior. Do you tend to lunge into a cleaning spree after fighting with a loved one? Do you obsess over word choices after feeling misunderstood by a colleague? Does it take twenty minutes to send a one-sentence email when you're preparing for a big trip? In general, do you tend to feel more anxious and destabilized after or in anticipation of a conversation or an event?

Don't try to fix anything; just notice it. Does a certain person or group of people tend to heighten your insecurities? When and where do you find yourself most harshly scrutinizing your language, behaviors, performance, or appearance? Who or what throws your identity into question or inspires self-doubt? Who or what triggers your impulse to try to gain a greater sense of control and authority over your life?

To get to the bottom of what's underlying your actions and choices, challenge yourself—in small, incremental ways that won't overwhelm you—to stop agreeing to the habituated action, and see what thoughts come up. For example, I went through a phase of compulsively applying makeup to align with my then version of what was attractive. It might easily have taken me twenty minutes to make "cat eyes" with black eyeliner or to put bronzer on my cheekbones. If I didn't make art of my face, the thoughts that came up for me were along the lines of *I'm not good enough. I'm unlovable. I'll always be alone.* Pretty extreme thoughts in response to pausing the action that made me temporarily feel safe (aka loved)!

These days, I rarely apply makeup at all, and if I do, it takes just a few minutes. I wear what will make me feel good about myself, not what I think other people want to see. Because there is no fear or expectation involved in the *why* of my choice to wear makeup, I don't perfect every stroke and blot. I'm not afraid of what I won't receive (attention, respect, love) if I don't look my sexiest or prettiest. I trust that my essence and internal glow will radiate in the world. Most importantly, I am more concerned with what I am experiencing on the inside than what I am presenting on the outside.

It is our underlying beliefs that lead to paralyzing behaviors. Instead of avoiding the upsetting feelings that accompany these beliefs, we can bravely—and with the support of loved ones and trained professionals—allow ourselves to experience the discomfort, fear, and pain caused by habituated thoughts. Eventually, with great courage and patience, we can release ourselves from the shackles of perfectionism and establish a new baseline for our lives that is rooted in freedom and love. Ironically, the pursuit of perfectionism is designed by our egos to create peace and a sense of safety, but in reality, it magnifies anxiety and the feeling of being out of control.

By letting go of perfectionism, we come to understand which relationships are based on mutual acceptance and appreciation. The people who do not truly value our authentic way of being will fall away. This is not a reflection of our worth or ability to be loved. It is an indication that some of the people we have surrounded ourselves with are clinging to an identity we have fabricated to feel safe, but are bravely outgrowing.

Turn to "Conscious Creation of Self" and "Journaling to Discover Authenticity" in the workbook.

PERFECTIONISM AND HYPERVIGILANCE

Hypervigilance occurs when a dysregulated nervous system makes it impossible for a person to discern between nonthreatening and threatening situations, and stress signals are constantly firing. A person experiencing hypervigilance actively seeks to identify potentially dangerous variables in their environment, and their response to stimuli is greatly elevated.[6] In my own experience, the compulsive looping thoughts that accompanied hypervigilance provided a constant supply of adrenaline that prevented me from ever letting my guard down. As long as I was analyzing the external world instead of scanning my internal world, I believed that I was protecting myself from potential harm.

Adrenaline crowds out feelings such as sadness, so while in a state of high alert, we aren't able to access murky and confusing feelings that may lead to a sense of hopelessness, helplessness, existential fear, or shame. Subconsciously, it's very likely that many of us categorize these experiences as unsafe. So, in addition to hypervigilance alerting us to external threats, it blocks us from experiencing the emotions that threatened the stability of our home when we were children. If our pain or discomfort was unmanageable in the presence of unstable caregivers, as adults, we may continue to wave a red flag and run from it the way we would from a tiger.

If a primary caregiver does not have the internal resources to put a child at ease, the child cannot relax. They may then attempt to control themselves, others, and/or their environment in order to feel secure. When a child feels taken care of, they know that they are safe, and their nervous system is regulated. But if, for whatever reason, a child views their primary caregivers as incompetent, inefficient, or unequipped to secure their emotional or physical safety, they will usurp the role of caregiver to ensure that the job will get done. This is problematic for many reasons, one of which is that children are too young to truly differentiate between real and perceived dangers. Some threats are clear: if every time a caregiver drinks whiskey, they hit their child, the child may internalize and predict this pattern. But if a caregiver unexpectedly scowls or walks away, a child may have no idea what's going to happen to them. And because children are born with an innate understanding that they must rely on adult caregivers and are biologically wired to remain in their good graces, children will bend over backward to ensure that they are loved, approved of, and cared for.

While hypervigilance is often the outgrowth of significant trauma, every time a caregiver behaves in a way that threatens a child's perceived sense of safety, stress signals fire. If this happens frequently enough, over time, a child may become generally anxious and learn to distrust the world around them altogether.

The first step I took to relieve my own hypervigilance was to notice when my anxiety was elevated. In what environments do you scan for threats outside of your standard realm of awareness? Under what circumstances do you find yourself unable to relax without accounting for everything around you? When do you find that you're most sensitive to stimuli? Some of my own personal triggers used to include getting into bed at night, entering a situation in which I might feel judged, and packing to go on a trip. The manifestations of these triggers ranged from intense stomach pain and sleeplessness to exhausting anxiety and OCD. Obsessing over what could go wrong often created the same physiological responses in my body as stress resulting from real events.

Somatic work was particularly helpful in training my body to process fear and anxiety. Please see chapter 6, "Healing Trauma," for a more thorough discussion of somatic work and its applications. Breathing deeply, slowly, and consciously in moments of tension is also a powerful tool to soften the feeling of being overwhelmed.

Turn to "Unpacking Triggers" in the workbook.

UNDERSTANDING HYPERFOCUS

One of the most standard fear responses is the hyperfocusing of attention. Consider the possibility that if children feel that the attitudes and behaviors of people around them are not in their control, they may compulsively attach to ideas, material objects, or tasks that are completely unrelated but which they feel they *can* control. My hyperfocus as a child became food and the aesthetic of the objects around me. When there was instability in my home, my first effort was to be a good girl and perfect myself in order to stabilize those around me. When those efforts failed, I sought to perfect things that I could more tangibly manipulate and quantify. If a person's attention is consumed by benign or superfluous objects and pursuits, the brain can detach from real events that feel troubling or threatening.

If your parents frequently erupted into volatile arguments when you were a child, or your caregivers were often but unpredictably moody and reactive, you might have employed hyperfocus as a way to avoid potential triggers or easefully navigate extraordinarily uncomfortable situations. Over time, this coping mechanism may have become a habit that influences what people perceive to be your personality (for example, "She is an anxious person."). In reality, you may not be an anxious person at your core. You simply may be a person who, at a very young age, used hyperfocus or hypervigilance to distract yourself from the pain of an abusive household. An adult whose hyperfocus results in behavior that might be perceived by others as snarky, short-tempered, intolerant, stressed, and so on fundamentally may be patient, kind, and warm. While our tools for survival tend to become intertwined with our personality, they are *not* our personality. Our personality is what remains when we strip away coping mechanisms and fear.

Deep down inside, we know that a true sense of safety is rooted in the belief that we are resilient and can manage all that does or doesn't happen to us and around us. We understand that real control means mellowing hypervigilance and navigating the world with trust and ease. But if when you were a child, your nervous system was programmed to always be on high alert and stress signals were constantly firing, you may as an adult have a hard time shaking anxiety—and chronic anxiety no doubt leads to the experience of adrenal fatigue and burnout. Those of us who did not feel safe as children may still feel like we are never really able to relax or enjoy where we are or what we are doing. We may always be waiting for the other shoe to drop, or trying to manipulate the many variables we think will guarantee us a sense of safety. We may even prevent ourselves from entering new situations or relationships where we anticipate not being able to control every variable related to the experience. This level of anxiety may create a life that feels restrictive, limited, and claustrophobic in our extreme efforts to feel safe. In reality, nothing dampens resilience more than living in a bubble or maintaining the status quo because we do not trust our fortitude, intuition, or adaptability.

In what ways are you equipped to self-soothe when you enter a mode of hypervigilance? How can you reassure yourself in ways that are calming? You can:

- Check your surroundings and take mental notes of actual versus perceived dangers and threats.

- Connect with touchstones that help you feel safe. This may mean digging your toes into the dirt, peering up at the sky, or glancing at the corners of a room. Notice how the world holds you.

- Bring your focused attention to the current experience of your body. How does the fabric of your shirt feel against your skin? What bodily sensations do your goose bumps cause? Is any part of you itchy? Which parts feel relaxed?

- Ask family, friends, and/or a therapist for help when you are feeling scared or alone.

- Imagine a place or person that brings calm and peace to your heart.

- Cultivate a soothing internal dialogue and speak to yourself the way you would speak to a scared child. Kind and simple words work best for me.

- Take a few deep and steady breaths.

All of these are beautiful ways to activate your parasympathetic nervous system and curb the fight, flight, freeze, or fawn instinct. Let's explore some other ways that have really helped support me on my own path.

DROP PERFECTIONISM

For me, perfectionism and hypervigilance are intertwined. To unpack one, I have to unpack the other. When one is present, the other is at work. To the best of your ability, allow yourself to be imperfect by reminding yourself that you are safe, loved, and lovable regardless of how you perform in life, what you do or don't do, or what your internal and external worlds look and feel like. Allow *good enough* to be your new standard of excellence, and redefine perfection as simply being in touch with how you are feeling and allowing yourself to move through it.

AVOID AVOIDANCE

Stop avoiding situations where you can't control everything, and practice loving yourself with compassion through new and potentially challenging experiences. I am not suggesting that you blindly and without caution enter situations where very real dangers exist. If you're aware that certain people or places pose a physical, mental, or psychological threat, avoidance may be the wisest choice. But in the case of hypervigilance, the issue is that we normalize manipulating conditions in an effort to ensure our safety, even when no real threat is present. This generalized fear affects every decision and makes it very hard to discern between real and imagined dangers. Even the inability to control conditions or guarantee perfection can be a perceived threat.

As tempting as it may be to try to curate an external world and cultivate an internal one that always feels safe, we cannot learn resilience without putting ourselves in uncomfortable situations. You may not know that you require a sweater if you never feel cold. By doing the things that feel impossible because you've grown accustomed to perfecting every variable relating to your mental and emotional safety, you acquire the skills that allow you to let go even more deeply. For you, the impossible could be getting on a stage to speak, or going to a party where you don't know anybody, or leaving the house without makeup, or going on a blind date, or traveling to a new city, or writing a book, or forgoing a sleeping pill. Whatever your version of impossible is, entertain for a moment the idea that you actually can do that thing and survive. Make room for the possibility that however being outside your comfort zone looks and feels, it is its own kind of perfection because it is authentic and real.

LET GO

If you're feeling ready and brave, choose one area of your life where you would like to let go, loosen the reins, or feel just a little more at ease, and make a plan for how you might support yourself through that experience.

Maybe you want to plan a dinner party for your birthday, but you know that you will obsess so compulsively over every detail that the event will create anxiety. Can you allow yourself to let go of *just one* aspect of this dinner? Maybe it's the food. Can you order pizza or organize a potluck instead of cook? Maybe it's the aesthetics of your home. Can you release the expectation that it needs to be sparkling clean? Maybe it's the conversation. Can you allow your guests to take responsibility for their own experience, and pause the urge to micromanage their interactions or the flow of conversations to ensure that everybody will have a good time?

A close friend of mine has the tendency to overeat all the wrong foods when he's stressed. After prolonged bouts of bingeing, he then does an extremely intensive five-day cleanse that involves restricting calories. I've seen this type of reset be extremely effective for people whose diets and attitudes toward food are otherwise balanced and healthy. But every time my friend fasts, he rebounds and eats even more of the foods he wants most desperately to avoid. I share this to make the point that too much change too quickly can result in even more toxic behavior.

If your goal is to mellow hypervigilance, but you throw yourself into uncomfortable situations without being properly resourced, you may find yourself feeling even more anxious. The body and mind know what they're ready for. In my experience, taking things slowly and gently is a kinder and more effective approach in the long run when it comes to hypervigilance. Therapies such as flooding (via which you "drown" yourself in an experience essentially to become immune to a trigger) may be effective for acute anxieties or phobias. But in the case of hypervigilance, your brain is flooded, and what you require is a mop, some towels, and a change of clothes to restore peace and balance. In other words, you need supportive resources that will allow you to unwind your defenses methodically.

Turn to "Feeling Relaxed" in the workbook.

THERAPEUTIC RECOMMENDATION: NEUROLINGUISTIC PROGRAMMING

Neurolinguistic programming (NLP) was developed in the 1970s and is commonly used to treat a wide range of issues, from anxiety and phobias to post-traumatic stress disorder and depression. Its goal is to reprogram the subconscious mind to overcome dysfunctional programming. In order to transmute beliefs that are preventing you from living your optimum life, it's necessary to know what you actually believe.

One NLP technique aimed at helping people discover hidden beliefs is to have them write down all of the feelings and associations related to a specific source of stress. Let's use math as an example. If math is a source of stress for you, was there a time when you miscalculated your budget and then your credit card was denied in public? Does the memory of a poor SAT math score still make you feel inadequate? Do you stress over filing your taxes because you made an innocent but costly mistake in the past? Over time, impactful experiences like these may lead to a negative belief about numbers or yourself in relation to numbers. Once a hidden belief is discovered, it can be addressed. Since memories are stored in the mind as pictures, sounds, and feelings, NLP techniques can change the representations of those memories and upgrade the emotions tied to them, along with your subsequent behavior.

Another technique used by NLP therapists is anchoring. Anchoring consists of turning sensory experiences into triggers for a desired emotional state or frame of mind. The anchor can be something physical (such as squeezing your thumb and index finger together) or verbal (a word that you associate with a positive emotion). The goal is to be equipped to immediately access the desired emotional or mental state through an anchor. Eventually, negative emotions can be replaced by positive ones by consistently utilizing learned triggers. For example, if every time I squeeze my thumb and index finger together, I visualize a glistening lake and focus on feelings of peacefulness and bliss, the simple act of touching my two fingers together may automatically trigger these emotions over time.[7]

Another very effective NLP technique is called a pattern interrupt. A pattern is any sort of process that leads to a certain outcome. It can be a habit, a ritual, or even an unconscious reaction to an event. Many patterns in our lives work well for us. You may arrange each night before bedtime for your coffee to brew automatically in the morning, so it's ready when your alarm goes off. Or maybe every morning, you carve out ten minutes for meditation before getting out of bed.

Let's imagine you've gotten into the habit of eating a pint of ice cream every night after dinner. Using a pattern interrupt, you might choose to store your ice cream in a harder-to-reach section of your freezer, or to not put it in your shopping cart the next time you're at the market. Another way to use pattern interrupts is to consciously alter your reaction to a triggering situation. If you usually get angry with a friend or family member when a particular topic arises, you can thoughtfully decide to interrupt that pattern simply by taking a deep breath and counting to ten before you respond. Instead of reacting automatically, you pause—which may enable you to release tension, recognize your pattern, and change course.

Turn to "Pattern Interrupt" in the workbook.

Have you ever felt super cranky or been immersed in dark thoughts, when suddenly you hear a song that almost instantly shifts your mood? It's incredible how impactful pattern interrupts can be, especially when we are whirling in thoughts and emotions that suck us in like a tornado. When I'm trapped in a vicious thought loop or ruminating excessively over past or future events, I make a conscious effort to shift gears both physically and mentally. My favorite pattern interrupt is a mini dance party in my bedroom (eighties music is my jam). Even just turning on a song that I can sing along to tends to break the cycle. From time to time, I interrupt my thoughts and ultimately my mood by watching ten minutes of stand-up comedy, listening to a podcast, or calling a friend. As long as the pattern interrupt doesn't foster another unhealthy habit (binge eating, drinking, drug use, or the like), it doesn't really matter what you do.

The more frequently you interrupt whatever negative state you are in, the more likely that your brain will come to understand that you won't allow it to live perpetually in a toxic and harmful space. This sentiment does not contradict allowing yourself to feel your feelings. With pattern interrupt, I'm referring to situations where you are consciously attempting to shift your mindset because you no longer want to dwell on negativity but are having trouble shifting gears. Our thoughts affect our mood, which affects our behavior, and at any time, we can question and reframe our thoughts. By doing so, we pave the way for both healthier choices and a personality that reflects our true nature.

INTERRUPTING PATTERNS IN REAL TIME

When I was taking singing lessons, my voice coach would command me to do all kinds of bizarre and spontaneous things with my body when I was overthinking a song. "Flap your arms!" he would shout. "Stand on one foot and rub your belly counterclockwise!" While attempting to use my body in new and unexpected ways, I couldn't obsess over how my voice sounded. You can play some version of this game with yourself by moving in ways that demand enough attention to break or at least soften your troubling thought patterns. Surprising yourself with what may feel like silly or outrageous choreography also may lighten the mood and invite moments of levity.

Another form of interruption is to engage in mental challenges. If your thoughts grow painfully redundant, try doing a crossword or number puzzle. Some of the same types of brain exercises that help with avoiding dementia, such as learning an unfamiliar language or practicing a musical instrument, also might be ideal pattern interrupts.[8] You don't have to take all day to do these things; even ten minutes of introducing new material to your brain can be beneficial. Memory games also require a lot of focus and may help extract you from repetitive or unhelpful thoughts.

If you are unable to stop and reset, or aren't in a position to hop like a kangaroo while scratching your head, listening to a podcast, an audiobook, or music may invite you into a new narrative. I subscribe to multiple podcasts, have dozens of Audible books in my digital library, and toggle between several Spotify and Pandora stations. Depending on my mood and the events of the day, I may require content to uplift and inspire me, warm my heart, or calm my adrenals. Whatever it is that my body and mind are craving is what I tune in to at any given moment. Accessing rhythms and storylines outside my own is consistently an effective way for me to recalibrate. Taking a walk while listening to something is a particularly powerful combination. You also may choose to be still and partake in a guided meditation using an app. The beauty of a guided meditation versus pure silence is that it allows us to hook into an external voice and effortlessly receive its guidance. Alternatively, you may find that creating space for silence is the antidote to a busy mind.

Creativity is another powerful way to bring us into a storyline that is less cluttered with anxiety and attempts to control. When I express myself through art, I release expectations of what should be and enter a state of presence that prioritizes how I feel. Art may look like any number of things: dancing or any other kind of physical movement, writing, painting, making music, or singing. It also may look like turning on a song and improvising with movement in your bedroom. You can make art of your body simply by following its lead and not questioning how it wants to move. Transitioning from the cerebral to the more expansive, curious parts of ourselves may have the power to calm or inspire us in ways that diminish fear.

RELEASING TENSION AND TRAUMA

When the body experiences trauma, its default stress patterns, which are designed to protect us, kick into action. The body produces energy and then looks for an escape. We tense up—often in the jaw, shoulders, stomach, or back—which can cause physical pain as well as affect our emotions and resulting behavior. One natural outlet is the automatic response of shaking, which resets the nervous system. Anecdotal evidence suggests that women who naturally shake after childbirth as part of the trauma response heal faster. After birthing my own children without drugs, I shook quite dramatically, and it turns out that animals in nature do this all the time to reset their nervous systems.

But what happens if the body doesn't produce this response automatically? The therapeutic modality of shaking, in basic terms, is not unlike the childhood Hokey Pokey dance, in which the participants consciously shake their feet, legs, hands, arms, and so on. Of course, no music is necessary for you to shake; you can simply stop and do so wherever you are.

Tension & Trauma Releasing Exercises (TRE) is another method of helping the body metabolize stress and release muscular patterns of tension and trauma. Through the activation of an innate reflex mechanism of shaking or vibrating, tension in the muscles is released, and the body is restored to a state of calm. There are ample books and videos available to help guide you through both the exercises themselves and the context for why these exercises are effective.[9]

RAPID TRANSFORMATIONAL THERAPY

Developed by therapist and author Marisa Peer, Rapid Transformational Therapy (RTT) combines elements of hypnotherapy, cognitive behavioral therapy, neurolinguistic programming, and psychotherapy to support people in achieving their personal goals. It emphasizes the use of hypnotic regression, based on the theory that the reason for problematic issues can be reduced to one of three causes: the feeling of being not enough, the feeling of being different, or wanting something that is unattainable. One main claim, as the name suggests, is that people can attain transformation quickly rather than over an extended period of time.

RTT practitioners regress their clients by using hypnotherapy, identifying the root cause of their issue, and providing positive affirmations and reframing to help heal toxic core beliefs and fears. The client then receives a recording of visualizations and affirmations deriving from their session, and they listen to it for three weeks following that session.[10] My experience with RTT was very positive, although for extremely severe trauma-based issues, I recommend having additional therapeutic support to help process memories that may surface while under hypnosis. It is a hard-and-fast deep dive, so having worked with a trauma specialist beforehand and speaking to a therapist the day after my session provided valuable support. The goal is to connect with the deepest part of the psyche without disassociating or disconnecting from the current reality after emerging from hypnosis.

If a trauma specialist is not affordable or available to you, consider practicing somatic work (explored further in chapter 6) before engaging in hypnotherapy. This will help ground you in your present-day life before and after sessions. Also consider in advance who you would call should you require emotional support of any degree. This may be a friend or family member, but in the case of a psychotic break, disassociation, extreme agitation or anxiety, or suicidal thoughts, please immediately seek professional help.

TAI CHI

When I was researching movement-based practices that might help curb perfectionism along with hypervigilance, tai chi made the top of my list. In this mind-body practice that began as a martial art in China, people move fluidly through a series of poses while breathing deeply and tuning in to their bodily sensations. The movements tend to be circular and encourage the body to remain in a state of relaxation.

Extreme perfectionism may lead to paralysis, whereby fear of making a mistake or excessive preemptive editing halts action. What I love about tai chi is that it encourages constant movement, which curbs the compulsion to overthink. And whereas some forms of more extreme exercise spike cortisol and adrenaline, which the body then interprets as stress, tai chi does not involve any level of bodily tension and supports calm.

While it is natural to lean on perfectionism and hypervigilance in an effort to maintain a false sense of control, we are truly safest when we let go. By experimenting with some of the therapeutic modalities described in this chapter, you may feel more equipped to soften any potential resistance to surrender. Nothing is linear or perfect, especially the journey of healing and the process of becoming more integrated. Slowly, gently, and with as much self-love as you can muster, celebrate your humanity by embracing every facet of it with as little judgment as possible.

— CHAPTER SUMMARY —

Perfectionism is a default setting for many of us who don't possess the skills to self-soothe or the freedom to operate authentically in the world. Unfortunately, perfectionism breeds other dysfunctional behaviors and inhibits us from expressing ourselves freely. By understanding why perfectionism isn't a helpful orientation and allowing ourselves to experience our full humanity, we liberate not only ourselves but those around us. A variety of beautiful therapies and practices have been designed to help ease the burden of perfectionism, so that we can, without apology, be who we really are and take ownership of all that is meant to be ours.

CHAPTER 4

REDEFINING YOUR SELF-CONCEPT

We all want to feel like a part of something (or many things): our culture, family, friend groups, natural environments, and team of work colleagues, to name a few. We want to feel accepted, chosen, and valued by these groups. We want to feel not only important but essential. We desire the confirmation that we are irreplaceable. Often, we look to others to reinforce our worth and validate our contributions. We look outside ourselves to ensure that we are safe in our communities, neighborhoods, and families. (In this context, I am equating safety with the feeling of having a secure place.)

But what would happen if you were to get fired from the job that has been the source of so much of your pride? What would happen if your lover or other romantic partner were to leave you for someone you deem to be more attractive, successful, or riveting than you? How would you be affected if you weren't invited to a certain birthday party, wedding, or night out with friends? What if you don't get nominated for the position you've been coveting, or if the friend you've been waiting to hear back from forgets to call you, or the date that made you believe you could love again were to turn out to be a dead end?

What if we were to take an honest look around and inside us and realize that many of the structures we've created for ourselves and that others have created for us don't actually resonate with our deepest truth? What if the labels and categories we've been assigned have never felt encompassing? What if the ways in which we define ourselves create a sense of limitation or suffocation, because we are bigger and broader than *any* definition? What if the words that most accurately and precisely describe us still put us in a box that we have no business being in?

Starting very early on in our lives, we receive feedback about what makes us valuable and to whom. Over time, this feedback heavily contributes to our self-concept, and we often carry that feedback into adulthood without questioning it. Sometimes it is overt, as in, "Good girl!" or "That was very bad!" At other times, feedback comes in the form of a gesture, facial expression, or lengthy pause. Feedback can manifest as a reward or punishment in response to certain appearances or behaviors. Screaming, praise, violence, silence, and a new toy are all forms of feedback.

From moment to moment, children look to the adults around them to approve or disapprove of their behavior. When they aren't looking, approval or disapproval descends upon them anyway. If a child draws a lovely picture of a rainbow, they might receive the response "Good job!" from a parent. If they throw their food on the floor or bite a sibling, they might hear, "Bad girl!" Grown-ups might clap for a child who sings the ABCs and frown at a child who spills a cup of milk. They might hug a child who walks without falling but shake their head in disappointment when that same child wets the bed. If a child expresses sadness, anger, or other emotions in ways that overwhelm, distract, fatigue, or annoy a caregiver, they might be sent to their room. That same child might receive a hug if they give their favorite teddy bear to a younger sibling.

As children, we learn from every interaction what is acceptable and what is not, what is beautiful and what is ugly, and what makes those around us happy or unhappy. We learn what makes them cry, what makes them rage, what disappoints them, and what leads to isolation, a spanking, punishing words, or a scowl. We learn what makes the adults in our lives stop crying, what makes them stop raging, what makes them proud of us, and what secures a hug, a treat, a smile, or applause. From a very young age, we learn how to survive.

When we are young and vulnerable, we instinctively associate the feedback of adults with who we fundamentally are and what we are worth. "You're a bad girl!" is a very obvious identity to absorb, but children don't require that level of specificity and clarity of language to come to that very same conclusion on their own. If a parent constantly sighs and rolls their eyes when a child can't figure out a math problem, the child's conclusion may not be "I am struggling with this math problem," or even "I am bad at math," it may very well be "I am bad." If a teacher cheers every time a child draws a realistic-looking sunflower, the child's conclusion may not be "I am good at drawing sunflowers," but rather, "I am good." Because children tend to generalize about *everything*, they all too often may make assumptions about their worth based on fleeting moments in which they please or disappoint authority figures. These moments are often *action-based*, and of course, the response of authority figures is loaded, because they almost always are projecting their subjective version of good or bad, success or failure onto the child, based on their own childhood experiences and biases.

Parents may raise their own children the way they were raised, instilling the values they absorbed from the authority figures in their own lives. Or they may war against the values that were upheld in their childhood and attempt to offer the opposite to their offspring. Either way, more often than not, we are not even clear about what the values we absorbed are, what we really stand for, what genuinely creates self-esteem, or what we believe about ourselves and how we've been trained to behave. Because we were taught specific ways of being and doing at such a young age, we are rarely even aware of how the feedback of others influenced and shaped who we are today.

Just as some of us have internalized the value systems, priorities, triggers, and pleasures of our caregivers and are living in an unconscious paradigm created by their moment-to-moment feedback, others have consciously rejected everything about the people who influenced them early on. If you became resentful of your early childhood caregivers and/or those who guided you through your teenage years, you may want nothing to do with the values you associate with them. Absentee and negligent caregivers also provide feedback by demonstrating a lack of care and presence. If your caregivers were materialistic and you perceived them to be vapid, unable to access deep emotions, or unable to truly see you, you might flee your capitalist life in favor of a humbler existence. If your caregivers pressured you to appear clean and polished, you might choose to not wash your hair regularly or wear fancy clothing. If your caregivers expected you to become a doctor and structured their entire lives to ensure that their dream was your dream, you might become a street artist. You might assume that because a parent didn't make time for you or left you at a young age, you are worthless or not valuable enough to receive sincere attention and love.

Whether you unconsciously mimic what you have learned from caregivers or you consciously defy it, these two approaches are equally dangerous because neither is necessarily authentic. It's possible that you're one of the very rare, lucky people who are able to weed through influences and early childhood experiences and construct an identity based solely on what *they* feel is right for them. Note that I use the word "feel," not "think," because overthinking our identity gets us into trouble. It creates space to justify, rationalize, explain, negotiate, and analyze, none of which generally gives us direct access to our truth. But I believe that the majority of us relate to others and make decisions based on value systems that may not even be ours, because we have internalized or rejected the value systems of others.

Culture is its own parent and also instructs us from before the time we can speak. It teaches us what is attractive, what we should want more or less of, how we should want to spend our time, what we should want to buy, whom we should want to spend time with, and what we should want to do for a living. Culture informs us of what is cool or uncool, acceptable or unacceptable, kind or cruel, elegant or unrefined, desirable or cringe-worthy. It lets us know which words and ideas are current and relevant, and which ones are lame or outdated.

Within each culture (of a religion, city, neighborhood, school, workplace, family, ethnic group, or the like), there are written and unwritten codes regarding manners, ideal philosophies to adhere to, and hierarchies of beauty and success. There also are spoken and unspoken expectations relating to how we should think, feel, behave, and represent ourselves. In reality, we all have been parented not only by individuals but by the laws, trends, fashions, languages, agreements, and assumptions of many different cultures and societies. Every subgroup you are subject to, indirectly privy to, or actively participate in is full of *shoulds*, some of which are boldly dictated and others of which are implied.

When we are young, we often assume that we are more valuable if we do and say the things that please others or conform to our culture(s). This is especially true if our actions and behaviors yield rewards, such as words of adoration and praise, a tangible prize, a boost in our societal rank, or the avoidance of punishment. The design of culture reinforces reward systems even once we grow into adulthood. Because of this, we continue to experience our value based on what we accomplish, create, and project into the world. "Correct" actions, behaviors, and appearances yield positive results, whereas "incorrect" actions, behaviors, and appearances garner negative feedback. In order to feel relevant, loved, and acceptable, we may work very hard to reinforce an identity that validates our sense of worth and secures our place in society.

When people consistently compliment us within the context of a single category, or notice something specific about us with regularity, we may form a concept of our identity that is quite binary and narrow. For example, if a young person hears over and over again that they're beautiful, they may assume that they are beautiful to the exclusion of intelligence. If a young person receives only the feedback that they are a math genius, they might doubt their more creative abilities. Likewise, if we hear other people receive praise that we don't, we might assume that we lack certain qualities or talents.

For instance, if your father is constantly commenting on how athletic your sibling is, you may assume that you're not athletic. If your mother frequently remarks on how talented at singing a friend of yours is, you may assume that your voice isn't as powerful. Comparisons are sometimes bluntly expressed by the people around us: "Your brother is so much smarter than you are." "The neighbor kid has such a better attitude than you. I wish you were more like him." But comparisons also can be implicit, and in our minds, we may create a contrast or divide that doesn't really exist.

If a person we respect, trust, love, or rely on consistently notices something positive about us, we may form an identity around what they are noticing. If they *don't* notice attributes or talents that we might objectively value, those parts of us may dim over time. Parents, caregivers, mentors, teachers, and culture constantly bombard us with versions of feedback that we interpret as praise or disapproval, and then we make conscious or subconscious assumptions about our value based on the collective feedback. We may come to believe that we are more valuable when we are doing or saying the things that receive praise, and less valuable when what we are doing or saying receives negative attention or no attention at all. Negative feedback may even lead to the false conclusion that who we are and how we express ourselves aren't worthy of love.

CORE VALUE VERSUS CREATED VALUES

It is important to differentiate between our core value as individuals and the personal value systems we create. Core value is the value inherent in each human being, and it does not change over time. At birth, we are 100 percent lovable and possess 100 percent of our value. But through culture and other influences, we may come to believe that our core value can shift and is dependent on a multitude of variables, ranging from how we look, what we wear, and what our job title is to who we are dating or married to, how many assets we have, how much money we make, how people perceive us, what we've accomplished, and so on. This is false.

As I said, our core value does not and cannot change over time. It is constant, unconditional, and not dependent on any external factors. It's also not dependent on our internal experience of ourselves, how we perceive ourselves, how other people respond to us, our mood, how we're feeling, or what we're thinking. We are 100 percent valuable at all times, because we are human beings worthy of love. There are no contingencies to our core value, and nothing can threaten it or take it away. We always possess 100 percent of our core value just by existing and being ourselves.

Our value systems are the most fundamental things we believe about ourselves and the world, and as I said, these beliefs are shaped largely by external influences, many of which we may not even be aware of. Because of this, it is important to question the values we've inherited and to actively contemplate what we truly and authentically value apart from indoctrination and feedback. How do you want to experience yourself and others in the world? What about yourself are you truly most proud of? What would you do or not do if you were to receive no feedback at all?

Let's for a moment contemplate a fictional person named Fiona. Fiona might think she values wealth, because she is part of a family that rewards material gain. These rewards may be delivered as words of affirmation, demonstrations of love or respect, attention, or tangible gifts. Because Fiona thinks she values wealth, she may pursue only jobs and opportunities that will earn a certain amount of money. By securing a specific income, she believes she also will secure whatever experiences she associates with financial success, such as familial support and a sense of emotional or material safety. But when she breaks down the concept of wealth and what it means to her, she may find that what she values is not wealth at all. It may be attention or love. It may be the feeling of validation or approval. It may be respect from high-achieving individuals.

Practically speaking, if you value wealth, it may be because financial resources provide access to extraordinary experiences, such as travel, or liberate you from a career path that feels predictable or imprisoning, or allow you ownership of more of your time. Perhaps material success contributes to a self-concept that includes competence, intelligence, power, and so on. If you are part of a family that values athleticism, you may pride yourself on being a champion soccer player. But do you truly love soccer? Maybe you do. But what would happen if you were to stop playing soccer and start painting or writing? How do you think your family might react? How might your decision to stray from your talent affect your self-concept? What might you gain or lose by redirecting your attention?

Turn to "Understanding Your Core Values" and "Identifying Your Positive Characteristics" in the workbook.

Furthermore, labels and categories don't account for the complexity of any human being, and they often reinforce a self-concept that is outdated or incomplete. In some cases, our descriptors may be totally inaccurate, especially if they were wrongly or prematurely assigned by caregivers, coworkers, and friends who were limited in their ability to see and know more of us. Or it's possible that the most common ways others define us may ring true but overshadow different qualities that we feel are equally or more important. When we and others reinforce an identity over and over again, the neuropathways associated with it grow stronger. In other words, our thoughts solidify into a concept of who we are that registers in our brains as true. And what we believe about ourselves and how we assume others perceive us affect our actions, choices, and willingness to take risks in the world. But at any point in our lives, we have the right to question and reshape the self-concept that formed as a consequence of the words that were chosen or not chosen to define us at every stage of our evolution.

Turn to "The What Does That Mean? Game" and "Identifying What You Truly Value about Yourself" in the workbook.

It's possible that the qualities people noticed and loved most about you when you were a child and that you once celebrated yourself don't feel relevant to your current adult life. If that is the case, it may be that core aspects of your being have fallen away or been drowned out over time by culture, responsibilities, struggles with managing time, expectations you've created for yourself, or values that you adopted from others but that aren't really your own. Consider how you can practically invite those parts of yourself to flourish once again. It may be as simple as taking out a pen and some paper and writing a poem, or as complicated as realizing that a job or relationship doesn't bring out the best in you and a big change is needed. Don't panic. Breathe. There is plenty of time to revisit the parts of your life that aren't working. For now, focus on understanding what you truly value.

What you value in yourself may be different from what you value in others. There may be crossover, but you also may benefit from and enjoy friends who have cultivated different interests and values. Those people may bring something unique to your life that might not be organic to your instinctive way of operating, thinking, or experiencing the world. For instance, my husband is very logical and tends to think about and solve problems in a linear, black-and-white fashion. While this sometimes drives me crazy, his approach also inspires me to question my relationship to a problem and has the potential to add valuable insights. His perspective, his skills, and what he chooses to focus on widen my lens, and my opinion is ultimately strengthened or modified as a consequence.

What you value in yourself may also change over time, as may the qualities and traits you prioritize. During one phase of my life, I might have been most proud of my capacity to listen to others, and during another phase, my bravery might triumph as a primary source of pride. At age twenty, you might lead with resilience or originality, and in your thirties, you might prioritize authenticity or the willingness to act on ideas. In your forties, you might applaud emotional stability, and in your fifties, you might celebrate your ability to connect deeply with friends. At one stage of life, you might desire to be romantically involved with men, and at another stage, you might prefer a female lover. One year, I might identify most consistently with my kindness, and another year, rely more on my outspokenness. In the same way that our lives are not static, what we place our attention on and the parts of ourselves that feel most vibrant and activated can shift over time.

"I AM" VERSUS "I FEEL"

Now let's take a look at the parts of ourselves that we would like to modify or that don't support our highest level of well-being. I've wrestled with plenty of these. Here is a short list of adjectives that we can use and play with for the purpose of this exercise:

Insecure
Anxious
Snarky
Compulsive
Controlling

Step one in modifying our self-concept when it comes to the parts of ourselves that we tend to judge or that we deem harmful is to separate what we feel and experience from who we are. We are not, at our core, any of the things that we struggle with. We are human, so our experience on this planet will no doubt represent and encompass the totality of the human experience. That will sometimes feel and look like joy, and other times will feel and look like grief, rage, or fear. It's okay and important to experience all of what it is to be human, but we don't have to define ourselves by these experiences. In other words, I am not insecure; I am a person who is feeling insecure. I am not anxious; I am a person who is struggling with anxiety. I am not snarky; I am a person who is overwhelmed, fatigued, anxious, and has adrenal burnout. I am not compulsive; I am grappling with fear. I am not controlling; I have trouble letting go, because in the past, when I did, I experienced pain.

Let's try deep-diving a bit into the first identifying word: "insecure." You may experience moments of insecurity, and they may feel overwhelmingly pervasive, but are you insecure 100 percent of the time? Is there ever a flash of confidence, self-knowledge, or pride? If you can't readily recall a time when you felt truly secure, was there a time when the tension and anxiety associated with insecurity were a bit mellower than usual? Are there any circumstances under which your feelings are, at the bare minimum, neutral? What we're doing here is trying to diffuse the belief that you *are* insecure by pointing out moments, even seconds, when that was not true. You are not what you experience, and what you experience shifts from moment to moment and day to day.

We grow accustomed to telling ourselves and others that we *are* certain things—funny, smart, or depressed, for instance. When we stop labeling ourselves, we can begin to identify the context within which a particular brand of experience occurs most frequently. If a set of emotions or way of being is chronic, break down the exact nature of the experience you are having, what it *feels* like in your body, and how it manifests visually.

Here is an example: "I feel insecure when X occurs or when I am in the presence of Y." State the exact type of incident, event, or environment that triggers your experience of insecurity, or the person with whom you feel most insecure. It could be twelve different instances in a day. It doesn't matter. We want to start separating our experiences from our concept of self. Other examples: "I feel insecure when my boyfriend glances at another woman." "I feel insecure when another woman in the room is prettier than I am." "I feel insecure when the person I'm having a meeting with has achieved more than I have in our professional field."

When you stop calling yourself names, your self-concept will invite you to be human without feeling guilty about your human experience or defaulting to self-judgment.

Turn to "Separating Experience from Identity"
and "Breaking It Down" in the workbook.

CORE IDENTITY VERSUS FLUID IDENTITY

Most of us are familiar with the concept of nature versus nurture. Nature is what we were born with, and nurture involves the many variables that influence and shape our personality, how we think, our perspectives, our skills, and even our self-perception. I conceptualize this distinction as core identity versus fluid identity. "Core identity" refers to the parts of us that really can't change, whereas "fluid identity" refers to the parts of us that can grow and evolve over time. Examples of core identity include physical attributes such as eye color and height, inherent personality traits, and extraordinary talents or gifts.

Our core identity is what we inherited—in essence, what our DNA assigned to us. Our fluid identity is malleable and may shift depending on our community, our cultural influences, our exposure, the goals we establish, and so on. It also may include interests, which sometimes but not always are an extension of our core talents.

More often than we should, many of us believe that our core identity is the same as our fluid identity. Because historically we might not have had access to certain opportunities or met the ideal mentors or teachers to guide us on our path, it can be hard to know what makes us feel fully alive and most authentically ourselves in the present. If we've never been encouraged to or had a chance to become skilled at something, chances are we won't be! Very few people possess the ability to teach themselves how to play the music of Beethoven, and even those who do would need access to a piano. In addition to what might have been lacking in the past, many of us have been inundated by feedback that contradicts our true nature and confuses the internal compass that directs our sense of knowing. Between what we were deprived of and the self-concept we unconsciously internalized, it is no wonder that as adults, we often feel lonely in our own company. In order for us to relish our relationship with ourselves, our identity must be rooted in the unapologetic truth of who we actually are.

When we were children, subtle or indirect messages from people in positions of authority also may have directed our energy and efforts. I was raised in a family where my mother didn't value math. Not only did she find it boring, but she frequently got flustered when I asked her for help with my math homework. "I'm just not good at math!" she would declare, exasperated. Based on how I watched my mother relate to numbers, I assumed that if I didn't immediately understand a math problem, *I* wasn't good at math. My mother valued and worked to master language, so that's where my own energy was directed. Would I have *loved* algebra if my mother had spent every afternoon solving mathematical equations on a whiteboard in our living room? Possibly—or maybe I would have despised it. The point is that I'm not really sure what my self-governed relationship with math is, because at a very early age, I watched the woman responsible for my survival cringe at numbers.

There may be things you are not currently doing because at one point you decided it was not "you" to do them, because you were made fun of for doing them, or because you lacked the exposure that would put them on your radar. Maybe certain activities or pursuits didn't garner feedback that made you feel positive about yourself and your choices. There also may be things you unconsciously continue to do or ways in which you habitually behave because at one point you were rewarded for particular actions and behaviors. This type of feedback loop infiltrates even the lives of adults as we sniff out what our romantic partners, bosses, family members, friends, and communities want and expect of us.

Ideally, children form an identity based on authenticity and continue to refine and reexamine this identity in a holistic way over time. Our own internal compass guides us toward or away from certain ways of thinking, being, and experiencing the world. Instead, most of us established a baseline identity as children that was fear-based and rooted in the instinct to survive, so the ways in which we adjusted our identity over time were fundamentally skewed.

Neuroscientist and Stanford University School of Medicine associate professor Andrew Huberman talks a lot about the role of the neurotransmitter dopamine in motivating and focusing people to pursue more of something. In a very famous experiment conducted at Stanford, children in preschool and kindergarten who innately loved to draw pictures and did so of their own accord began to receive rewards for their drawings. When the children stopped receiving rewards for their artwork, their natural impulse to draw plummeted.[11]

Huberman's explanation for this is that dopamine peaks when we receive a reward but plummets below its baseline level afterward. Because of this, the mind believes over time that the motivation for achieving a goal is the reward, versus pure enjoyment of the process. When we routinely receive a reward after we complete an activity, over time we are cut off from higher levels of dopamine while actively engaged in the endeavor, which gradually lessens the pleasure associated with engagement. When our reward system is generated from within, our pursuit of something meaningful is sustainable and not reliant on external variables or reinforcement.

Psychologist Carol Dweck builds upon this data with the theory that the reward we all should be striving for is the satisfaction and pleasure associated with effort versus the reward that follows completion. She calls this the growth mindset, which values effort and the tension of striving as the end goal.[12]

Consider the application of these principles to your own life. How willing and able are you to support your own internally generated reward system? Can you agree to the effort and tension inherent in striving without banking on an end result? What kind of internal dialogue will best support you as you grow and evolve as your authentic self? What kind of pleasure can you derive from the challenge of becoming the truest version of you? I imagine that many of us will never fully arrive at a version of ourselves that feels satisfying and complete at all times. The more comfortable we become with the growth mindset in relation to tasks, projects, and goals, the more likely we may be to apply this mindset to the evolution of our souls.

Turn to "Encouraging a Growth Mindset" in the workbook.

EXTERNAL EVENTS DO NOT DEFINE YOU

While certain events may seem to demand a specific set of reactions and feelings, we always possess the power to interpret them as we choose to. Our concept of self can be completely autonomous, and yet we often experience who we are based on what does or does not happen to or for us. And quite often, we attach judgment to events that are outside of our control. After one of my friends, a very gifted kindergarten teacher, communicated to her employer that certain aspects of the school's culture were uncomfortable for her, she was asked not to return the following year. Truthfully, she was completely fed up with the school and didn't have any real desire to return, but she instantly felt disposable when she was asked to leave.

When she called me with the news, she said that she felt like a loser because they didn't want her back. "I get it," I told her. "It was a breakup, and you wanted to be the one to call it off on your chosen timeline. But what matters is that this school isn't the right match for you, and now you're being forced to move on and create or find something new." But however much we dissected the culture of the school and deemed it dysfunctional, my friend kept referring to herself as a failure. Despite her yearning to be part of a professional community that welcomed feedback and perhaps even healthy pushback, the fact that she hadn't been asked back made her feel unwanted and therefore unworthy. Even though my friend had been extremely unhappy in her job and wanted to leave, being let go threatened her sense of self. In reality, this event was unrelated to her job performance and potential, but even more importantly, it was not a reflection of her fundamental being. It simply revealed that she wasn't the right match for one particular school. She is an excellent teacher who was enmeshed in a work culture that wasn't compatible with her personality. And yet my friend could not separate the event of not being asked back from her self-concept, and she insisted on feeling undesirable.

Compare this reaction to that of my husband, in a conversation we had before we were married. Early on in our relationship, it became clear that he had been the one to end basically every romantic involvement before me. I scrounged and probed for an exception until a story finally surfaced involving a girl he had dated twice. Round one, he ended the relationship. Round two, she ended it. "That must have hurt," I said, eager to secure some semblance of vulnerability from him. "Not really," he said. "She was the one missing out by not being with me. I felt kind of bad for her, because the guy she ended up marrying was really self-involved."

My husband's perspective blew my mind. The one time a boyfriend had broken up with me, it took me years to fully regain my sense of self. A feeling of rejection swallowed me alive, and my conclusion, despite tons of evidence to the contrary, was that I was not good enough for him. My husband's conclusion after his breakup was that the other person was losing something really valuable (him), and he felt sorry for her. In his mind, it was her loss. But in the case of my friend who got fired, her conclusion was that she wasn't valuable.

Shaming and judging ourselves and others are distractions from true introspection as well as deeper feelings. They limit our compassion and do not allow us to see or love ourselves with full integrity. They minimize our capacity to feel free and shrink the ability of those around us to feel unencumbered. Judgment is an indicator that deeper feelings of unworthiness and doubts regarding our ability to be loved are lurking beneath the surface.

BE WHO YOU WANT TO BE IN THE WORLD

We all define success differently, and every person has a right to determine the terms, parameters, and measures of their own success. I currently consider my life to be a success if I am making an active effort to be as authentic and kind as possible. That's it. Do I have measurable goals? Yes. But whether I accomplish these goals or not does not define whether I am a successful human being living a successful life. Practically speaking, what prevents us from being as successful as we want to or can be? What gets in the way of our ability to fulfill our vast potential? Here's my short list:

Perfectionism
The desire to please others and/or feel accepted
Doubt regarding our chosen path
The fear that we could do it wrong/the fear of failure
The fear of losing something
The fear of gaining something
The fear of being seen
The fear of judgment

What is it that you're afraid of having *less* of? Consider some of these possibilities: privacy, opportunities to isolate, knowledge of what you're actually capable of versus what you hope to be capable of, the ability to live in your head versus having to take action, the ability to dream versus experiencing reality, the armor you employ to shield yourself from exposing your true self, your current lifestyle, financial security, and/or time. Are you afraid of upsetting the status quo of certain relationships? Do you fear that people may become jealous of you, that you may outshine them, or that you will have less time for those you love?

What is it that you're afraid of having *more* of? Consider some of these possibilities: responsibility, pressure, witnesses to the job you are doing or the life you are living, and/or exposure. Are you afraid of having too much on your plate? Do you fear the abundance you might receive? Might that abundance contradict deeper beliefs about your identity that are intertwined with shame or a sense of unworthiness? Do you prefer to remain comfortable rather than stretch outside your comfort zone?

Notice how frequently fear factors into your unwillingness to expose yourself, take risks, and step into your power. According to social worker, researcher, and author Brené Brown, it is not fear that keeps people from being courageous leaders; it is the armor that shields them from vulnerability. While Brown's research focuses on individuals in a position of leadership, consider the application of her research findings to your own life. We are all called to be bold, courageous leaders in some capacity, even if only in our family units or our own hearts. So, what is the armor you personally employ to keep you from being brave?

Another barrier to being who we desire to be in the world (which starts with an internal experience) is being too hard on ourselves. Do any of these thoughts feel familiar?

I'm not enough.
I'm too much.
I'm still in the same place after all these years.
I'm not evolving fast enough.
So-and-so has accomplished way more than I have.
My contribution is so tiny.

The mentality of not doing or being enough (or being too much!) crushes our potential to grow internally and to change the world. Change doesn't need to be profound to be monumental, nor does it have to be recognized by many to be valuable. The experience you have of yourself in quiet, unseen moments determines what you will project into the world and how you will create. And what you have to offer is unique and irreplaceable, because you yourself have those things, regardless of where you are in your evolution.

AUTHENTIC CREATION VERSUS REACTIVITY

When I was fourteen, I had debilitating ulcers in both my large and small intestines as well as my stomach. Repressed trauma and habituated voicelessness raged within my body and literally made me ill. At the time, I was attending a highly competitive high school that was all-consuming and left little time to decompress, much less heal. Day after day, I imagined myself in a world reminiscent of a time when there were no cars, there was no rush, and people wrote poetry at night by candlelight. Of course, my fictionalized imaginings were highly idealized and a blend of multiple eras from which I plucked utopian highlights, but these fantasies were messages to my body and soul. They provided useful information about what I was wanting more or less of and where I was wanting to be. In my imagination, I always positioned myself outdoors or in a cozy, dimly lit indoor space. I was never competing with anyone or trying to prove my intellect or worth. I had ample time to process my surroundings. Stimulation was tempered by the absence of electronics and speediness, and there was a spaciousness that allowed for an abundance of creativity.

I did not know how or where I could have the experience I was craving, so my first intuitive step was to consciously break down the components of what I desired. My short list went something like this: the ability to spend more time in nature, the absence of academic pressure and competition, and more time to read and write poetry. I surmised that the foundational components of my healing would secure freedom from stress and space to realign myself with what felt real and true for me.

One evening, I came to my mother and stepfather with this intense ache in my heart for something I could not even name and a life that did not even seem possible. All I had ever known was setting an alarm for a time before I was ready to be awake, driving in incredible traffic to get to school, sitting in classrooms for the majority of the day, and returning home to piles of homework.

"My body wants something different," I told my mother and her husband. "It *needs* something different."

When I described my experience of sitting beneath fluorescent lights while reeling in pain, my stepfather suggested homeschooling. While homeschooling is now a widely accepted and legitimate option for many kinds of people, in the nineties and in my particular social circle, it was unheard of. When my stepfather described the nature of homeschooling and the profound level of flexibility it offered, I instinctively knew it was the right choice for me. This unorthodox way of learning would allow my creativity to flourish and dim the cerebral, fearful part of my brain. Within a couple of months, I was unenrolled from traditional school and learning at home.

Many people are born into families and circumstances that preclude a certain level of flexibility. If you are raised in poverty and get recruited into a gang at age twelve, or if your parents don't allow you to receive an education or even learn how to read, the notion of starting from scratch may feel like a pipe dream. The ability to make opportunities materialize that extend beyond the power of imagination is to some degree contingent on privilege. But if your life allows for even the tiniest sliver of divergence, and the machine in which you are churning is not working for your body and soul, then diverge. If you can gather with your community and dream up a kinder and more beautiful way to exist, then gather. If you can peel off in your own direction and find a way to attain the resources and freedom you desire, then peel off.

Some people enjoy the luxury of designing their life from the perspective of infinite possibility, while others face severe practical and logistical limitations. Actively imagining a more liberating and satisfying future is step one for everyone, regardless of where they are coming from. If you don't have a clear vision of where you're headed, simply allow yourself to meditate on the feelings you want to experience more of. You may find that this exercise puts your whole body at ease.

If you are in a position to take action, don't underestimate the power of incremental steps. Carving out a few moments a day to engage with whatever it is you fantasize about will calm potentially false narratives about being "stuck," challenge paralysis, cause the neuropathways associated with engaging with your genuine passion(s) to blaze, soothe your nervous system, bring calm to your body, invite joy, ease the burden of continued obligations, and hopefully, reinforce the belief that more dramatic life changes are possible. Today, ten minutes of painting may be possible. Two years from now, owning your own gallery may be possible. Every inch of movement toward what you imagine reinforces the message to yourself and the world that you are serious about living a life full of passion and growth.

Authentic creation is different from reactivity. When you create authentically, you begin to identify the dreams of your heart with your senses. You may not even be able to name your dream, just as I was unable to attach a label to the kind of education and life I desired. That is more than okay. Start with the basics. Where do you see yourself? What does your environment look like? Who are you with? What are you doing? Using your senses, envision yourself living the life of your dreams. What do you see, smell, hear, taste, and touch? What do you *feel*?

Now let's step away for a moment from the bigger picture of your life to focus on self-concept. Who you are as an individual is more than just a collection of reactions to conversations, events, and other individuals. But often we surrender our power to authentically craft an identity, instead defining ourselves based on how successfully our bodies and psyches have metabolized the outside world. Each one of us is constantly processing and integrating external information. And while some folks are more naturally adept at interpreting their relationship to this information in ways that elevate their identity, none of us does that 100 percent of the time, because we're human. In a perfect world, we would always filter and interpret the variables that impact us in ways that promote a sense of well-being. But when we don't, we can:

- Remind ourselves that who we are at our core is different from how we experience the world.

- Call our perceptions and interpretations into question, especially if they are harming our sense of self.

- Return to the concept of core value.

For most of us, life is pretty rocky, and over time, the imperfections of our experiences mingle with our sense of self. Internalizing layers upon layers of external influences can make it nearly impossible to identify who we are at our core, but know that our fundamental being is completely distinct from how we process the outside world. As years pass, we often develop dysfunctional patterns and unproductive coping mechanisms in our best efforts to navigate an unpredictable world, and we wrongly assume that who we are is the same as how we feel and behave. I invite you to pause, take a deep breath, and accept that who you truly are may not be the same as who you have become as a consequence of living life. At your core, you are kind, peaceful, joyful, and full of hope.

Now, let's circle back around to the concept of reactivity. As we discussed, it is essential to not conflate what we've absorbed from external influences with who we fundamentally are. Our identity requires careful deconstruction as we pull apart these influences to reconnect (over and over again) with who we are at our core. A similar process is helpful when it comes to relationships with others. When I review many of my most significant romantic relationships, it is evident that my choosing a romantic partner at any moment in time was, in great part, a reaction to the partner who came directly before him. When I was with someone whose heaviness and emotional turmoil dragged me down, I rebounded with an upper of a partner whose buoyant spirit was a breath of fresh air. When I was with someone flighty who I felt might abandon me, my next partner was eager for commitment.

In relationships, as in all areas of life, it is limiting to perceive our future strictly through the lens of our past. While it may be wise to learn from each relationship what we desire more or less of in our next one, ideally the people we choose to invest in on a personal level are not simply a reaction to what we have received too much of or were thirsty for in past relationships. The more clarity we have on who we genuinely are, the easier it is to attract people who more objectively bring light and inspiration to our lives.

Many of us have habituated to creating our identity from the outside in versus the inside out. We begin with the context of our culture and subcultures, and from there we determine what is reasonable, appropriate, and acceptable. We internalize norms and trends and attempt to inject some shred of individuality and preference into preestablished paradigms. The identity of every culture and establishment possesses its own set of expectations that are generally accepted, and only rebels on the fringe differentiate themselves from them. But in reality, even the ways in which so-called rebels distinguish themselves are often a reaction to preexisting paradigms versus conscious creations.

To be the person I truly desire to be in the world, my goal is to hush preconceived notions—at first simply by acknowledging that they exist—and to become increasingly aware of the unconscious narratives and cellular memories that drive my life. I then reverse the default pattern of creating my identity from the outside in by imagining my life from the inside out. How do I want to *feel* in my daily life? What type of people do I want to be in the presence of? What does my ideal day look like?

Turn to "Questions for Reimagining
Your Life" in the workbook.

Even in the context of romantic partnerships, many of us tend to insert ourselves into predetermined blueprints that actually may not reflect our inner life and desires. Instead of automatically agreeing to norms, what if you were to scrap traditional concepts of family and partnership and consider experimenting with the relationship style that best suits you? This may look like a classic nuclear family, or it may look like three women raising a child together. It may look like two people sharing a home but enjoying separate bedrooms, or being in partnership but not living in the same location. It may look like two women who are romantically involved but who occasionally enjoy male attention, or choosing to not be in any formal commitment. Embedded in every culture are societal norms, and choices that contradict these norms may be stigmatized or involve potentially dangerous repercussions. But if there is freedom (even within your own heart), apart from explicit danger, to explore arrangements and opportunities that call to you, why not explore? You may experience pushback from your family, and friends may question your choices. But ultimately, you are the boss of your own life.

Sexual preferences or inclinations need not dictate the structure of our lives, but all too often they do. Who we choose to love and who we choose to make love to may or not be the same person or people. The life that feels most expansive and honest for you may look nothing like the life you were raised to believe is valuable, or even any life you have ever seen before. There are many ways to love, to make love, and to create a home and a community. When you close your eyes and imagine the flow of your life, what does it look like? Are you a woman living in a home with several other women who are co-raising children? Are you a woman who is married to a man but requires the consistent nurturing and collaboration of other women to feel fully supported? Are you a man who would like a for-ever partnership without being legally married? Are you in a monog-amous same-sex partnership? Is there freedom in your relationship to explore other connections? When we commit to a lifestyle that has been designed from the outside in, it may preclude a version of reality that more fully represents who we are and what we require to thrive. And because inherent to all structures are expectations that lead to specific roles, we may find ourselves playing a part that feels false or incomplete.

UNDERSTANDING WHAT WE WANT MORE OF IN OUR LIVES

When you gain clarity about who you are based on your authentic natural inclinations and the guidance of your heart, you may find yourself reevaluating the life that you have or have not created. It is never too late to claim the essence of whatever you feel you have missed out on. Of course, you cannot go back in time, and it may not be appropriate to abandon the current structure of your life over-night. But at any point, you can identify the feelings you associate with the lifestyle, experience, person, job, trip, or whatever else you

»•«

Prompt: Your Identity at Home

Grab your journal or a piece of paper and a pen and jot down answers to any of
the following questions that resonate with you. When you're finished, reread your
answers. Are you surprised by the picture they paint? What are some small adjustments you can make to be more aligned with a fulfilling daily life?

Within the context of your home life:

What do you enjoy doing, and what do you find to be a bore?

Where is your talent shining through, and under what circumstances is
it suffocated?

How do you feel about your use of your time?

How much of your time is spent in ways that feel purposeful, useful,
valuable, and/or pleasurable?

Do you often find yourself spinning your wheels or silently agreeing to a
hamster wheel of obligations?

How often do you feel taken advantage of or underappreciated?

Do you feel fulfilled?

To what degree are you being seen, heard, and valued by the people in
your home?

To what degree do you believe the people in your home are honoring
their commitments and obligations?

In what ways are you supported and not supported in your home (financially, emotionally, and practically)?

Under what circumstances and in whose presence do you feel the most
authentic?

What about yourself are you most proud of?

Who or what do you avoid in your home?

What do you want and need more of?

Who or what do you feel desperate to let go of?

What are you ready to say yes to?

What are you prepared to say no to?

What is missing?

Do you have the freedom to listen and respond to the prompts and cues
of your body, heart, and mind?

How able and willing are you to break free from established roles in
your home?

»•«

believe you missed out on and strategize how to incorporate them into your present life. Maybe you're craving emotional freedom, fun, a sense of adventure, or the feeling of being sexy, valued, and alive. Perhaps you want to eliminate anxiety, expand access to different emotional states, or have the ability to be spontaneous and improvise. Whatever it is you want to experience more or less of may be available to you within the context of your current reality. You could try an improv acting class, watch a master class on painting, or start hiking every morning before work. It's even possible to transfer the experience of fun and play to your overall attitude or to a relationship or hobby. Sometimes, to carve out a new life, we require a clean break from our current one. At other times, we can creatively revise the paradigm of what already exists and infuse it with satisfying textures and dimensions. Begin to connect the dots between how you want to feel and what activities, hobbies, and interests might connect you to that feeling.

If you feel like something is missing in your life, or you are craving something more, but are not sure what that something is, consider who you most enjoy spending time with. Who we choose to be in the presence of provides clues about what we desire more of in our lives. If you love being around a friend who is funny, do you want to laugh more? Do you wish you could generate a higher level of positivity, energy, and humor yourself? If your favorite work colleague is the one who shows up every Monday morning with elaborate tales about their crazy weekend, does some part of you feel stuck in your predictable life and patterns? If you are obsessed with a new lover because that person notices all that is unique about you, do you desire a more generous view of yourself or more frequent opportunities to be seen? The question I ask myself when I'm drawn to people is "What do I recognize in this person that I want to experience more of within myself or my own life?"

Turn to "Manifesting Desirable Qualities" in the workbook.

A friend of mine has a pattern of dating men who are deeply absorbed in their own lives and don't consider her needs. It is possible, and not uncommon, to be attracted to someone because they remind you of other significant people in your life (a caregiver or former lover, for instance). Without even realizing it, you may be trying to recreate a dynamic that is familiar. Even if a relationship is causing pain or discomfort emotionally or even physically, you may still be drawn to what you know.

In the case of my friend who has been dating men who always put themselves first, it dawned on me recently that she never puts herself first in relationships or prioritizes her needs and desires. When I asked her why she's drawn to her current beau, I realized she actually may be envious of the fact that he prioritizes himself, because that's what she really wants to do for herself. In essence, he is a mirror that reflects back to her what she doesn't have enough of in her own life, and by association, she feels empowered just by being near him.

Ironically, she is suffering as a consequence of involving herself with people who are focused solely on themselves. But since that's secretly what she wants to do for herself, she views them as powerful, sexy, and self-possessed. No one actually wants a romantic partner who treats them like crap or a friend who is too busy to call back. But there may be qualities in others or some version of how they operate that represents what we are missing in our own lives, be it happiness, contentment, confidence, freedom, and so on.

Who we are outright jealous of also can provide clues about a part of us that is not accessing or in touch with our core, authentic selves. Jealousy is rooted in the perception of being less than, but it's impossible to ever be less or more than anyone else. Accomplishments are separate from identity; they are the outgrowth of identity, but the full value of who we are is present at birth and remains intact without ever fluctuating until we die. Jealousy is a fabulous indicator, however, of what you may want more of in your life, where you may want to be, who you may want to be with or without, and what you may want your life to look and feel like. It provides information about how you want to be perceived in the world and how you want to perceive yourself.

Use your jealousy in service of determining what you desire more of in your life. Jealousy itself may not propel you in a healthy way, but it can be used as a tool to create a framework or vision for your future. What you want is not to be someone else or even to have what someone else has. It is to be more entirely and authentically yourself, experiencing all that you were meant to experience and possessing all that is meant to be yours.

Turn to "Reframing Jealousy" in the workbook.

WHAT *IS* WORKING?

If you have done anything at all that you are proud of, celebrate this. You have come so far and done so much, even if it doesn't feel like enough. Every task you complete, every time you pick your kids up from school, every phone call you return, every moment you smile at a stranger is a win. Start celebrating what *is* working in your life, the moments when you *are* experiencing peace or you *do* laugh, the actions that *are* propelling your life forward or supporting the lives of those around you. As you examine what doesn't feel complete, recognize what *is* working and what *does* feel good. Just by showing up for this wild and unpredictable life, you are winning. Just by agreeing to be present and making an effort to move forward, you are doing an incredible job.

There is wisdom in balancing what you are striving for and what already is complete. If you are reading this book, you are actively participating in your personal evolution. You have committed to taking steps to support your growth and agreed to reframe punishing thoughts, or at the very least, you have contemplated a kinder and gentler way of experiencing yourself. Since you already are striving, give yourself permission to turn your attention again and again to beauty, delight, and what invites a sense of ease and joy. You will always return to your pursuits and desires, but as often as you can, breathe deeply and glory in the miracle of who you already are. Your soul is already what your personality is striving to become, so allow for magic and ease to offset the effort of being human.

Turn to "Drawing from Inspiration" in the workbook.

It's important to remember that the beliefs we form about other people and their lives usually say more about us than them. We rarely, if ever, have access to the deep struggles and internal worlds of the people we superficially observe, especially if we know them only in passing or through social media. More often than not, the unseen experiences of those we envy are every bit as convoluted as ours, because we are all human and want the same things: to feel safe, loved, and accepted, and

>> • <<

Prompt: Write a Letter of Gratitude

Gratitude is a beautiful way to honor your spirit, release stress, shift your focus away from negativity, and combat fear. The more stressed and fearful I am, the more gratitude I express. While I often give thanks (in my mind, out loud, or on paper) for people and privileges that exist outside of my being, every now and then I write a letter of gratitude to myself. These notes remind me that I am special and valuable, and steal my attention away from all that I am working on in terms of personal development in favor of all that which is already is working.

Today, try writing a letter of gratitude to yourself. Just for now, set aside everything you wish were different about yourself and your life, and just give thanks. Honor yourself for your attributes that you admire, for the effort required to be alive, for your hopes and dreams, and for the fundamental value of your existence. Reaffirm specifically what you are proud of, what you are doing well, and what you love and respect most about yourself at this moment in time.

>> • <<

that we belong. What the lives of acquaintances, celebrities, and even friends look like on the surface doesn't necessarily indicate what those people are feeling inside.

It's also important to differentiate between people's accomplishments or achievements and the characteristics that support their success. For instance, if you wish to publish books, you might be jealous of a bestselling author such as Gabrielle Bernstein or Dan Brown. Using "bestselling author" as a benchmark, see if you can identify some of the characteristics, actions, and other attributes associated with this title.

Here's an example:

Gabrielle Bernstein (Bestselling Author)

Honest, authentic, kind, intelligent, deep, confident, bold, outspoken, prolific.

Writes impactful stories, philosophizes, shares life experiences, supports the internal transformation of others, speaks to audiences, communicates through numerous avenues, is on podcasts, speaks the truth.

Dedication, focus, patience, creativity, the ability to let go of perfectionism, resilience, fortitude, ambition.

By making this list, you will begin to identify the deeper layers of what you desire and recognize what is required to attain it. If you wish to take it a step further, break down each characteristic, action, and attribute in terms of how it directly relates to your life. In other words, what would you need to do or believe to make all of those bullet points your own?

Here's an abbreviated example:

Honest. "I will practice telling the truth, even when it's uncomfortable or I feel exposed and vulnerable."

Authentic. "I will follow my inner guidance. I will question who I am doing things for and why I am doing them. I will work to ensure that what people see and experience in my presence reflects my internal world."

Deep. "I will begin to ask others questions that may help me understand them more deeply. I will talk to people about how I'm really doing without the fear of burdening them."

Speaking to audiences and supporting the internal transformation of others. "I will carve out time to write a book that will lead to public speaking opportunities. I will share my goals with close friends who will encourage me and hold me accountable."

Writing books that are impactful. "I will limit myself to thirty minutes of television and social media scrolling daily to create space to write. I will create an environment that is conducive to writing, even if it's in my bedroom. I will set my phone to Do Not Disturb mode while I write. I will limit additional distractions in advance."

WHAT DO YOU DAYDREAM AND FANTASIZE ABOUT?

This may seem obvious, but understanding what you desire more of in your life may come simply from paying attention to what you daydream about. When you find yourself visualizing potential realities or harkening back to old memories, what kinds of images and fantasies show up? How do you feel in the scenarios that you are playing out in your mind and heart? What are you doing or saying? What are you *not* doing or saying? Who is with you? Where are you geographically? Which of your senses are activated? How do you feel about yourself in these daydreams?

A dear friend of mine often fantasizes about a boyfriend from her past, despite being generally content with the partner she has chosen to build a life with. When we dug into her fantasies, we realized it wasn't the guy she was missing, it was the version of who she was when she was dating him. As a mother of three young children, my friend hasn't prioritized feeling or looking sexy, but every time she recalls her ex, she reconnects with the part of herself that felt desirable, sassy, energized, and spontaneous.

In regard to life pursuits, a simple and straightforward way to gain an understanding of what you may want to do more of is to track what you read, listen to, or yearn to know more about. Is there a class you want to take or a potential job you can't stop thinking about? Do you find yourself googling a certain topic, or watching TV shows or movies relating to a certain theme? What kinds of podcasts do you listen to? What do you love to read? Which conversations do you wish would never end? What intrigues you? Asking yourself these questions can help direct your energy toward pursuits that ignite passion and curiosity.

Turn to "Questions to Help Clarify Your Self-Concept" in the workbook.

CONSCIOUSLY OBSERVING THE SELF IN RELATION TO OTHERS

Notice times when you withhold parts of yourself, and when you are more willing to shine a light on your vulnerability. Do you tend to be more reserved and less forthcoming about your ideas when you're around a particular family member, because you perceive them to be a know-it-all, and they shame you for having bold ideas? Are you funnier than usual around a coworker who laughs at your jokes?

It's very hard to express yourself genuinely in a romantic relationship if you are afraid of losing something that feels essential and life-giving, such as respect, love, or attention. Do the following thoughts ever enter your mind?

What if they don't like me?
What if they desire someone sexier or more successful?
What if they get bored?
What if I'm not enough?
What if I'm too much?

If you have any of these thoughts, what do you do or say to calm and reassure yourself? Do you tend to keep these thoughts private, articulate them with self-compassion, or act out? Notice your patterns.

There's a difference between giving from a place of authenticity and working to please others in order to secure love and attachment. As often as possible, ask yourself, "Who am I really doing this for, and why?"

— CHAPTER SUMMARY —

Many of us have defined ourselves based on the expectations and feedback of cultures, families, and friends that reassure us that we are safe, acceptable, and worthy of love. But no one can truly define us except ourselves, and by peeling back the layers of our influences and uncovering our true desires, we have the opportunity to connect with and express ourselves in ways that are genuinely satisfying. The world needs you as you truly are; it does not deeply benefit from the version of you that you were trained to be. At any point, you possess the right to question your level of authenticity and reconnect with the parts of your being that bring fulfillment, peace, and joy. The degree to which you are able to express yourself authentically may be the most powerful defining factor in your ability to access emotional freedom and joy.

CHAPTER 5

HONORING SLEEP

Of all of the things I think about, dream about, and covet, sleep is at the top of the list.

Sleeping deeply and for the number of hours our bodies require is essential to well-being, and yet many of us grapple with sleeplessness as a consequence of being dysregulated. Fascinating books have been written about sleep, and apps have been created to help facilitate deeper sleep and create greater awareness around sleep hygiene. Although I am not a sleep expert, I spent much of my life tossing and turning in the cruel hands of insomnia and sleeping only a few hours a night. Eventually, I became addicted to sleeping pills, and for eleven straight years, I did not go a single night without relying on them. Suffice it to say, as the expert on my own life, I've learned a thing or two about sleep.

Almost half of all Americans report feeling sleepy during the day three to seven times per week. That might be because about 35 percent of American adults—especially single parents, working adults, and active-duty members of the military—report sleeping fewer than seven hours a night.[13] Narcolepsy, sleep paralysis, sleepwalking, talking in one's sleep, sleep apnea, and night sweats are all disturbances that interfere with sleep, but far and away, the most common is insomnia. In fact, 237 million people globally struggle with the condition, and between fifty and seventy million Americans are affected each year.[14] To break this down further, it has been reported that one in five adults experiences nightly struggles associated with sleep, and half of adults in the United States grapple with insomnia at least once a month or more.[15] Women have a lifetime risk of insomnia that is as much as 40 percent higher than it is for men,[16] with 78 percent of them experiencing insomnia during pregnancy. Those with medical or mental health conditions also are at risk. Additionally, 35 percent of those with insomnia appear to have a family history of the condition.[17]

Insomnia can be broken down by duration of the condition.

Transient insomnia is temporary, lasting less than one week.

Acute or short-term insomnia lasts fewer than three months and is likely to be caused by a stressful life event. The resolution of that event relieves the condition.

Chronic insomnia is characterized by trouble falling asleep or staying asleep at least three nights per week for three months or longer.

Insomnia also can be categorized by how it manifests nightly.

Sleep-onset insomnia indicates trouble falling asleep at the beginning of the night.

Sleep-maintenance insomnia indicates the inability to maintain sleep throughout the night.

Early morning-awakening insomnia indicates waking up well before needed in the morning.

Lack of sleep over the course of a short period may leave a person feeling cranky, but it is hardly a life-changer. The effects of chronic insomnia, on the other hand, can lead to mental health problems such as anxiety and depression. In fact, findings reveal that people with insomnia are five times more likely to suffer from depression and twenty times more likely to develop a panic disorder than those without insomnia.[18] Moreover, research shows that while an occasional night of poor sleep does not lead to a significant difference in overall mortality risk, both sleep duration and sleep regularity are influential factors in the long run.[19]

Treatments for insomnia are varied and have varying rates of success. Charlene Gamaldo, the medical director of the Johns Hopkins Center for Sleep at Howard County General Hospital in Columbia, Maryland, has stated that people who engage in at least thirty minutes of moderate exercise will notice an immediate benefit in their quality of sleep.[20] (However, exercise should be avoided close to bedtime, or it will have the effect of revving up the body rather than winding it down for the night.) Cognitive behavioral therapy (CBT) is a particularly effective treatment for insomnia, with up to 75 percent of patients seeing improvement in their symptoms. Sleep routine changes, acupressure, meditation, hypnosis, and alternative therapies such as yoga also are recommended to treat the condition.[21]

Sleep is not a one-size-fits-all type of deal, and there are as many potential solutions to sleeplessness as there are reasons why people struggle to sleep soundly. The most common frustration those of us who have struggled with sleep share is why something so basic and essential feels out of reach. We look at people who nod off mid-sentence or on airplanes in the midst of chaos, and we think, *Why is it so easy for them? Why can't I sleep when other people just close their eyes and dream?* It doesn't seem fair. We feel out of control. And the feeling of helplessness only heightens our anxiety, which reinforces our fear, which makes peaceful sleep even less likely. It is a vicious cycle that I am about to help you break.

While you may feel you are the only person in the entire world who lies awake at night with spinning thoughts or in a muddled haze, you are not alone. In fact, I guarantee that on any given night, when you are experiencing the pinnacle of your anxiety while tossing and turning or staring up at the ceiling, thousands of people all around the globe are sharing some version of this experience. They, like you, are sleepless and feeling entirely out of control and want nothing more than to let go and surrender to their dreams.

While I could spend days unpacking the sensations and psychological torture relating to my own experience of insomnia in an effort to ease any sense of aloneness you may have, my primary goal here is to equip you with practical information that may help relieve your burden. The following paragraphs discuss some of the most common reasons why people don't sleep, and provide some potential solutions. As you read them, remember that you are not alone and that countless others are grappling with the very same feelings of isolation and angst that often accompany sleeplessness. If your ultimate goal is emotional freedom and a joyful, fulfilling life, nourishing sleep should be a priority.

ROOM TEMPERATURE

Your room might be too warm or too cold. For most adults, the ideal temperature for sleep is sixty to sixty-seven degrees Fahrenheit. (For babies and children, the range is sixty-five to seventy degrees, and for the elderly, it's sixty-six to seventy degrees.) My internal body temperature consistently has been below average, and I happen to sleep best when my thermostat is set to sixty-nine degrees. That being said, I keep a blanket at the edge of my bed should I want an additional layer during the night or in the early morning, when my internal temperature drops.

In addition to ensuring that your room is the right temperature, you also want to make sure that your bedding provides the ideal level of warmth. I have found that down comforters are too hot for me and have opted for a layering system that involves a sheet, a slightly warmer blanket, a quilt, and an optional throw. Experiment with your room temperature and bedding, and notice when you are more restless or toss and turn more frequently. If you identify that your sleep is disrupted when you are too hot or too cold, adjust accordingly. Also note the nights when you've slept soundly. What temperature was your thermostat set to on those nights? What were you wearing? In addition to tracking variables relating to temperature, note other factors that might have affected your sleep. What did you do or not do preceding sleep? Did you take a bath, skip your evening cocktail, drink more wine than usual, exercise, or not exercise? Did you get a disturbing phone call or go to a concert? You may even choose to keep a sleep journal that documents the quality of your sleep and the factors contributing to it.

YOUR MATTRESS

Many of us have been sleeping on the same mattress for years without ever questioning when or if we should replace or upgrade it. If your mattress is uncomfortable (too hard, too soft, lumpy, or uneven), you may find yourself shifting around in a state of shallow sleep without ever attributing your restlessness to the very thing you're sleeping on. I cannot urge you enough to invest in a mattress that makes you look forward to getting into bed and that properly supports your body and its specific requirements and preferences. An organic mattress, meaning it is free of potentially toxic chemicals, is an ideal choice. Mattresses are a large financial investment and one that most of us put off because we feel we have more immediate concerns. But creating an environment that is conducive to sleep may offset bigger issues, such as the inability to function at full capacity and the plethora of health problems that result from sleeplessness, including depression and anxiety.

During sleep, our body heals, restores itself, processes, and decompresses, and we owe ourselves the best shot possible at a good night's rest. Because a quality mattress may be financially burdensome, many companies now offer monthly payment plans to make the purchase more affordable. It is ultimately far costlier (financially, mentally, and psychologically) to not invest in your sleep than it is to commit to the staples that will support it. Sleep is, after all, inevitable and unavoidable. I highly recommend going to a physical store where you can try out mattress options before choosing your ideal match. And just as our emotional and environmental needs shift over time, so do our physical needs. Every five years or so, evaluate the integrity of your mattress to determine if it can meet you where you are.

UNWILLINGNESS OR PERCEIVED INABILITY TO PRIORITIZE SLEEP

I cannot tell you how many of my closest friends claim that they're jealous of how many hours I sleep (eight) and can't believe that I never use an alarm clock or wake up feeling sluggish and lackluster. But when I claim that sleep is just as accessible to them as it is to me, they push back. I have a few dear friends who work late into the night and then want to be present during the day for their children. With these women, the conversation is more about how to steal pockets of rest intermittently through meditation and catnaps.

For those of us with some flexibility, the goal is to organize our lives in a way that more frequently than not ensures that we get the amount of sleep our bodies require. (Of course, there are always exceptions.) To get eight hours of sleep, I generally require nine hours in my bed. This additional wakeful hour provides the buffer to unwind, fall asleep, wake up in the middle of the night to use the bathroom or drink water, and gradually emerge from dreams in the morning without having to catapult out of bed. Some people require as few as six hours of sleep, and others require ten or more. There is no judgment regarding what your body requires; it's simply a fact. Honor and plan for it. It's not a miracle or a mystery that I get eight hours of sleep. I have created a life that prioritizes all aspects of my well-being, and sleep is nonnegotiable.

If you would like to try getting the amount of sleep your body requires, you most likely will need to plan ahead. For many of us, the number of hours we need to sleep fluctuates depending on our levels of emotional stress, physical exertion, and hormones, our diet, the degree to which we exert mental effort throughout the day, and so on. The key to creating a healthy sleep window is to allot for the *maximum* number of hours your body may require. You may end up not spending as many hours in bed as you have planned for; the advantage of that would be having an early morning that is productive and full of ease.

YOUR IDENTITY IN RELATION TO SLEEP

I am amused by friends who brag about how little sleep they get, as if they're competing to see whose life is the most frantic and busiest. When I reminisce about each phase of my life, I realize that my relationship with sleep has been skewed heavily by my age and identity. As teenagers, my friends and I thought it was cool to stay up all night because finally, nobody was enforcing a bedtime. In my twenties, I equated being up all night with flourishing socially and working hard. In my thirties, I recognized that my mental and physical health were so greatly influenced by the quantity and quality of my sleep that I began to equate good sleep with self-care. Currently, I conceptualize sleep as a period of total surrender and healing that allows me to pursue my waking dreams at full throttle when the sun comes up. Alternatively, some of my peers seem to unconsciously associate being up all night with productivity or having a strong work ethic, and they view sacrificing sleep as evidence of their devotion and commitment.

*Turn to "Examining Your Relationship between
Sleep and Identity" in the workbook.*

ATTACHMENT TO THE PERCEPTION OF STRUGGLE AND THE JUDGMENT THAT FOLLOWS

One of the most common traps of those who struggle with falling or staying asleep is worrying about not getting enough sleep. This may happen prior to getting into bed, as soon as their head hits the pillow, or once they recognize that they are not asleep and want to be. Generally speaking, the more time that passes in a state of anxiety, the more fear the body generates. The body produces cortisol and adrenaline in this fear state, which stimulates us to feel even more awake, which compounds our fear about not falling asleep, and on and on the counterproductive cycle continues.

In Buddhist philosophy, there is no right or wrong way to feel or experience life. Everything just is what it is. There is no judgment attached to any given emotional state or frame of mind; there is simply the reality of what is happening in the moment. As I see it, by removing judgment, we remove fear. And by removing fear, we eliminate the need for categories such as right and wrong. The struggle we may have while trying to fall asleep is never wrong; it just is. By believing that we shouldn't be struggling, we are communicating to ourselves that we are having a wrong experience. We are not only judging the experience but labeling it as bad, stressful, awful, and so on, which are all experiences we wish to avoid.

When we judge our emotional state, we tend soon after to judge our fundamental being. Emotional experiences that we deem stressful and that we believe are out of our control can make us feel powerless, weak, and sometimes even stupid. By judging them, we almost always end up judging our core selves. Emotionally charged states also catalyze the instinct to attach labels to ourselves, to others, and to circumstances and experiences. Instead of our experience simply being what it is—something that doesn't even require words to be felt—judgment tempts us to define and categorize all that may feel uncomfortable as bad. We interpret the experience of struggle as scary and bad and attach ourselves to a narrative that we are crazy, helpless, or scarred. In our effort to contain and control a situation that feels out of control, we make it wrong. We also attempt to control our own human nature by making ourselves wrong.

In reality, what happens when we judge and label things is that our earnest desire to avoid danger kicks up. If enough fear enters the scene, fear itself becomes the primary experience versus whatever it is we claim to be afraid of. In other words, we forget what we actually are afraid of or hoping desperately to avoid—or, conversely, to grasp or attain—and focus exclusively on fear. This is ironic, given that our primary desire is generally to feel safe.

In alignment with the Buddhist way of thinking, there are no wrong experiences, just as there are no wrong people; there are simply experiences and people. Because we are so accustomed to overthinking in an effort to distract ourselves from feeling or to feel safe, it can be helpful to briefly name experiences as a starting point. This may sound like a contradiction, based on my comments about the tendency to judge and label, but naming things may temporarily relieve the anxiety and provide a moment of comfort by way of acknowledging the state rather than denying it. The issue, as I see it, is that we attach ourselves too heavily and for too long a stretch of time to words, which keeps us in an analytical state rather than allowing a more sensorial experience. Once we name our experience, the goal is to drift away from language and into a state of full surrender. If need be, from time to time we can gently remind ourselves that we are safe, valuable, and lovable exactly as we are in the moment and regardless of what we are experiencing.

Turn to "Naming Your Experience" in the workbook.

Here's an example of how this might play out for me. I'm in bed and notice that my mind is spinning with anxious thoughts because my landlord has just told me that our family needs to move. I cannot comprehend even finding the time to relocate, the prices of homes are inflated, and I am working full time while taking care of my children. First, I name the feeling: "I am feeling scared." Next, I become consciously aware of my physical experience: "My breath is shallow, my palms are sweaty, my mouth is dry, my legs are restless, and my heart is pounding." Then, without judging or labeling my experience or myself, I drift away from language to the visual representation of what it is I desire to experience.

I imagine myself feeling lighthearted and free, sitting in my new home that is organized, cozy, and full of joy. As soon as words enter, I focus on the positive feelings associated with the fantasy that I have created. I notice myself breathing with more ease as I move deeper and deeper into the experience of lightness. *Everything is where it should be*, I think. *We are where we are meant to be.* In my vision, my children are playing on the floor. We are listening to jazz. If fear creeps in, I may choose to speak the word "light" in my mind to bring me back to the scene where I feel joyful and content.

Overthinking provides a false sense of control that clouds true understanding. By quieting the inner dialogue that keeps you awake at night, you will gain access to the wisdom that knows you will be provided for and that you are acceptable exactly as you are. Rationally, you are aware that you cannot solve problems by trying to control yourself, others, or the world, and that you should not wait until you feel that everything in your life is stable to surrender to peace. But often, our minds assume that to be responsible, we have to "make" things happen, ensure our future success, ward off potential obstacles, and worry our way to whatever emotional or tangible resolution we crave. As you drift off at night, remind yourself that the desire to control and the feeling of fear block you from the peace you are trying to secure through thinking.

Instead of believing that you will acquire ease and feel safe once everything in your life makes sense and is lined up predictably, allow peace to be your starting point. It is from a place of surrender that the truth offers itself to us like a gift, and we realize it's not contingent on anything outside of ourselves. Just as your core value is forever unwavering, so is your access to peace. Peace is a choice, not a privilege.

Some of the things I say to myself to facilitate wordlessness are:

"It's safe to let go."

"My body knows more than my mind knows."

"There is nothing I need to describe, create, understand, narrate, or guarantee right now."

"Without language, my most profound wisdom, inner guidance, and direction emerge, and healing can take place."

"In the silence, all of my answers will come."

"Everything I require will be provided at exactly the right time."

"What is meant to be mine will be mine."

The answers to your burning questions may appear as an image, be plucked from the lyrics of a song, or be recited to you in the form of a kindergarten poem. In your bed, your only job is to surrender to the vast spaciousness that allows you to dream, so that when you wake, you will be available to receive all that is meant to be yours. Whatever feels unresolved, incomplete, punishing, ambiguous, or terrifying when you lay your head on your pillow at night will not feel more resolved, more complete, lighter, clearer, or less terrifying because you obsess over it. What brings relief is the healing and processing that occur while we sleep and dream. And when we allow ourselves to surrender to sleep rather than trying to control our lives by resisting it, ideas come more fluidly, and we are in a sharper frame of mind to take action if and when it makes sense to.

YOUR PROXIMITY TO ELECTRICITY

Everything that is alive contains an electrical charge. And while modern society has come to rely on and enjoy revolutionary technology, there is no doubt that our bodies are not meant to absorb the impact of genius inventions such as cell phones, computers, microwaves, satellite dishes, and so on. Human beings are intended to exist in a natural environment that is far less stimulating and that supports the natural vibration of our cells. Our bodies were not designed to be activated by artificial charges, and those of us who are sensitive to input may be greatly impacted by them.

To help regulate your nervous system and offset electrical disruption, you can practice grounding. Also known as "earthing," grounding involves connecting the body's electricity with Earth's energy. Benefits reported by devotees include reduced bodily inflammation, lowered cortisol levels (less stress), increased energy, and decreased pain. People report looking, feeling, and sleeping better.[22]

>•<<

Practice: Grounding Throughout the Year

The simplest and most natural way to experience grounding is simply to walk barefoot outdoors on grass, dirt, or sand. Wet substances in particular make for better conduction of electrons. Whenever you are able to do so, pop off your shoes and walk on any of nature's surfaces, even for just a minute or two.

Grounding indoors is a bit trickier, since surfaces such as wood, glazed tile, and vinyl are not conductive. However, items such as a specially designed mattress and pillow covers, along with sleeping mats that connect to a wall outlet, enable your body to connect to Earth's energy. Wearable bands and special footgear also make grounding accessible indoors year-round.

>•<<

At night, unplug as many appliances and devices as is convenient for you, and if possible, charge devices (phone, computer, and the like) in another room while you sleep. I personally make a point of unplugging myself from technology two hours before I plan to fall asleep. This may seem like a stretch for some of you, but try turning off your computer and phone just thirty minutes earlier than you normally would and see what happens. Challenge yourself to set devices aside earlier and earlier with each passing night, in increments of thirty minutes, until you have reached the two-hour mark. If, for whatever reason, you absolutely must be on a device, make sure to wear blue-light-blocking glasses or activate a blue-light-blocking app on your phone as often as possible to support your circadian rhythms (your sleep and wake cycle). Also, dim the level of brightness on your screen as you edge toward bedtime.

A very close friend of mine scrolls Instagram nightly to decompress, then has a hard time falling asleep. I understand that scanning social media can feel borderline hypnotic, but I'm pretty sure that it's not helping my friend truly unwind. If anything, it's stimulating her brain and activating a series of emotions in quick succession that she then has to process, even if not consciously. So, I encouraged my friend to conduct an experiment for forty-eight hours and cut herself off from social media before dinnertime. The results were astonishing. She felt less anxious and depressed and fell asleep faster both nights. I'm not encouraging anyone to ban social media altogether, as it can be a profound way to connect, communicate, and receive. But I do suggest that in the hours preceding sleep, you cultivate rituals that are less stimulating and more in touch with your natural rhythm.

YOUR CIRCADIAN RHYTHM

Circadian rhythms are the internal processes (mental and physical) that regulate the sleep-wake cycle within a twenty-four-hour time frame. Because of modern technology, our bodies are no longer inclined to sleep when the sun goes down and rise at dawn. In fact, it seems that the majority of us have lost touch with our innate rhythms and are not even sure how to reconnect with them. The field of epigenetics suggests that our genetic blueprint is heavily influenced by the experiences and struggles of our ancestors. If this is true, I imagine that the effects of modern technology on the body are being wired into our DNA, making it more and more difficult with the passing of time to connect with our natural internal rhythms.

Simply put, if you are surrounded by bright lights at night, your body believes that it's still daytime. Because we are meant to be alert and energized during the day, if our surroundings suggest to our bodies via bright lights that it's daytime, we may find ourselves activated at night. Melatonin is a hormone that our brain releases at night in response to darkness. It helps regulate our sleep-wake cycle, and exposure to light at night inhibits melatonin production. Many of us go and go until the moment it's time to sleep, then abruptly turn off all the lights in our house. While this may work for some, those of us whose circadian rhythms are thrown off course by bright lights may benefit from gradually dimming the lights concurrent with sunset. This may sound exhaustive or extreme, but I assure you that it's a pivotal part of resetting your nervous system and aligning yourself with your circadian rhythms.

For me, dinnertime is the turning point at which I begin to dim lights. As the evening progresses, I do my best to match the level of brightness inside my home with the level of brightness outside. During summer months, when sunset occurs significantly later than at other times of the year, I determine what time I want to go to bed, and close curtains or dim lights to encourage melatonin production accordingly. While this may sound burdensome, I do it automatically at this point, without any real conscious effort involved. Anything that becomes a habit requires less mental energy than something that occurs only occasionally. If you dim your lights nightly, it will just become part of your routine.

The hormone melatonin decreases during the day as we are exposed to light and stimuli, and increases at night, as our exposure to light lessens and eventually disappears. Now think about the course of nature and how our exposure to light dissipates gradually as the sun rotates around Earth. It's not sunny until bedtime, and then the sun abruptly turns off, and *bam!* It's time for sleep. A slow and steady dimming takes place, whereby the strong light of the sun fades into late-afternoon light and then the gloaming and sunset before, finally, it is nighttime. Nature's design is genius, as it allows us to understand the way in which our own bodies and minds are meant to function. If we were to mirror the sun, we would be full of energy and light in the morning, and then, as the day progresses, our brightness would dim slowly into something slightly less vigorous and potent, until finally we surrender to sleep.

If you'd like to try winding down more gradually before retiring for the night, practice dimming the lights in your home around dinnertime or shortly thereafter. Try to avoid overhead or track lighting if possible, and favor lightbulbs that provide softer, warmer lighting. As the evening progresses, see how few lights you can comfortably exist with until it's time for you to sleep.

To support your circadian rhythms further, see if you can step outside in the morning soon after waking up. I'm not asking you to open your bedroom window and leap out of it at dawn. But the sooner you step outside, the better. The sun will regulate your melatonin levels, and your body will understand more fully that it's time to be awake.

HORMONAL IMBALANCES AND THYROID ISSUES

I am walking evidence that hormones affect sleep, because for the two days preceding my menstrual cycle, I tend to toss and turn more, and my sleep is shallower and less predictable than at other times of the month. Because I know this about my body, I compensate for it by drinking a cup of chamomile tea and taking some supportive supplements. Mostly, the awareness is helpful because I don't get anxious about the sleep disruption and can accommodate it by getting into bed a bit earlier.

If you consistently struggle with sleep, hormones may very well be a factor. From time to time, I have lab work done and order hormone panels to make sure that all my levels are within a normal range. If you can budget for lab work, it's an extraordinary way to receive concrete feedback about what's happening in your body. Functional doctors, who look at the body as a whole versus focusing solely on individual parts, are particularly skilled at understanding and interpreting lab work, as there are often deeper layers and more complicated variables impacting results.

PARASITES

I've had these! They're no fun. Ask your doctor to test you for parasites, and make sure to test for SIBO (small intestine bacterial overgrowth). Parasites can negatively impact sleep, but there are treatment plans for every kind, ranging from dietary restrictions, supplements, and herbs to antibiotics.

LACK OF ESSENTIAL NUTRIENTS AND DIETARY IMBALANCES

Lab work may help confirm that you are not only consuming but also absorbing a full spectrum of nutrients. The majority of us favor feel-good or convenient food choices instead of prioritizing balancing our blood sugar and making sure we're consuming adequate amounts of the vitamins and minerals that help support our bodies and balance brain chemistry. In some cases, undiagnosed food sensitivities and allergies can contribute to inflammation, which also disrupts equilibrium.

Vitamin D deficiency is prevalent (especially during winter) and can dampen mood and energy, so make sure to check your levels and get some sunshine or take a supplement if they're low. Vitamin D is technically a hormone and also helps regulate our circadian rhythms. If you feel you may not be eating a mineral-rich diet (most of us aren't, because of poor soil quality, among other factors), consider taking a comprehensive mineral supplement. If you might be suffering from food sensitivities or allergies, try an elimination diet. In brief, this involves eliminating potential allergens from your diet (wheat, corn, gluten, soy, dairy, eggs, sugar, and so on), and then slowly reintroducing them one by one and noting your reaction.

TIMING YOUR LAST MEAL OF THE DAY

If your body is busy digesting food—in particular, a meal that is fatty or high in protein—it's harder for it to do its miraculous job of healing and repairing. If you have blood sugar irregularities that require you to consume food at specific intervals, this may not apply to you. But for most of us, sleep comes faster and is deeper when we can time our last meal of the day to give us plenty of time to digest before delving into dreams. You may consider keeping a food journal if what you eat for dinner seems to affect your sleep, noting indigestion, acid reflux, blood sugar imbalances, and the like.

CAFFEINE AND ALCOHOL CONSUMPTION

It can be tempting to reach for a steaming cup of coffee or an ice-cold latte in the afternoon, when our bodies feel sluggish and we're looking for a quick pick-me-up. Know your body and experiment with how late in the day you can consume caffeine without it disrupting your ability to fall asleep, stay asleep, or sleep deeply. My husband is one of those ridiculously unencumbered people who can eat, drink, and do just about anything at any time and then conk out. But the *quality* of sleep we experience is just as important as the number of hours we sleep, and maybe even more so. So, if you suspect that caffeine may be interfering with the quality of your sleep, try indulging only before lunch and replacing your afternoon splurge with high-quality snacks, such as nuts, fruit, a protein shake, or an electrolyte drink. The rituals we come to rely on for emotional comfort or a quick energy burst can feel imperative to us, so if sipping something hot later in the day feeds your soul, try choosing a caffeine-free option, such as herbal tea or warm milk with turmeric and spices.

Recent statistics reveal that 20 to 30 percent of adults in the United States use alcohol to help them fall asleep.[23] While alcohol may relax us and help us fall asleep faster, it generally prevents us from entering the deep sleep phase known as rapid eye movement (REM), which is crucial for maintaining normal brain function, physical health, and emotional well-being. Consuming alcohol prior to sleep also may affect blood sugar in the middle of the night. So, if you enjoy an evening cocktail, try not to splurge too close to bed-time, or indulge moderately.

FOLLOWING YOUR BODY'S GUIDANCE

Everything we do and think about during the day affects our night-time sleep: what we eat or don't eat, how we move or don't move, what we meditate on or stress about, and what we celebrate or let go of. As often as possible, consider the way you move through the day. Are all of your needs being met? Are you prioritizing move-ment as part of how you work through stress and struggles, be they emotional, psychological, mental, or physical? Whether the body contains the energy of fear and anxiety or the energy of excitement and exuberance, all of our intangible experiences require an out-let and a way to be processed. We can talk about our feelings and channel them through creative mediums such as art, books, songs, sharing and receiving wisdom, innovative work projects, and so on, but everything we think, believe, and feel still needs to work its way through and out of our bodies.

In this very moment, what is required of your body to free what is imprisoned within you? Maybe a walk around the neighborhood or a living room dance party is what your body needs to shake off or integrate all that you are processing. Maybe you need to sprint, lift weights, do jumping jacks, or lie still and meditate. The way your body prefers to move or not move may change from day to day and even moment to moment, depending on your workload, your fear level, and how rested you are. It may be influenced by where in your body you are storing anxiety and stress, and how they are manifesting. Listen and respond to the demands of your body today, which are different from the demands of your body yesterday and the demands that will come tomorrow.

Our body and mind require different experiences each and every day, so respond to what is happening right here and now, and claim with full integrity and in full truth the revelations of this moment.

Following the guidance of your body may look like flapping your arms around wildly like a scared pigeon, or gently stretching on the floor, or streaking like a maniac around your home, or rolling your neck in slow, meticulous circles. Your body knows what it needs. Follow its guidance as often as possible, so that when you lay your head on the pillow at the end of the day, you will be emptied of the emotional and physical energy that otherwise might haunt you at night.

Turn to "Intuitive Movement" in the workbook.

EXCESSIVE EXTERNAL STIMULATION

If you are a sensitive person, and especially if you have experienced trauma associated with nighttime, you may turn to hypervigilance as a safety mechanism when the sun goes down. Grounding yourself in the reality of the *now* and reminding yourself that in this very moment you are safe make a great foundation for sleep. You also may require support in blocking out external stimulation so that your body and mind can let go more fully. The tendency of hypervigilant people is to obsess over and fully absorb all the details relating to their safety, which is the opposite of what sleep requires us to do.

Because I am a person whose antennae go up at night, I sleep with earplugs, a white noise machine or an air filter, and a sleep mask. These resources help me block out light and sound so that I can relax more fully. If you prefer to shut out external stimulation as well, you may benefit from a mental reminder that you're safe to let go, along with practical actions such as locking your front door or setting a security alarm. If you have children in your home, it is important that you or another caregiver are still able to respond to them in the middle of the night should they need you. If my kids call for me while I'm asleep, my husband wakes me up so that I am able to go to them. If he is out of town, I sleep with the door open and keep the white noise machine off but still utilize earplugs and a sleep mask. Experiment with what works for you, and always make sure you can hear important sounds such as fire alarms.

External stimulation also includes what you watch and listen to before bedtime—basically, anything you absorb from the outside. If you're committed to being informed about world events and are having trouble sleeping, maybe carve out time earlier in the day to read local and international news or watch TV that might trigger compulsive or worrisome thoughts.

LACK OF CONNECTION TO SLEEP

My seven-year-old son, Max, is one of those delicious and quirky boys who sleep and eat only because it's a functional part of staying alive. He always would rather be dangling from the top of a tree or hunting snakes than eating a sandwich or sleeping. While my husband loves to sleep and is consciously aware of how pivotal it is for his body to recharge, I'm a bit more like Max. The knowledge that sleep is something I *have* to do is irritating to me, unless I consciously frame sleep as something that is extremely active and productive—which it is!

Our relationship with sleep is one that, as with any other valuable relationship, may require some peeling back of layers and reframing. Do I wish I could always be awake? Yes, honestly, I do. But I know that what happens while I sleep may in some ways be even more important than what I do during my waking hours. I understand that boatloads of research suggest that sleep is one of the most pivotal, transformative keys to longevity, presence, and health. And because I am aware of the value of sleep and its positive effects, I prioritize it. By making it a central and irreplaceable part of how I care for myself, I no longer feel that sleep is something that is happening to me. I choose it. And inherent in every choice is a degree of the unknown.

I cannot know in advance what dreams I will have on any given night, at what point I may wake up, or how I will feel in those moments of midnight consciousness when I rouse briefly to take a sip of water. I cannot predetermine the exact nature of those experiences, just as I cannot predict what it will feel like to be with my partner, my children, or myself from day to day. But in the midst of all the unknowns, I trust in my resilience and core strength. And part of core strength is the willingness to be vulnerable and open, as well as available to the influence of external variables.

The stillness of sleep, the surrender required to fall asleep, and the aloneness of shutting out the world can be absolutely terrifying. Without the distractions, chatter, schedules, and sunshine of the day, we are left to breathe deeply into the knowing of our own psyche and souls. To not only agree to sleep but also celebrate and look forward to it, we must first believe that we are safe in our own bodies and minds and can exist peacefully in our dreams. We must be willing to let go and see what happens. We must be comfortable without the noise that deflects deeper feelings and make us feel less alone. Ultimately, we must trust ourselves.

Culturally speaking, despite all the talk about how and why sleep is so important, American values don't holistically reinforce the power of sleep and its influence on mood, perspective, behavior, productivity, mental clarity, and physical health. We are blatantly encouraged to work hard, make money, buy things, do things, pursue things, and create things. But what if sleep were considered an exquisite and profound offering to ourselves and the world? What if we were to reverse the paradigm of action and movement as indicators of ambition and success, and instead celebrate the possibility that in doing absolutely nothing but surrendering to our innate wisdom, we are doing absolutely everything? When we are sleeping, we are not only nurturing our brain and every other vital organ that keeps us alive, we also are processing the truth of who we are and how we truly feel. We are, even for a brief moment in time, divorcing ourselves from the propensity to want to control everything.

When I turn off the light, I expect my sleeping hours to heal the parts of me that require healing, restore the parts of me that require restoration, replenish the parts of me that feel thirsty and dry, and thread together the parts of my life that feel disconnected. I ask my psyche to provide dreams that nourish my soul and reveal significant truths, even if those truths may feel uncomfortable. I can handle the occasional awkwardness or discomfort of my dreams, because I know that I am safe. And I can disconnect from the bright, stimulating world, because the world within has just as much to offer and teach me. In the quiet moments of aloneness, I transform and evolve even without having to work and push for change. Some of our deepest healing and integration occur while we sleep. If we frame sleep as the deep and meaningful work that it is, we position ourselves to prioritize and respect it.

STRESS, ANXIETY, AND FEAR

It is almost impossible to unwind and rest when we are amped up with adrenaline. Unfortunately, many of us are so busy over the course of the day that we don't pause to process the stress and tension that accumulate in our bodies. Alone in the dark, we are flooded with everything that is bothering us. Our minds become crowded by the deadlines and medical diagnoses and relationship dramas that we are able to avoid when there is external stimulation and activity. If possible, set an alarm to go off two or three times throughout the day as a reminder to check in with yourself and assess your level of stress. Then name the potential source(s) of that stress, if you can.

By checking in with yourself throughout the day, you periodically will provide opportunities for awareness and relief instead of storing up all your anxiety for the moment you turn the lights off. When I do my check-ins and recognize stress, I often immediately do something physical to move it through my body. I may shake, bob my shoulders up and down, or roll my head in gentle circles. Always, I breathe deeply. In conjunction with my physical release, I sometimes create a sound that represents what I am feeling and embodies the quality and textures of my stress in real time. It may be a yelp, shriek, breathy whimper, or groan, or musical scales. It doesn't matter. If you do this, don't overthink it. Just let the sound exit your body as you move.

Turn to "Releasing Stress through Movement
and Sound" in the workbook.

A friend of mine is a university professor and prolific global activist, and she is highly qualified to worry about the problems of the world. Her profession requires her to ruminate about war, disease, famine, slavery, genocide, human rights, and endless other essential and weighty topics. But because the work she does centers almost exclusively around the pain of others, I wonder sometimes if she is creating the space to connect with her own personal struggles. Often, the things we worry about most frequently in the external world mirror some aspect of our internal experience and may keep us awake at night.

Turn to "Managing Anxiety before Sleeping" in the workbook.

When thoughts that feel pressing dart in and out of my mind as I'm trying to fall asleep, I remind myself that I'm equipped to handle everything that might come my way in the daytime. In fact, by being well-rested and having a fully functional brain and body, I am exponentially more prepared to respond to my fears from a place of confidence and objectivity. When I've slept peacefully, I have access to all of the internal resources necessary to navigate challenges strategically, intuitively, and with compassion. In order to let go more fully at bedtime, I jot down all of my fears on a piece of paper, then remind myself that the best time to address them is in the morning after a good night's sleep.

HUSHING OUR INTERNAL NARRATIVES

Do you ever find yourself ruminating on certain aspects of your life, rehashing past events, or rehearsing future ones when you wish to be falling asleep? When you are entangled in the storylines of your life, consider providing your brain with content that is alluring enough to capture its attention, but not so captivating that it overstimulates you. This content may take the form of a quiet mental game (recalling every country you've been to, imagining the names of all your friends spelled backward, thinking of as many words as you can that involve hyphens or digraphs such as "sh," "th," "ck," and so on). I used to work my way through the alphabet, imagining a needle and thread inscribing words into my mind's eye. Beginning with *A*, I would spell out things I was grateful for, watching the needle and thread move elegantly through my imagination: "A chance to live again tomorrow. Breath. Cold weather that makes me feel cozy. Dogs…" I rarely made it past *F*.

WORDLESSNESS

Anxiety can often lead to repetitive and stressful thoughts without relief. If you find your mind buzzing with excessive words at night, set the intention of wordlessness. Quietly and gently make the sound "om"[24] in your mind for a couple of seconds, then visualize something from nature, such as a leaf, tree, or flower. Take a few deep breaths to reset your nervous system, and then repeat this cycle of alternating between the *om* sound and something visual. You may change the visual as you go, but the idea is to soften the influx of words.

Another way to potentially bring yourself into wordlessness is to create a melody in your head. By internally humming the song of how you feel, you will be without the need for language. If creating your own melody feels far out of reach, try to silently hum the tune of a familiar song.

What other ways can you come up with to put words to sleep? What wordless place or scene can you travel to in your mind to connect more fully with peace? If you cannot think of one that exists in reality, you can always create one.

»•«

Practice: Implied Resolution Through Gratitude

Much of what we fear at night relates to the unknown—what *could* happen in the future. For many of us, the unknown can feel vast and daunting, especially when something significant is at stake. One of the ways you can calm yourself at night if you find yourself worrying is to preemptively give thanks for the desired resolution of whatever it is you are stressed about or anticipating. Here are some examples:

"Thank you that my interview went so well."

"Thank you that I am in perfect health for giving my speech."

"Thank you that I slept so beautifully."

"Thank you that I have the resources I need to buy my children their schoolbooks."

Claim the ideal outcome of whatever it is you fear or are unsure of even before you experience closure. The more you anticipate positive outcomes, the calmer your body should feel. If I'm struggling with wanting an answer to an important question, I usually state the question and then say, "Thank you, higher consciousness, innate wisdom, and the universe, for answering this question at exactly the right time." There is so much pressure attached to unanswered questions, and in my experience, the best way to access our highest truth is to ask our questions and allow the answers to come to us in a natural, organic way.

»•«

NEGATIVE ASSOCIATIONS WITH BEDTIME

I will never forget a sleepover at the home of one of my best friends when we were eight years old. Her parents were going through a rocky divorce and began to viciously fight right after tucking us into bed. Thirty-three years later, I still remember the gist of the fight—and they weren't even my parents. My friend's home felt emotionally violent, and we squeezed our eyes shut in an effort to block out her parents' words of resentment and rage. Not surprisingly, my friend became sleepless around the age of her parents' breakup, and to this day she struggles with falling asleep at night. A sort of dark, uncomfortable feeling overtakes her body when she crawls into bed, and she feels eerily unsettled when she turns off the light. The feeling is vague but very real.

If your parents fought in close proximity to your bedroom when you were growing up, or you could hear a drunken parent stumbling into things at night, or the sound of things breaking abruptly disrupted your sleep, or you were privy to crying, yelling, tension, or the impending threat of physical danger, it's very possible that you have post-traumatic stress disorder (PSTD). And the trauma of those memories exists within you on a cellular level. If someone in your home was being abused physically, emotionally, or sexually, and you were privy to the abuse but unable to stop it, there's a very good chance that this trauma lives in you today, along with the perception of helplessness it incurred. If your body and psyche have not integrated former trauma, most likely it continues to influence your present-day behavior and impact your current version of reality.

If you yourself were abused, there is no doubt that you are carrying the great weight and burden of having been unsafe with the people who should have protected you. If any of these things happened in your life, I am so sorry. Please know that you are not alone and that there are trained and compassionate professionals who can gently and effectively support your healing process. There is no right way or one way to heal, but we all deserve freedom from the legacy of our past and how it continues to shape us and our lives today.

Even worrying about a parent who has lost their job and can't pay the bills is incredibly stressful for a child. There is no doubt that instability of any kind impacts the nervous system and imprints in a person the feeling of being unsafe. The context of a child's life should always be one of physical, emotional, mental, psychological, spiritual, and material safety, so anything that threatens any one of these categories puts a child's well-being at risk. Most often, these threats overlap, so if a child is compromised in one regard, there is a good chance that they feel unsafe on a broader level.

If you are experiencing sleeplessness due to traumatic memories, please consult a trained professional who is equipped to counsel you through the process of addressing, integrating, and releasing your past. Often, a turbulent or violent childhood splits a person into two parts as they grow older. One part is the helpless, vulnerable child who is at once overstimulated, neglected, and traumatized, and the other part is the rational, cognitively inclined adult who thinks they can talk or explain their way out of trauma, or simply ignore it in the hope that it will resolve naturally.

In my experience, integrating the scared and rational parts of our being often requires that we do less thinking and more feeling. The good news is that there are loving and well-trained therapists who are available to walk through the fire with you. Again, you are not alone. I myself have been there. Many of the people I love have been there as well. You are capable of healing and will at some point experience more of the emotional freedom and sense of safety you deserve. Please be patient with yourself.

Neglect and abandonment can be as impactful and disconcerting for young people as outright abuse. When a child receives the message that they are unworthy of being properly cared for, the result is often shame. If you have night terrors and the grown-up in charge of you chooses to not hold you in the middle of the night, you are left alone to hold yourself. The issue with neglect such as that is that children don't necessarily know how to regulate their own nervous systems or intuitively comfort themselves in ways that create a true sense of safety. We learn these skills from adults through modeling and the experience of being held by them.

As we watch the adults we love and trust self-soothe, we learn how to self-soothe. As they rub our backs, stroke our heads, and comfort us with words of reassurance and hope, we learn to comfort ourselves physically and emotionally as needed. If that instruction and guidance are missing, we may resort to coping mechanisms that in the moment provide a false sense of safety, but that don't actually regulate our nervous systems or provide a solid foundation of trust in ourselves and the world. These coping mechanisms may include worrying, having superstitious thoughts, drinking, condemning ourselves, shaming ourselves when we feel vulnerable, creating emotional walls, numbing ourselves, and punishing ourselves physically, mentally, and/or emotionally when we feel out of control. They also may include micromanaging our external and internal worlds in order to maintain a false sense of safety. What hasn't happened to us or for us may be just as powerful and harmful as what has.

PAIN OR DISCOMFORT FROM INJURIES, IMBALANCE, OR ILLNESS

When I was in the third trimester of my first pregnancy, I had to get up every few hours in the middle of the night to stretch, because my hips were expanding. Because of this, I have incredible empathy for people who experience physical discomfort that keeps them awake at night. Any level of disruptive discomfort can be overwhelming, whether it's from a broken ankle, chemotherapy treatment for cancer, or something else. Fortunately, there are doctors, psychologists, and others in the medical field who write and talk about pain management. If chronic discomfort is an issue for you, I suggest you consult pain management experts, who can provide resources, tools, and perspectives to help reframe your mindset and inspire hope.

One of the most helpful tidbits I gleaned from the parents in my son's baby group was to frequently reinforce the reality that all our experiences on this planet are brief and inevitably will pass. Every time an exhausted new mother said something such as "He's waking up every thirty minutes!" or "I'm so tired, I can't even see straight," or "I'm feeling really depressed and anxious," our mentor would swiftly tack the words "for now" onto the back end of the declaration. "He's got acid reflux." "For now!" "I feel like I can barely function." "For now!" "I don't have the wherewithal to make dinner." "For now!" Those words, "for now," echo through me all these years later whenever I feel down or am in a rut without a definitive end point. If you are in bed and are overcome by the thought that what you're experiencing might never end, try out those two simple words. See what it feels like to entertain the notion that your fear and/or physical discomfort are present now, but won't be forever.

Also, if you are too distracted by your discomfort to fall asleep, see if you can pinpoint just one part of your body that isn't in pain. Does your pinkie nail hurt? How about your belly button? Focus your attention on the non-struggle experienced by your hair or the tip of your nose, and breathe into that part. Accept the relief that comes when you focus your attention on what *is* working and full of ease. Now try out these words and see how they land in your heart: "I do not need to be free from physical discomfort to live in peace."

EXTERNAL DANGERS

If you are in a radically unsafe environment, my sincere hope is that you will be able to seek safety at a shelter or in the home of someone who can provide at least temporary protection and relief. If you are subjected to war, political or social unrest, systemic violence, or natural disasters, my prayer is that you will be able to relocate to a city or country where staying awake is not required for staying alive. If you are in a neighborhood where gun violence, domestic violence, and/or break-ins are rampant, you may never feel fully safe in your bed. If you are experiencing physical violence in your own home, I imagine that you are at all times prepared to spring into action, hide, or respond to the demands of your abuser. If you or someone you know is a survivor of domestic violence, please seek support from the National Domestic Hotline. Since internet usage can be traced, immediately delete your history of consulting this resource, but know that internet searches can never be permanently deleted. Calling or texting the hotline may be a preferable option.

> National Domestic Hotline
> https://www.thehotline.org/
> 800-799-SAFE (7233)
> Text START to 88788.

EYE MOVEMENT DESENSITIZATION AND REPROCESSING

Eye movement desensitization and reprocessing (EMDR) is a form of therapy developed in the late 1980s for the treatment of PTSD. EMDR is guided by the adaptive information processing model. In simple terms, the concept is that if the brain does not properly process a disturbing event, it retains the thoughts, emotions, and physical sensations that occurred when that event took place. At any point when the memory later resurfaces, the individual experiences those negative impressions.

During an EMDR session, a person is directed to focus on a disturbing memory and simultaneously use bilateral stimulation (BLS), commonly involving eye movements. Working with a clinician, the participant evaluates and rates their reaction to the memory of the unpleasant event after engaging in these eye movements. Treatment sessions typically occur once or twice a week for six to twelve weeks until the memory or memories are no longer disturbing.[25]

INTERNAL FAMILY SYSTEMS MODEL

The internal family systems model (IFS) is an approach to individual psychotherapy developed by therapist Richard C. Schwartz in the 1980s. Some find it very effective for integrating the parts of the psyche that have become fragmented as a result of trauma. Adherents suggest its appropriateness for the treatment of a variety of issues, including trauma, abuse, anxiety, phobias, alcohol and other substance dependency, and body image concerns. Its fundamental tenet is that the mind is made of various parts, and the system focuses on the relationship between those parts—all of which have a positive intent, as set out in Schwartz's book *No Bad Parts*—and the core self.[26]

According to IFS, the three general parts of the mind are exiles (representing trauma, pain, fear, and the like), managers (protectors who influence interaction with the outside world), and firefighters (helpers when exiles overwhelm the individual). The way in which these parts interact can also be broken down into three parts: protection (provided by managers and firefighters), polarization (as the word suggests, this occurs when two parts are at odds about how to feel or behave), and alliance (the opposite of polarization).

An IFS practitioner assists the client in accessing the self to unburden exiles (remove painful emotions or negative beliefs), permitting managers and firefighters to step down from their protective roles.[27]

COGNITIVE BEHAVIORAL THERAPY

Some forms of psychotherapy encourage delving into the past to understand current feelings. In contrast, cognitive behavioral therapy (CBT) focuses on a person's present-day thoughts and beliefs. CBT rests on the assumption that the way people think affects how they feel and behave.

Here are some basic principles associated with this form of therapy. First, automatic thoughts are an individual's immediate interpretations of an event. They shape both emotions and behavior in response to that event. For example, a friend may pass you on the street and not say hi. If you have the automatic thought *I've done something to upset her*, you may feel upset (emotion) and perhaps avoid her in the future (behavior). On the other hand, if your automatic thought is *She must be preoccupied today*, you will neither feel stress nor avoid that friend moving forward.

Next, cognitive distortions are irrational or extreme thought patterns that lead to false conclusions. For instance, dichotomous thinking involves the creation of two mutually exclusive categories with no shades of gray in between. This is commonly referred to as all-or-nothing thinking. Another common distortion is mind reading, in which individuals assume they know the thoughts and intentions of others. A third is catastrophizing: focusing on the worst possible scenario or viewing a situation as impossible rather than just difficult.

What skews people's perceptions is the underlying core beliefs (or central ideas) they've formed about themselves and the world. During therapy, an individual brings conscious awareness to negative automatic thoughts, compares them with reality (by asking themselves if their reaction is rational or irrational, proportionate or disproportionate), assesses how those negative thoughts make them feel, and modifies them. Typical treatment involves weekly sessions of approximately sixty minutes for eight to twelve weeks.[28]

THE INSOMNIAC IDENTITY

For years, I told people I was an insomniac. I thought of myself as an insomniac, believed I was an insomniac, and lived as if I were an insomniac. Then one day, a dear friend suggested that I stop telling myself I could not sleep. She encouraged me to tell myself that I *could* sleep, and that I was the best sleeper on the planet. "Tell yourself that you can sleep anywhere," she said. "On a plane, in the middle of a grassy field, on a train, in your bed, in a hotel room. You are the most flexible and adaptable sleeper around. You are not an insomniac. You are the queen of sleep."

My initial reaction was to tell my friend that she had no idea what it was like to be someone who couldn't sleep anywhere without pills, and that her Mary Poppins suggestion was making light of my struggle. Then, after my defensiveness and fear softened, I allowed her words to sink in. What if my body *was* capable of sleeping any-where at any time? What if my mind *was* capable of shutting off, and by identifying with the label of "insomniac," I was actually reinforc-ing my limitations surrounding sleep?

So, I started to imagine myself as a fabulous sleeper. I imagined what it would be like to step onto an airplane, shut my eyes, and sleep. I imagined what it would feel like to get into my own bed at the end of a long day, pull the covers over my tired body, and surren-der without a fight. And I stopped telling people I was an insomniac. If it was relevant to talk about sleep, I would say things like "I'm working on becoming an amazing sleeper," or "Sleep doesn't come as easily for me as it may for others, but it will one day," or "I'm putting together an incredible routine to help support my sleep."

Replacing my identity of insomniac with words that described my struggle but invited optimism into the equation was absolutely life-altering for me, and it can be life-altering for you too. You are not an insomniac; you are a person who is working on developing healthy sleep hygiene. Once you separate your struggle from who you are, you'll be able to craft a new self-concept. If you are a human being with a history of trauma who is deeply invested in quality sleep, you must work at it as you would any other relationship in your life that is meaningful to you. You are not what you feel or what you experience. You are a human being, period. And you are capable of growth and change.

»•«

Tip: Redefining Your Experience with Sleep

Let's consider how to reframe your sleep challenges and eliminate the identity of insomniac. What language can you use to describe your struggle without blending the line between identity and experience? What statements can you make to yourself and others that allow for growth? How can your words support the possibility of a future that looks and feels radically different? Here are some ideas:

"I am working on my sleep hygiene and will one day be a fantastic sleeper."

"I've been wrestling with some sleep issues, but it's important work that will yield beautiful results."

"It feels really exhausting to not be able to sleep deeply, but on the other side of my fatigue is freedom."

"I'm tired today, but my body and mind are working together to create change. I will not feel this way forever."

»•«

SLEEP QUEEN

I am now going to walk you through my sleep routine, which is one that I rely on and cherish. Everyone's routine is different, and some people are able to be far more flexible with their ritual than I am; this is just what works for me. In general, creating a sleep rhythm is an extremely powerful way to train the body. I try as often as I can to get into bed around the same time nightly, to maintain a strong internal clock. If you struggle with falling asleep, consistency is key.

I love rituals, so regardless of what comes before, my bedtime ritual begins with the gradual dimming of lights in my house. About fifteen minutes before I get into bed, I stretch on a yoga mat in my bedroom with only the lamp on my nightstand turned on. This lamp provides soft, warm lighting as I stretch. I then mix a single serving of Alaya Naturals' Calming Blend powder (containing magnesium carbonate and L-theanine) into water and drink it. This relaxes my body and provides a sense of calm.

160

Years ago, when I was trying to wean off Ambien, I worked with a hypnotherapist who asked me to recall in great detail the sensations that I experienced when I took Ambien. In brief, my body grew heavier and heavier as if it were laced with metal, my sharp thoughts mellowed into nothingness, and eventually blackness took over. While under hypnosis, I reenacted the experience of taking Ambien, using a natural stress relief remedy called Bach Rescue Pastilles as a substitute. Now, I keep a tin of these pastilles on my nightstand, and if I'm feeling particularly activated, I suck on a pastille while I'm winding down for sleep.

Over many years, I have practiced training my brain to have Pavlovian responses to all kinds of things. By my believing that something will impact my body, it often does—the placebo effect. Imagination is its own unique brand of magic. If you've never taken sleeping pills, maybe you can imagine a time when you were severely jet-lagged or missed a night of sleep and were a zombie the next day. Utilizing all of your senses, recall an experience of feeling impossibly drowsy. Now draw on that memory to create a similar Pavlovian response to the one my hypnotherapist helped me generate while sucking on a Bach's Rescue Pastille. You don't even need to put something in your mouth; you could touch two fingers together, lay your hands across your heart, or do whatever feels natural and comfortable for you. If you do choose to put something in your mouth, just make sure not to fall asleep before it has fully dissolved.

Interestingly, on nights when I'm hesitant to put something in my mouth because I suspect that I might fall asleep before it will have fully dissolved, I find that gently resting my tongue against the roof of my mouth creates almost instant relief from racing thoughts. I've associated the pressure of a pastille against the roof of my mouth with relaxation for so many years that now even the pressure of my own tongue does the trick.

Every time I get into my bed, I understand that there will be a period of time dedicated to fidgeting and thinking. Yes, I allot time to fidget and think. Regardless of how many times I have checked in with myself over the course of the day and made efforts to alleviate stress, new thoughts and feelings pop up when the lights go out. This is why I carve out a window of about fifteen to thirty minutes to decompress and to exfoliate the residue of the day.

While I consider my bed to be a safe, nurturing space in which to ruminate, I don't want it to be a place that I associate with over-thinking. Once hot topics and emotions have surfaced, I give myself a little time to unpack them, and if necessary, make a list of all that feels unresolved. For efficiency, I keep a pen and paper on my bedside table to avoid having to get out of bed. After I've scribbled down the subject matters that feel activating, I tell myself that I can address them after a peaceful night's sleep.

If mental processing begins to create or heighten anxiety, that is the point when I encourage myself to drift away from language and into a state where words are no longer useful or welcome. If visualizations or access to imagination feel elusive, then I practice Emotional Freedom Techniques (EFT, also known as tapping) in relation to every troubling thought or fear. (Read on for an explanation of EFT.)

Every night, I also play with which positions help my body feel relaxed and grounded. When you get into bed, do you notice that your thoughts stop racing when you're lying on your left side, but your mind gets activated when you're lying on your right? Do you unwind faster on your back, your belly, or your side? I personally shift around in my bed until I settle into a position that supports the process of letting go.

I also feel supported by what my friend Serena refers to as Upstairs. Her concept of God, the Divine, Spirit, or Source is some-what undefined, but she prays to Upstairs, and in her belief that there are unseen forces guiding and lovingly protecting her, she feels held. Some people pray to God, and others to ancestors, spirit guides, angels, nature, or to their own higher consciousness. I refer to my higher consciousness as my knowing, and I often call upon this part of me to provide answers or relief when I cannot sleep. Whatever or whoever you pray to, including your own majestic capacity to nurture and comfort yourself, may invite a feeling of peace. When you are in bed, wondering how you are going to pay your taxes or nail your work presentation or break up with your partner, try speaking (internally or out loud) to your version of Upstairs.

Turn to "Creating Your Bedtime Routine" in the workbook.

When I can't seem to let go of specific sources of anxiety at night, I do EFT, which has at its core the ancient Chinese philosophy of *chi*, assumed to be the life force flowing throughout the body. Therapist Gary Craig developed the technique in 1993, based on what he learned about Thought Field Therapy (TFT) from psychologist Roger Callahan. Advocates of EFT claim that it can treat a wide variety of physical and psychological disorders. Even the ritual itself is soothing and may provide a sense of comfort. The process is simple. First, identify your emotional or physical source of pain or other issue. Second, assign it a value of distress on a scale of one to ten. Then prepare a setup phrase. A common one is "Even though I have this [state the problem], I completely accept myself." Theoretically, you are targeting the emotional component of the issue, even if the issue is physical pain.

Next, focus on that specific issue while tapping on certain areas of the body (meridian endpoints, as used in traditional Chinese medicine), such as the top of the head, eyebrows, sides of the eyes, under the eyes, chin, collarbone, under the arms, and wrists. While tapping each point, repeat your phrase. After each round of tapping, reassess your degree of emotional distress. Would you say you went from a level eight to five, for example? The goal is to continue the tapping cycle until the trauma level has been lowered adequately, ideally to zero.

It may take practice to use this technique effectively, but some adherents report success simply by imagining themselves tapping when in a situation where physical movement is not possible. Because I consistently use this technique, I no longer assess my stress level between rounds if I do more than one. The assessment piece tends to bring me back to language and analytical thought, so I simply tap and trust that the effort is successful. A detailed breakdown of meridian points is included in a free manual from EFT International. While it is helpful to work with a trained practitioner for the sake of accuracy, it is entirely safe to attempt EFT on your own. Please consult the EFT Tapping Training Institute's website (www.efttapping-training.com) along with the Tapping International website (www.tappinginternational.com) for additional guidance.[29]

Here are a few final ideas for inviting sweet sleep and surrender:

Imagine all the words that enter your mind as colors. If a scary, unsettling, or stressful feeling enters your body, assign it a color and a shape. Now assign a color and shape to the word *peace*. Imagine your representation of the icky feeling morphing into the representation of peace. Do this for as many feelings as you need to.

Imagine yourself as part of nature. You may be an ancient, looming pine tree in the middle of a forest. Peaceful and still, you embody wisdom in your state of wordlessness. You may be the ocean, fluid and transparent and shifting without thought. You may be a leaf, or a stone, or the wind. You have no taxes to file, no one to report to or consciously take care of, and no money to make. Soak in the harmony and ease of having nothing to do other than be, and nowhere to go besides where you are. As part of nature, you are free from requirements, pressure, and stress. You have no expectations, agenda, or plans. You simply are.

Imagine yourself as a baby with wonderfully nurturing and thoughtful parents. You are cared for, every single one of your needs is met, and your only job is to surrender to sleep. Curled up in your bed, you drift off without a care.

— CHAPTER SUMMARY —

Sleep is not just a good idea, it is essential to the emotional, mental, and physical health of every human being. By examining your relationship to sleep, the beliefs you've subconsciously formed about who you are in relation to sleep, and the barriers that may be keeping you from sleeping soundly, you will pave the way for prioritizing thoughtful sleep hygiene and enjoying the benefits that will follow. As someone who spent years struggling with sleep, I know the extent to which good sleep can positively influence a person's outlook on life and support their ability not only to function optimally but to heal.

CHAPTER 6

HEALING TRAUMA

As defined by the American Psychological Association, trauma is an emotional response to a terrible event, such as an accident, a crime, or a natural disaster.[30] When I was considering my personal definition of "trauma," here's what felt right: trauma is the resistance to what is real, based on a period of time during which one's vulnerability led to feelings of extreme terror or shame. Trauma may result from a single incident or be the product of an entire relationship that threatens or crushes one's sense of safety emotionally, physically, and/or psychologically.

The reason I frame trauma in terms of resistance to what is real is that a person who has been traumatized most likely will have one of the following reactions: shock, denial, disassociation, behavioral addictions that block true emotion (such as self-cutting, disordered eating, or drug or alcohol abuse), or emotional patterns that also block core emotion (such as codependency, intimacy avoidance, anxiety, or depression). Whether you are numbing yourself through denial, drug use, sex, violence, rage, or depression, one thing is true: none of these reactions to trauma is you. Your feelings and behavior while trying to process and heal from trauma are coping mechanisms. They are meant to block you from the reality of what has happened to you and prevent you from experiencing similar levels of pain in the future.

Unfortunately, in order to fully heal, we must consciously experience to some degree what our bodies and minds most resist feeling. But once we have processed the (at times agonizing) emotions we've buried, we will have deeper access to the experience of emotional freedom. I believe that the true essence of every individual is at least partly defined by peace, ease, love, and joy. To experience and relish our core identity, we must understand and let go of who we are not. At our core, none of us is anxious, fearful, depressed, or full of rage. As a way of trying to protect us from overwhelming pain and grief, our trauma response thrusts us into thought patterns, emotional states, and behaviors that block genuine relief and contentment. But freedom is always and already ours; all we have to do is peel back the layers of who we are not in order to fully embrace the reality of our stunning nature.

Trauma is an incredibly sensitive topic that many of us avoid for numerous reasons. When we speak, hear, or write the word "trauma," what comes to mind may be severe physical, emotional, or sexual abuse; war; extreme destitution; or undeniably radical suffering.

There may always be a person or group of people who challenge your right to feel that you have experienced trauma, or who compel you to disregard or minimize your experiences. This person may very well be yourself. And while some people have no doubt survived horrific and virtually unbelievable levels of trauma, when we begin to compare our experiences to those of others, we are essentially shaming ourselves out of our feelings. While we may assume on a superficial level that there is something heroic, humble, appropriate, or reasonable about disregarding our own experiences because others have experienced "real" trauma, all trauma is real trauma and impacts every one of us in deep and significant ways.

TRAUMA CANNOT BE MEASURED

Trauma is trauma, regardless of how "big" or "small" it is. All levels of trauma incur a sense of shame, dysregulate the nervous system, and interrupt our ability to actively engage with life in a way that feels meaningful and satisfying. As much as we are in the societal habit of wanting to measure and quantify things, there is no way to empirically define how deeply a traumatic experience impacts a person or how. Because of this, I am going to suggest that we stop trying to quantify our trauma or the trauma of others and just let ourselves feel it. If we are busy processing our internal world and equipping ourselves with the resources to self-soothe and rewire ourselves, we will have less interest in trying to determine what qualifies as trauma. Nor will we feel entitled to judge what other people interpret as trauma. If a baby flings mashed potatoes against the wall and is sneered at by a tired mother, that child may experience a level of trauma as a result. A lover ending a relationship is a traumatic experience, as is losing a job or pet or loved one. Trauma might result from finding out your partner is having an affair, or being in a car accident, or getting fired unexpectedly.

Furthermore, two people who experience the exact same event might respond entirely differently. The same experience might feel only mildly traumatic to one person and catastrophic or life-ending to another. There are many factors that influence a person's potential response to a triggering event: their genes, their level of resiliency and adaptability, how they perceive the event, what they fundamentally believe about themselves and the world, the meaning or purpose they ultimately assign to the event, how they consciously use the event to evolve or help others evolve, and what other traumatic events have occurred in their life, to name a few. How you personally metabolize the world is important, relevant, and legitimate simply because it is your experience. You do not need to dismiss or disregard it because other people are also struggling, or because you yourself have struggled before in what you feel were more significant ways. Everything you experience is important. *You* are important. Take time to acknowledge whatever it is you have been through or still are grappling with, however much you would like to wish it away or ignore it.

I highly recommend that everybody who is in the midst of unpacking trauma have reliable, consistent friends or family members they can count on for emotional support. Our society encourages people to frequently ask how others are doing. Unfortunately, most communities are not equipped with the emotional or tangible resources to encourage individuals to respond to this question with any level of depth. Because of this, many of us have habituated to providing superficial responses to the question of how we are doing, so our emotional state remains a mystery to others, and possibly even to ourselves. We all benefit from accountability and support, so I encourage you to select one or two trustworthy people in your life with whom you can commit to being completely transparent about your psychological state. Even if they aren't specifically equipped to help you, it is important for at least one person to be aware of your struggles (to whatever degree feels reasonable) and to check in. This may not only help you feel less alone but also provide objective feedback about ways in which you might require additional support.

Additionally, you may deeply benefit from interviewing and connecting with qualified professionals who are trained to respond to whatever potentially scary or overwhelming feelings may come up. Remember that you are not alone. Every single person in the world has experienced some level of trauma and is grasping to feel safe, loved, accepted, and held, not despite what they've been through, but because of it.

There are several reasons why a person who has experienced trauma may not speak freely or readily about it. Below, I am going to list some of the possible reasons. I personally relate to all of them, which is how I came up with this list: they were once *my* reasons. Shame is an awful, disorienting experience, and pretty much everyone I know who has experienced trauma of any kind can relate to it. What we want people to believe about us is that we are more than our diagnosis. We want our loved ones to accept that we cannot be definitively labeled. We want them to know that we are not, at our core, what we struggle with. But as hard as this is, we cannot control what other people think or how they feel about us. We can in no way manipulate their reactions to our stories. All we can do is own our stories as if they were our children and nurture them with compassion, grace, forgiveness, and love. Freeing yourself is one thing; claiming ownership of your freed soul is another.

My story is my child, and I don't punish it for being complex and confusing and for occasionally bringing out the worst in me. When the grittiest and darkest parts of my past cause me to react to current events in ways that are self-punishing, rigid, or judgmental, I try not to let shame run the show. Instead, I take a deep breath and speak to myself the way I would to a scared child: "Wow, you seem to be having a really hard time right now. What can I do to help you feel better? How can I support you? What do you need from me in this moment?" The less you punish yourself for all that you have been through and are currently experiencing, the less you will fear the judgment and condemnation of others. You are, after all, just a human being having a human experience.

Do any of the following reasons for avoiding the exploration of your trauma resonate with you?

FEAR OF BEING TRIGGERED

The fear of being triggered—experiencing the emotions associated with trauma—without the internal resources to self-soothe and stay present is very understandable. More often than not, addressing trauma will catalyze deeply uncomfortable feelings, which may include intense sadness, rage, terror, and/or a sense of helplessness and feeling overwhelmed, to name a few. You also may experience the instinct to run, hide, numb yourself, compulsively people-please, or act out. So, why even go there? Because as tempting as it is to avoid tapping into these feelings, you are already feeling them deep down inside. Awareness may temporarily heighten feelings, but if you haven't consciously connected with them, you are an unconscious slave to them.

Think about it. If underlying your peppy, functional, productive adult self is a scared or angry child, that child ultimately will dictate the degree to which you may ever be able to experience unencumbered freedom and joy or receive love without stipulations. Whatever you aren't consciously acknowledging will surface and manifest in one way or another, be it through a short temper or a propensity to snap at people, the pursuit of perfection, compulsive tendencies, inexplicable depression or physical ailments, an inability to connect intimately with others or yourself, or an unhealthy reliance on others for positive affirmation or validation. It also may affect the level of success you allow yourself to achieve; the nature of your self-talk and internal narrative; how you interpret external events; what you believe about yourself, others, and the world; or how you define and are available to the experience of feeling safe.

Regardless of how terrifying or humiliating it may feel to access the parts of yourself you want so badly to separate yourself from, accepting yourself in your totality will allow you to experience the full spectrum of emotions—including freedom, joy, peace, and contentment—more radically and completely. You are not required to feel anything you don't want to feel, but you are allowed to. And I promise you that on the other side of fear is freedom. On the other side of anxiety are allowance and surrender. On the other side of sadness are compassion and joy. And on the other side of repression is the bold, beautiful truth.

SHAME

At the heart of trauma is shame, which is perhaps the most elusive and insidious yet pervasive experience of my lifetime. At certain times, it felt like an emotional fog that never lifted regardless of where I was, who I was with, or what I was doing. In the words of Brené Brown, "Shame needs three things to grow exponentially in our lives: secrecy, silence, and judgment."

SELF-BLAME

People who have experienced traumatic events sometimes feel that they have failed by allowing themselves to be traumatized. Self-blame is a common coping mechanism, since children assume that when a primary caregiver behaves in ways that are erratic or neglectful, it is because of something they've done wrong, or because fundamentally they *are* wrong. By believing that their behavior is the problem, and that *they* are the problem, a child is able to maintain faith in their caregivers and the world. When self-blame becomes habituated, children may grow into adults who continue to blame themselves not just for their trauma but for everything that ever goes wrong in their lives or in the lives of those they love. Even minor imperfections or mistakes may incur a sense of shame.

RELUCTANCE TO SHARE

Sometimes, a person who is suffering doesn't want to inconvenience, burden, or disappoint others by sharing their trauma. Additionally, when we expose parts of ourselves that feel damaged or wounded, we are susceptible to the shame, sadness, and fear associated with potential judgment. Because of this, it is natural to create excuses as to why we should not or cannot be vulnerable with others. Many young people also are aware of all that their caregivers are managing (jobs, finances, other siblings, and so on), and they may wish to avoid feeling like an additional source of stress. The fear of being burdensome or "too much" may cause people to suffocate their feelings and stories even into adulthood.

DESIRE TO PROTECT VERSUS NEED TO ESCAPE

An individual's trauma may implicate a person or people they love and/or want to protect. Trauma can occur in countless ways. We may witness or overhear something disturbing, such as a car accident, violence, or a statement that rocks us to our core. We may be subjected to circumstances outside our control that threaten us physically and/ or psychologically, such as war, living in a crime-ridden village or neighborhood, becoming homeless, or lacking basic necessities. We also may experience some kind of abuse from an absolute stranger, which strips us of our sense of safety.

But what if the abuser is our mother, stepparent, or neighbor? What if it is our cousin or uncle? What if it is the father of a childhood friend? The instinct to protect those we love, fear, or feel obligated to respect and protect puts the survivor of abuse in a very confusing situation. On one hand, they may feel compelled to protect their abuser in order to maintain important relationships or remain fundamentally safe. On the other hand, they most probably wish to be rescued from danger and expose the truth. In cases where a stepfather or a mother's boyfriend is the abuser, young people may wish to protect themselves or their mother by remaining voiceless. The perceived benefits of secrecy may be related to the child having received a direct threat from their abuser, the nature of the mother's romantic involvement with the abuser, the mother's unwillingness to protect the child, or the fear of how the mother would react if she were to find out. Even when a mother is ignorant of her child's abuse, she is vicariously implicated when the truth emerges. This is a reality that some children wish to avoid.

DISBELIEF AND DENIAL

The truth can be terrifying, overwhelming, and saddening. It also can cause us to question ourselves, those we love, and even the integrity of the whole world. When certain events feel too overwhelming to process, we may block them out or repress them. We also may accept certain portions of reality, but not the totality of what we have experienced, so that the experience is more digestible. Some people rewrite history altogether, or skew and distort the past so that it mirrors a version of reality that makes it easier for them to survive. Disbelief and denial are common ways for a person to remain functional when they don't believe they are properly resourced to handle the truth.

OUR IDENTITY

The majority of people I know who have experienced trauma—myself included—have worked very hard (at least for some period of time) to delete any traces of their dark past as it relates to their current identity. We want people to view us as confident and in control, and we wish to view ourselves that same way. Confessing our trauma opens the door to vulnerability and potential judgment, which, on a superficial level, negates our efforts to appear "together." But the reality is that nothing makes people more truly confident than owning their whole story and consciously claiming their life.

Just as we cannot eliminate body parts and still have a whole body, we cannot eliminate parts of our past and still have a whole life. By admitting to and having compassion for the entirety of what we've been through, we are essentially saying yes to everything that we are. While it may feel more comfortable to describe ourselves in purely flattering ways, none of us are loyal, kind, or patient without occasionally acting stubbornly, reactively, or fearfully. It is the full acceptance of how our humanity gets expressed that creates true self-love and emotional freedom.

We may always seek to consciously evolve, but there is no need to condemn or slash any part of who we are. Likewise, we should not attempt to exile any part of what we've been through but rather integrate it into a framework that allows us to live an emotionally free and joyful life. When we stop running from the parts of ourselves and our past that we feel others will reject, we experience deep relief. The truth is incredibly liberating once we move past the fear of being abandoned and unlovable.

FEAR OF PUNISHMENT

The fear of being persecuted or punished by loved ones, caretakers, people in the workplace, people on social media, and so on is very legitimate. If you let authorities know that your father has been abusing you, your mother may fly off the handle. If you are entrenched in a community or religion that is concerned with reputation, and you report abuse, people may gather to bring you down. If you anticipate a genuine backlash that poses a threat to your physical or emotional safety, it is wise to put a support system in place should you choose to share your trauma. This may include a shelter of some kind, a crisis hotline, a person you can stay with, or someone—even just one person—who is willing to advocate for you.

Often, we imagine the backlash of sharing our truth and try to predict how people will feel and think about us. Our first assumption—rooted in fear—is that they will shame us. "They" could be your Instagram community, folks at the office, family members, friends, and so on. As challenging as it may be to stop layering expectations onto potential responses to your truth, try. You are responsible for one thing and one thing only: freeing yourself. Other people are responsible for their own reactions to you and your story. And while we often resist relinquishing control, control is an illusion anyway. We cannot manipulate people's responses to us by remaining in a state of stress and anxiety, curating the perfect monologue, or strategically contextualizing our abuse to help others understand and metabolize it. Since these types of efforts aren't ultimately helpful or persuasive, drop them. Focus instead on yourself and your healing. The more generous you are with the many parts of your being, your experience, and your story, the less externally imposed shame will resonate with you.

OPPOSITION TO LABELS

Nobody wants to be defined by, labeled, or judged according to what they have survived. Being given a label, even a positive one ("brave," "stable") can feel limiting and create suffocating expectations. I have spent my entire life crawling out of boxes that other people have constructed and that I have reinforced. In an effort to create a more objective self-concept, I now try my best to disregard words that encourage me to believe I can be defined at all. Most of us desire to be respected and loved for who we are at our core, not what we've been through. It is natural to want to avoid language that narrows the scope of your identity.

AVOIDING THE HARD WORK

On a superficial level, trauma feels easier to ignore than to face. Let's say you're presented with two bowls of walnuts. One bowl is full of shelled nuts, and the other is full of nuts in their shells that require cracking. Which bowl are you more likely to reach for? If you've ever cracked a walnut, you know that it is an arduous, laborious process. Some of the nut gets lodged in the crevices of the shell. There's a sort of protective skin surrounding the nut that you have to peel off even after you've extracted it from its shell. The graininess of these textures may be less enticing. The whole thing can get messy! Doing the work of confronting your trauma is a process that requires a lot of patience and the willingness to peel back each layer until you've arrived at some semblance of acceptance, and ultimately, peace.

FEAR OF BEING MISUNDERSTOOD

Many of us possess a deep fear of being misunderstood. Since fundamentally, we all want to be known, trauma may threaten our confidence that people will recognize and experience the totality of who we are. It also may produce the fear that people will associate our trauma with weakness. In reality, the survivors of trauma hold the potential to emerge stronger and more empowered than ever before.

FEAR OF NOT BEING BELIEVED

Nothing is more excruciating than the notion that we might share our trauma and not be believed. *What's the point of telling the truth if no one is going to believe me?* a survivor of trauma may think. If you were molested by your father's favorite nephew, you may fear that your father will accuse you of making up a story. If you were abused by a faculty member at a prestigious school, you may assume that the school board will call you a liar if you come forward. A child may anticipate that the adults in their life will accuse them of lying to seek attention. You might imagine that people will assume you have an ulterior motive for speaking your truth. Maybe you wonder if too much time has passed since your trauma occurred, and you don't want others to question why you're finally speaking out at this moment in time.

LACK OF RECALL

You may have a lack of clarity regarding the details surrounding your trauma. Your trauma may have occurred years ago, or it may have happened very recently. It's also common for people of any age to dissociate during traumatic experiences. The human brain is brilliant and knows how much it can tolerate and consciously process at any given time. If an experience is too painful, overwhelming, or scary for us to be fully conscious of it, we may either black out completely, or remember just enough to know that an event occurred but not possess the ability to recall the details. Even if we can remember some level of nuance, we may disconnect from the psychological and emotional torment associated with the memory. When this happens, recall tends to be purely factual and intellectualized. This fuzziness and/or emotional detachment may make the trauma feel less real or legitimate to yourself or others.

Because we move through the world with tangible bodies, earn money, acquire stuff, bump into the edges of furniture, and so on, we are accustomed to thinking about life in a concrete way. Dreams, love, longing, imagination, feelings, and memory are more elusive than what can be touched, seen, or understood tangibly. We cannot quantify or measure memories. We cannot always fully verify which aspects of our memories are accurate. Memories may morph and evolve over time. They often are incomplete and may leave us with a feeling or sensation in our bodies rather than verifiable evidence or images. Even if we were to videotape or in some other way document a traumatic event in real time, our internal experience of that event is subjective and cannot be documented.

If you cannot recall the nuances of your trauma, that doesn't mean it didn't happen. The reality that our experiences are subjective and we may not remember all of them doesn't make them any less real. Your body is the vault that holds all of your secrets, and you may experience the truth of your trauma as back or hip pain, tense shoulders, chronic fatigue, an eye twitch, issues with intimacy, the tendency to escape into your imagination, rage, perfectionism, or disease. Trauma may manifest itself in any number of other ways to help distract you from immense emotional pain. In essence, you may be displacing the psychological and emotional torture associated with your original trauma so that your focus remains exclusively on the symptoms. As clever as the mind is at fragmenting and creating distractions (aka coping mechanisms), some part of your psyche is deeply aware of all that you have been through. Even if you do not feel safe enough to consciously connect with the full extent of your trauma, it will live in your body until it is seen, recognized, and given a voice.

FALSE COMPARISONS AND DISQUALIFICATION

Consider the possibility that you are (consciously or subconsciously) comparing your trauma to the trauma of others. Comparisons of this nature are inherently judgmental and minimize or even invalidate your very real, completely legitimate experience. They disqualify you from recognizing and sitting with your own pain, and they perpetuate the avoidance of harder-to-access feelings. It is rarely, if ever, helpful to relativize your trauma before you've even allowed yourself to process it. There is a spectrum, a range, for everything. It is not your job to determine how your trauma compares with the trauma of others or to judge whether it is more or less severe. Judgment has no place in the world of trauma. You cannot objectively evaluate your struggle relative to the struggle of others, nor should you try. Any focus on the experiences of others should only serve the purpose of inspiring you to feel your own feelings and express your truth more honestly.

Furthermore, nothing is more powerful than using our pain to help transform the pain of others—but not before we've given ourselves permission to acknowledge and heal the tragedies of our own lives. Regardless of your age, gender, socioeconomic status, ethnicity, race, or circumstances, you deserve access to all that exists within you. If you dedicate your life to helping others without first processing your own internal landscape, you may find yourself exhausted and depleted. By directing focused attention to healing yourself, you ultimately will be far better equipped to help others learn how to heal themselves. By recognizing the textures and colors of your disappointments and practicing the art of self-soothing, you will gain the skills to teach others how to comfort themselves. Even by modeling love and care for yourself, you will inspire others to reframe their inherent worth.

Because revealing trauma can heighten insecurity, trigger repressed memories, and create an overall sense of vulnerability, I recommend that if you plan to share and work through your trauma, you begin with a safe person or group of people. By "safe," I mean people who are emotionally prepared to hold space for you, who you believe will not judge you, and who care for you deeply. Once you have done a significant amount of inner healing work, you may choose to speak freely about your trauma, post your experiences on social media, write and publish your story, speak to audiences, host workshops, or counsel others. But doing so before you have healed may intensify anxiety, cause you to plunge deeper into hiding, or exacerbate unhealthy coping mechanisms.

Turn to "The Imagined Healing of Those Who Have
Hurt Us" and "Rewriting History" in the workbook.

THERAPEUTIC RECOMMENDATIONS

In this section, we'll explore some therapeutic recommendations for addressing trauma, including Internal Family Systems, somatic work, and neurofeedback. These particular approaches to therapy have personally benefited me, but there are many other therapeutic approaches that may support your healing journey. Dialectical behavior therapy (DBT), for example, has been valuable to some of the most meaningful people in my life.

INTERNAL FAMILY SYSTEMS

As we discussed in chapter 5, "Honoring Sleep," IFS is an approach to individual psychotherapy founded in the 1980s by Richard C. Schwartz. It may be helpful in processing trauma, abuse, anxiety, phobias, alcohol and substance dependency, and body image concerns. Please refer to chapter 5 for a more thorough explanation of Internal Family Systems.

SOMATIC WORK

Using the Latin word *soma*, meaning "body," philosopher and educator Thomas Hanna coined the term *somatics* in 1970 to describe a healing therapy that explores the relationship between body and mind.[31] There are variations on somatic work, such as somatic experiencing, developed by psychotherapist Peter Levine in the 1970s. This theory suggests that when a person experiences trauma, energy is trapped in the body during the fight, flight, freeze, and/or fawn response to threatening stimuli. The fight response ignites in us an active, aggressive reaction. The flight response urges us to run. The freeze response paralyzes us. The fawn response causes us to pacify and please in order to avoid conflict or danger.

Because it has no outlet, trapped energy interferes with a person's ability to feel balanced and centered. Not only the brain but also the cellular structure of the body stores memories. In other words, it's not just all in your head. That is why you might feel unsafe or anxious in your body even when no anxious thought is present or you can't identify a clear trigger. The book *The Body Keeps the Score* by Bessel van der Kolk beautifully illustrates the ways in which cellular tension and stored memories complicate a person's sense of emotional freedom.[32] Key elements of the therapy are body awareness (tuning in to what your body is feeling and where), resourcing (accessing people you can trust and who support you), descriptive language (speaking out about what you feel. For example, "I feel trapped"), and movement (even something as simple as shaking your foot to demonstrate that you can escape your trap).

Titration is a feature of somatic work that introduces stress to participants in small doses rather than encouraging them to be inundated with it. The concept of pendulation is tied to titration. Think of a pendulum swinging back and forth. During this therapeutic process, there is a focus on stress, and then on something pleasant or calming, followed by stress, and then again on the calm focal point. Gradually, anxiety softens. Treatment techniques incorporate deep breathing, relaxation exercises, and meditation. Some physical techniques that may be used in conjunction with somatic therapy are dance, exercise, yoga, Pilates, judo, tai chi, qigong, massage, and physical therapy.

Somatic therapy was created to help trauma survivors gain relief from symptoms such as flashbacks, insomnia, dysfunctional patterns, and other related issues. Over time, it also has proven to be effective in assisting people with relationship struggles, insecurity, anxiety, depression, and more.[33]

NEUROFEEDBACK

In the simplest terms, neurofeedback involves measuring brain activity (EEG waves) and training the brain to positively adapt in response to a feedback signal (visual and/or audio). The technique was developed in the 1950s and has been effective in treating attention deficit hyperactivity disorder (ADHD), learning delays, anxiety, depression, sleep disorders, migraines, drug addiction, and more. What differentiates this method of treatment is that no active participation is required.

During neurofeedback, electrodes are gently placed on the person's head in relation to the category of brain function that is being focused on, for example, the ability to pay attention. The wires are then connected to a computerized monitoring system that measures brain wave activity. A participant might then view a video, and while the brain is producing a certain level of beta brain waves, indicating alertness, the movie is clear. But when those brain waves shift, the screen begins to fade. On its own, the brain then automatically determines the optimum thought pattern to get the movie to play without interruption. Once those patterns are learned, the brain tends to remember them. Alternatively, a person may be asked to play a game with a specific goal that requires the brain to reorganize and regulate its frequencies.

Treatment generally calls for twenty training sessions, lasting from twenty to thirty minutes each, two to three times a week. The participant's progress is then reassessed to determine whether further treatment is required or desirable.[34]

— CHAPTER SUMMARY —

Trauma is a complex and delicate topic that many of us avoid for a multitude of reasons. While our survival instinct may prompt us to avoid the stress and pain surrounding traumatic memories and events, holding trauma in our bodies impairs our ability to navigate the world with physical and emotional ease. The burden of stored tension, which we may not even be consciously aware of, can impact every area of our lives, from our energy levels to our ability to form deep, intimate bonds. Since trauma has a profound impact on the brain and other vital body parts, it is best to work with a skilled therapist who can support the process of integrating mind and body and distinguishing between past and present. The ideal therapist would not only help you cultivate an internal sense of safety but provide you with meaningful resources and tools as you explore potentially overwhelming feelings.

CHAPTER 7

FEELING IT ALL

One of the most miraculous, stunning, and mind-blowing privileges of being a human being is having the capacity to experience complex emotions. Of course, this capacity can also be extremely overwhelming. I have spent much of my life trying to manage myself and my feelings, only to realize that what I truly require is not management, but rather the opportunity to be seen, heard, understood, loved, and validated as I am. And while I historically looked to others for validation, the feedback I received was inconsistent and incomplete.

Parents, loved ones, lovers, and friends may not be in a position to reflect to us the level of love and acceptance we would ideally offer ourselves. This is especially true if they struggle with providing these things for themselves. But at any point, we can learn how to parent and care for ourselves, regardless of what those around us say or do, or don't say or do.

HIDDEN EMOTIONS

Quite often, buried emotions are at the root of our most confusing and exhausting behaviors and compulsions. After my parents split when I was three, I packed a suitcase every Sunday night. During this packing process, I anticipated leaving one parent for an entire week to live with the other parent, which caused deep pain and sadness. Progressively, I became more anxious and compulsive rather than sad: folding the same shirt two or three times, angling objects very specifically, counting and recounting the pairs of socks I might require.

My explanation for this, by the time I was five or so, was that I feared forgetting something and inconveniencing or burdening one of my caregivers. But underlying this explanation was a deeper fear: that I would miss a parent. Obsessing over material details distracted me from the deeper feeling of sadness and the anticipation of separation and loneliness. The next time something is bothering you, and your reaction feels disproportionate, ask yourself what may be lurking beneath the surface. During what other times in your life have you experienced a similar feeling? Stream-of-consciousness journaling is a wonderful way to dig deeper and unpack the true sources of your fixations, preoccupations, behaviors, and fears.

ANXIETY AS A DISTRACTION FROM THE DEEPER EXPERIENCE OF PAIN

It is highly possible that becoming compulsive and eventually developing OCD was my way of elevating anxiety to block access to deeper, more painful emotions. At the root of my anxiety was fear, the fear of losing something or missing someone. But anxiety served the miraculous role of overshadowing and blocking out the more vulnerable experience of pain, because it became so overwhelming. Anxiety was my way of self-medicating, because I did not feel safe exploring or exposing my grief for fear of hurting my parents' feelings. Because I was not equipped to explore my grief internally, I never learned how to self-soothe in a healthy way. My only tool was to create so much anxiety through compulsions and fixations that I drowned out all other emotions.

What intensified and reinforced the coping mechanism of anxiety was the perception that I did not have a voice. I did not want to share my sadness with my parents for fear of causing them anguish, but I also had no say in where or when I went, or which parent I was with. Consistent silence in conjunction with the perception that I had no control made me fixate on inanimate objects that were equally voiceless and that I *could* control. If I could not speak, I would arrange and rearrange. If I could not decide where my own body was to go, I would decide where every stuffed animal or T-shirt would go. If I could not bear to feel the discomfort and pain of saying goodbye to a parent, I would lose myself in anxiety.

Sadly, I believe that habituated anxiety leads to adrenal burnout, which may result in chronic fatigue and/or depression. It requires an incredible amount of energy to suppress our emotions and keep them from surfacing. Some of the functional medicine doctors I consult with also cite inflammation as a potential catalyst for depression, as there seems to be a correlation between depression and higher levels of inflammatory markers. Persistent stress leads to the chronic release of inflammatory compounds such as cortisol, and inflammation may lead to imbalances in mood-regulating neurotransmitters such as serotonin and dopamine. Since it causes an imbalance in neurotransmitters, it's possible that inflammation also may be a predictor of future depression.

The correlation between depression and anxiety is undeniable. According to David Prescott, associate professor, chair of Social Science and Humanities at Husson University in Maine, there is a causal relationship between stress and depression whereby one can both trigger and exacerbate the other. This feedback loop is referred to as being bidirectional. In other words, stress can cause depression, and depression can cause stress. Lifestyle choices (both conscious and unconscious), social consequences, chemical imbalances, and thought patterns that accompany depression may lead to anxiety and vice versa.[35]

Clinical psychologist and bestselling author Becky Kennedy presents a unique and compelling perspective on anxiety. During an interview with Goop founder Gwyneth Paltrow, Kennedy states that in a child's world, "aloneness is the enemy of building emotion regulation.... It's not so much ever at any stage in life a feeling that dysregulates us as much as feeling alone in that feeling." She goes on to state that adult anxiety is "that memory of aloneness next to another experience." In other words, when we are triggered by an unsettling experience as an adult, our body remembers the aloneness we felt as children when we were abandoned during moments of dysregulation. According to Kennedy, this memory of aloneness is what generates anxiety, not uncomfortable experiences in and of themselves.[36]

If it is true that it is not necessarily the awkwardness and challenges of pain that cause emotional turmoil, but rather the feeling that we are alone in our pain, then the ability to self-soothe becomes imperative. If our nervous systems were not calmed by supportive and present individuals when we were young, we must learn as adults to encourage and calm ourselves through the quality of presence that was missing in our childhood. For adults who lack the tools to self-soothe, the instinct may be to clamor for external sources of comfort. I personally believe that at every age, genuine connection with others is at the heart of emotional health. But if our sense of aloneness becomes all-consuming, and we have no ability to contribute to our own experience of emotional relief, we may enter into codependent relationships whereby we look to others to constantly regulate our nervous systems and upgrade our internal narratives.

EMOTIONS AND EPIGENETICS

To complicate matters further, scientists and psychologists are exploring the very real potential that we may inherit the trauma and emotional experiences of those who came before us. The field of epigenetics is providing increasing evidence that our emotional patterns are heavily influenced by those of our ancestors, and that the feelings we are most vulnerable to internalizing as our own essentially have been passed down from previous generations. In other words, we are not a clean slate even at birth; our genetic blueprint is intertwined with those of relatives who were challenged by the political, economic, social, and cultural realities of their time. They may have lived through famine, war, or slavery, or survived extreme poverty or loss. They may have been taken by genocide, or lost a child, or lacked basic resources such as food and clean water. They may simply have been raised in a home without love or where verbal abuse was the default way of communicating and controlling. Your blood is the blood of those who came before you, and in your DNA are traces of their struggles and legacy. Psychoanalyst Galit Atlas said the following in an interview: "In therapy, I sit not only with you but with your parents and with your grandparents. So, we have many generations in the room with us."

While this may seem like daunting news, it is also enlightening and explains a lot about why we are the way we are and why we feel the way we feel. According to Galit, in addition to the inheritance of trauma, babies and young children desperately seek connection with their caregivers at all costs. If a parent is depressed or emotionally dead, children may go so far as to emotionally deaden themselves in order to retain the connection with their parent and avoid isolation.[37] Fortunately, the human brain is extremely malleable, and we have the potential—through conscious awareness alone—to shift patterns and claim productive new ones.

I am going to tell you a "woo-woo" story that you can take or leave. I have no agenda whatsoever in sharing it, other than to suggest that the ecosystem of the unseen world, along with the consciousness of souls that permeate it, is far more complex than we often realize. When I was eight months pregnant with my first child, Max, I went to see a massage therapist whom a friend had referred to as "very intuitive." I assumed he meant intuitive about the human body, which thrilled me, because my hips were rapidly expanding and I could barely (if at all) sleep due to aching ligaments. About twenty minutes before the session ended, the massage therapist asked me if I would like her to work on the baby. I said sure, assuming she would rub coconut oil onto my belly in circles as if she were painting a moon. Instead, she asked me to lie face down with my tummy sinking into the hole of the massage table, which was designed for doing prenatal work on sleepless, hangry women like me. Then the massage therapist did something completely unexpected. She crawled under the table and stretched her hand toward my belly without touching it. We remained in this position for the duration of the massage while I toggled between fantasies about her digging into my hips and a sense of wonder at the miraculous acrobatics going on inside me.

When the treatment was over, the massage therapist emerged from under the table and shook her head slowly in what appeared to be a state of awe. "This little soul is very clear about what he wants coming into this life."

I froze. Soul? She was communicating with my son's *soul*? It sounded lofty and absurdly abstract.

"Wow," I said, wishing she had spent our final twenty minutes kneading my thighs like pastry dough.

"Would you like to hear what he communicated with me?"

I was suspicious but curious. "Sure," I said.

"First," the woman said, "he showed me a series of images related to a kidnapping. Does your husband happen to be Jewish?"

Now she had my full attention. "Yes," I said, "he is."

"Is his family from Israel?" she asked.

I nodded yes.

"Your son showed me snapshots of Israel and of children being taken. He explained that the tragedy occurred in the family of his father's mother."

I knew the story and understood the imagery. "So, what is it that he wants?" I asked, my heart now eager to know.

"It's not just what he wants; it's what he *doesn't* want. He said he does not want to be born with the fear of persecution in his DNA. He said he wants to be born fearless."

This event occurred far before I had even heard the word *epigenetics* or knew that it was possible to connect with a soul that had not yet been born. And yet, in a few moments, I came to realize that what comes before us is part of us, and that the conscious choice to want or not want certain things can influence our trajectory, along with the trajectory of the children we bring into the world. Apparently, simply by acknowledging my son's request and supporting the energy of his determination to be born different, to be born free, he was freed. By his cutting ties with the past in some intangible yet undeniable way, I believe that my child was liberated from a legacy that may have condemned him to a life of fear until he became brave enough, conscious enough, exasperated enough, or desperate enough to heal himself by differentiating the journey of his soul from that of the souls who had come before him.

Max was unwilling to be oppressed by the tyranny of persecution his ancestors had suffered for thousands of years; emotional freedom was nonnegotiable. And by refusing to be a victim of fear or haunted by the legacy of those who had come before him, he defined new terms for his life that featured joy, a sense of possibility, a willingness to take risks, an astounding level of resilience, and limitless potential to experience all that comes with being fearless.

BEFRIENDING YOUR FEELINGS

If we can wrap our brains around the fact that the web of interconnectedness on Earth extends far beyond biodiversity and environmental ecosystems to include the interconnectedness of souls, we begin to view ourselves and others differently. I believe that our connection to other souls has three distinct branches. Branch one is the epigenetics piece: we have come from our ancestors and are influenced by their genes and experiences. Branch two is the concept of oneness (or universal consciousness), whereby the thoughts and beliefs of each individual permeate the larger world (even if only energetically) and affect the nervous systems and cells of those around them. Branch three is the possibility that through prayer and conversation, we can engage with souls that have come before us. Based on my experience with my second child, Maya, I believe that it is possible to communicate with souls who have yet to enter the world tangibly—in particular, those who intend to enter our lives in a meaningful way (a biological or adopted child, for example).

After my prenatal massage experience, I became so passionate about the idea of transformation on an energetic and soul level that I became a Reiki practitioner. Reiki is a healing therapy based on the principle of life energy flowing through the body. It takes its name from two Japanese words, *rei* and *ki*, meaning "universal" and "energy." Mikao Usui developed the most widely practiced Reiki techniques in Japan in the 1920s, but in essence, Reiki has been practiced for thousands of years.

During a session, the participant lies on a table while the practitioner places their hands on or above what are believed to be the body's energy centers, like those used in acupuncture and acupressure treatments. Energy is exchanged between the practitioner and the participant, who may or may not experience a warming or tingling sensation as the session proceeds. The participant may experience any number of subtle or more powerful physical or emotional releases throughout a session, and they generally feel lighter afterward.[38]

In working on others, I came to realize that the magic of Reiki is stillness. Simply by quieting the world around us, it allows space for us to hear our own thoughts, see imagery, and become aware of the cellular tension we hold in our bodies. In the safe, loving, gentle pause that is a Reiki session, we have the opportunity to be seen and held, and to see and hold ourselves. That is all the magic. That is the kindness and healing and repair. The exchange of energy between two people is extremely powerful, but so is the message that you are important and valuable enough to receive.

WHOLE-BODY LIVING

My practice of Reiki has led me to a new understanding of how to be in the world. I call it whole-body living. When I listen, I listen with my whole body. When I speak, I speak with my whole body. When I receive, I receive with my whole body. When I feel, I feel with my whole body. Embodiment is a practice in and of itself that many of us take for granted, because we are able to function without accessing all of our senses, honoring all of our body parts, or oxygenating our entire being, both literally and metaphorically. But when we live with our whole bodies, we allow them to feel, know, and experience all that they are capable of feeling, knowing, and experiencing. We are not holding our breath, embracing the mind to the exclusion of the body and soul, disconnecting from any parts of ourselves emotionally or physically, or believing that if we access pain or uncomfortable feelings, we may shatter.

Conversely, we trust that access to all that we are and all that we feel and believe is the ticket to freedom. We breathe deeply. We value our minds, bodies, hearts, and souls as equal partners. We trust that they are working for us and not against us. We are aware of what every part of our bodies is experiencing or not experiencing. Do you allow yourself to feel pain in your shoulders but not your hips? When you experience anxiety and sadness, does your entire body bear the burden, or do you concentrate tension in specific parts? Which parts of your body do you not allow to feel certain things, and why? Where do you hold your anger, sadness, grief, and anxiety? Why there?

Imagine that each part of your body has a brain. That's right, picture your pinkie, nose, shoulders, and chest all having a mind of their own. Now scan your body from head to toe and pose these questions to the "brain" of every body part: "What do you know about my anxiety? What do you know about my sadness? What do you know about my fear? What am I not allowing you to feel? Why do you feel the way you feel? What do you need me to know? How can I help bring you relief? What do you find comforting?"

In order to live with your whole body, first breathe. Then be open to believing that it is safe to feel all that you are feeling and to consciously receive the messages of your body. Your mind, body, heart, and soul can (and should) work together to create abundance, invite healing, and activate joy. Invite them all to the game. Value each of their unique roles. Scan your body and see which parts of you are cut off from feeling, and which parts are bearing the burden.

Just as you asked each body part what it wants and needs you to know, you can engage in a similar line of questioning for situations in your life that are muddled and require clarity. When you are seeking answers to important questions or deciding which way to turn, I recommend that you ask yourself what I refer to as the Questions.

THE QUESTIONS

"What does my mind know about this?"

"What does my body know about this?"

"What does my heart know about this?"

"What does my intuition know about this?"

"What does my higher consciousness know about this?"

"What does my soul know about this?"

"What do my ancestors know about this?"

"What does a future version of myself know about this?"

Each part of you contains distinct wisdom, but is inextricably bound to and fundamentally reliant on the other parts. The ocean cannot exist without the sky, and the sky cannot exist without the land.

Just as there is a bidirectional relationship between anxiety and depression, there is a bidirectional relationship between the mind and body. One informs and affects the other and cannot be considered to the exclusion of the other. Your shoulders may know what your conscious mind does not, or the manifestation of your thoughts may lead to tension in your neck. Every physical symptom your body experiences provides clues about what you may be believing, thinking, and feeling. Ask the discomfort and pain of your body what they know.

Looping, obsessive, or negative thoughts may be a sign that there is a disconnect between your body and mind. It also may mean that you are not allowing yourself to experience feelings such as anger or sadness. If you sense that this may be true for you, ask your mind why it's a container for your grief or rage (or whatever feelings you are harboring) to the exclusion of your body. Why is it safer to live in your mind than your body? What happens when you feel your feelings instead of just thinking about them? If you were to give your thoughts permission to morph into feelings, what would they become? Anger? Disappointment? Sadness? Anxiety?

Our minds, feelings, and bodies are part of a tapestry, working together to facilitate whole-body living. If you allow your emotions to work their way through your body in the act of crying, shaking, or movement, it will be much harder for them to live exclusively in your mind. Some part of you already is in touch with your deepest and most concerning beliefs and feelings. The goal of whole-body living for you is for all of your parts (mind, body, heart, and soul) to be aware of the same things and communicate about how to best support you.

LISTENING TO YOUR DREAMS

Apart from the healing work that occurs in moments of stillness and focused attention, you can learn a lot about how you're feeling from your nighttime dreams. Some people have dreams that unfold like movies, with developed characters and scenes and a colorful storyline. Others barely remember their dreams. The easiest way to remember your dreams, if you care to, is to jot them down in the morning when you wake up.

Turn to "Dream Journaling" in the workbook.

For many years, I kept a dream journal, documenting in great detail versions of a nightmare that began in my childhood. This nightmare resurfaced with unrelenting intensity after I welcomed my daughter into the world, and my psyche practically forced me to address any remaining trauma associated with the sexual abuse that had occurred when I was very young. While I had zero interest in continuing to shine a light on any element of this dark part of my life, I had to in order to thrive. What I wasn't acknowledging and processing during daylight hours was torturing me when I was asleep. One way or another, the truth of your feelings will surface. They may reveal themselves in the job you choose, the lover you commit to, the way you communicate when you feel threatened, or the dreams you have when the sun goes down.

CONNECTING WITH YOUR TRUTH

Some of my most honest, raw feelings did not surface until I was nineteen years old and in the psychiatric ward. It took me completely disassociating and having a mental break to reveal the full truth of my past. Some refined, culturally acceptable part of me did not believe it was appropriate to experience and express all of my feelings, so I had psychotic episodes instead. As I said, the truth will surface in one way or another. If you choose in a conscious and loving way to access all that exists inside of you—even the parts you deem ugly or unacceptable—you are far less likely to break. While it may feel as if our survival depends on our holding it all together, what we are holding together is often a limited version of ourselves and our lives. How can we experience the breadth and scope of love and joy that are possible when we dim, hush, and deny our grief and pain? How can we fully access the parts of ourselves that create connection when we are disconnected from our own truth? In my experience, the more deeply I lean into the chaos and darkness of what feels hard, the more expansive my experience of beauty becomes.

We may temporarily create more rigid boundaries or shield our hearts more actively when we dip into pain, but once we have moved through it and are on the other side, the experience of emotional freedom is incomparable. This is not just because we have recognized, integrated, and healed our pain; it is because when we trust ourselves to access all that lives within us, we stop judging all that exists within others. By exorcising our emotional demons, we learn that nothing can break us—not even our grittiest, most vulnerable parts. In fact, we begin to celebrate those parts, because removing the dam from one set of emotions and experiences often inadvertently removes the dam from other sets of emotions and experiences. In freeing our buried emotions, we free ourselves to connect more deeply with joy and with everyone around us in ways that create mutual compassion, concern, and an eagerness to elevate.

When people are clinically depressed, they often cannot access *any* of their deepest emotions and feel numb. The beauty of our pain and discomfort is that they indicate that we are not so overwhelmed that we have shut off our capacity to feel altogether. As tricky and challenging as it may be to keep the feeling channels open, by doing so, we continue to have access to happiness, peace, and a sense of security and purpose. As you explore buried emotions, please do so gradually and gently, preferably with the oversight of a trained professional, depending on the nature of what you are unpacking. Too much too fast can lead to feeling overwhelmed, which may shut down a broad array of feelings.

There is no rush to heal. If your intention is to clarify parts of your past or allow repressed emotions or events to surface, you have ample time to do so. While suffering may lead to a sense of dire urgency regarding resolution and make deep diving feel like an emergency, it usually is not. You can kindly, lovingly pull yourself out of the well with the help of those who are rooting for you. Please be patient. Everything you desire to feel, you will feel. The peace you crave will be yours. As life coach and author Martha Beck reassures us, we were born to live in peace. Another way of conceptualizing this is that we were born to feel free.

DANGER OF REPRESSION

When we suffocate anger, sadness, disappointment, fear, or whatever else we are experiencing, those critical feelings may strategically morph into other feelings we secretly believe are more permissible. They also may manifest as dysfunctional thought patterns or behaviors, such as perfectionism, hypervigilance, recklessness, self-sabotage, controlling tendencies, destructive habits, negative thought loops, disassociation, addiction, judgment, and so on. These are all *normal* reactions to not permitting ourselves to feel.

Additionally, fear and anxiety may support the false belief that we are acting responsibly by actively staving off the possibility of getting hurt. While stress hormones do serve the very real purpose of protecting us at critical moments when our lives actually may be threatened, they are meant to spike and then subside. Healthy stress of any kind catalyzes important and timely actions for a brief period of time, and then vanishes. But in modern society, stress has taken on a new meaning altogether. Instead of being acute and critical to survival, stress defines the majority of everyday moments for many people. It's almost as if our brains have lost the ability to distinguish between a tiger and a broken pencil. And since the chemical reactions associated with stress are meant to be brief, all the systems of the body are negatively impacted when they are sustained. If stress hormones are constantly firing, even relatively benign moments may become intertwined with anxiety and a sense of panic. Ultimately, if we are unequipped to tame the constant perception of threat, to self-soothe, or to relativize sources of danger, we may accept a chronic state of anxiety as the status quo.

Let's conceptualize this paradigm more visually. Imagine a flat line that is your baseline stress level. Every time you experience a stress response in your body, that line spikes a little or a lot, depending on the level of threat your brain is detecting. If every few minutes, your baseline stress level spikes more significantly than it should in response to a benign trigger, it may become elevated over time. Once you habituate to this new baseline level of stress, your brain will have to become even more alert, and your body will have to produce higher levels of stress hormones to detect more significant threats. In other words, your stress response will become more and more intense over time as it adapts to new baseline stress levels, in order to ensure that legitimate threats are not overlooked. As long as your mind is overactivated in its effort to distinguish small dangers from big ones and protect you from all potential dangers at all costs, this cycle is likely to continue.

The threat may be an Instagram post that makes you feel bad about yourself. It may be a traffic jam or financial fear. It may be watching the news and absorbing tragedy. The threat may occur in real time, or you may anticipate what you fear: a conversation, a bill, a change of employment, a breakup, insomnia, and so on. Threats may be tangible or intangible; it doesn't make a difference to your mind. But unless you breathe deeply and question your initial response to a perceived threat, your mind processes all threats as real and legitimate. And the more danger it feels you are in, the greater an effort it will make to protect you. Unfortunately, habituated fear and anxiety actually distort our perceptions in ways that are not useful and prevent us from discerning between reality and fantasy. If we perceive everything as a potential threat, we are actually less effective at responding to real threats.

Existing in a chronic state of suspicion or fear not only doesn't protect us or guarantee freedom from pain, it impairs the innate instincts that *do* protect us when healthy stress is warranted. We are far more capable of effectively coping with every situation, including dangerous ones, when we trust ourselves and feel *emotionally* safe. Our ability to discern between real and perceived threats is sharpest when hypervigilance does not obscure our intuition and instincts. Hypervigilance is also fatiguing. It tires our adrenals and other bodily systems that are designed to comprehensively protect us should a concrete threat arise.

While it may feel practical to build fortresses around our hearts by living in our minds and overanalyzing even mundane situations, we are not effectively able to cope with danger if we are cut off from the raw and spontaneous communications of our bodies. The well-intentioned purpose of living in a constant state of anxiety is to prevent pain and protect ourselves from feeling physically, emotionally, mentally, or psychologically overwhelmed. But in reality, the opposite occurs. Instead of protecting us, anxiety fatigues our nervous system and makes it virtually impossible for us to differentiate between what is truly dangerous versus what is safe. Situations that might warrant only a small amount of healthy stress may end up feeling catastrophic. We may even end up interpreting potentially supportive people and opportunities as threatening, because our physiological responses have become so obscured by fear. In my experience, as counterintuitive as this may seem, open-heartedness and vulnerability are what allows me to sniff out potentially harmful people and situations. By allowing your body to relax through deep breathing, reminding yourself that you are safe, and trusting in your resilience, you will be fully equipped to discern between reality and fantasy and make decisions accordingly.

When my reaction to an event, a person, or an exchange feels disproportionate, or my emotional charge is confusingly intense, I try to remember the very first time I experienced that particular feeling. A heightened reaction may be reflecting old, unprocessed memories and emotions that magnify or distort current realities. When I overreact, I am replaying a situation that occurred in my youth more often than not. In essence, I am reliving the experience of helplessness I felt when I was technically at my most vulnerable and lacked the tools and empowerment to claim my feelings and voice. If a feeling rises up in you that is overwhelming or borderline unbearable, it may have been living inside of you for many years; maybe it just needed a catalyst to surface. In your moments of feeling overwhelmed, talk to yourself the way you would communicate with a scared, helpless child, and reassure that child that they are safe, loved, and well-resourced.

PERMISSION TO FEEL

Children who learn how to please, pacify, inspire, and comfort their caregivers leave little room to explore the complex world of their own authentic emotional lives. Simultaneously, they seek to behave in a way that is helpful and that alleviates or temporarily resolves their caregiver's feeling of being emotionally overwhelmed, even if this means acting in a way that feels completely insincere. When this pattern extends into adulthood, the result may be what is referred to as codependence.

Also consider the internal world of a deeply sensitive child whose primary caregiver does not seem actively engaged in understanding that child's experience. The unwillingness of a caregiver to ask questions about a child's inner world no doubt leads to an extreme sense of aloneness, abandonment, and emotional isolation on the part of the child. Perhaps the caregiver is disinterested in understanding the child's internal world, or fears what they may not understand or relate to, or is simply oblivious to the possibility of digging deeper, since that has never been modeled for them. Maybe a caregiver is an introvert who favors privacy, and questions regarding their emotional life feel like crossing boundaries. Whatever the case may be, children who crave being known and understood more deeply may assume that their feelings are to remain clamped, because there's no inquiry about them and/or no one even seems to notice them.

Additionally, a caregiver may be reserved about expressing their own emotions or experience discomfort surrounding confusing or layered feelings. A child who never sees their caregiver dig deep emotionally or open up may be inclined to think that complex feelings are off-limits, overwhelming, ungraceful, unfit for public consumption, or indicative of them being weak or out of control. Also, if a caregiver hasn't learned to communicate with patience and self-compassion during moments of emotional strain, a child may associate a state of exasperation, defensiveness, anger, depression, or exhaustion with the generalized concept that it is unsafe to feel their feelings.

When we don't feel safe expressing our inner worlds openly and honestly, we may attempt to manipulate, alter, or extinguish our feelings in an effort to receive positive feedback. The conflict of feeling one way and expressing ourselves in the opposite way has numerous implications, including compromised self-trust, the inability to be truly known by others, and the feeling of betraying ourselves. When we act over and over again in a way meant to ensure attention and love from the external world, the basis of our identity is inauthentic. Over time, we may truly begin to believe that we are the persona we feel compelled to project outward for survival purposes. This is why it's valuable to deconstruct the identities we've assumed under pressure, in the hope of understanding our true nature.

An example of manipulating our feelings (consciously or subconsciously) is replacing them with feelings that we or others deem more palatable. In essence, we choose to express the feelings that we believe in the moment will protect us from a negative outcome, such as being yelled at, punished, abandoned, disrespected, or unloved. Many of us transmute our core feelings to ones that will keep us emotionally or physically safe and/or are societally acceptable. If you were pissed off at a parent who allowed you to be mistreated, that rage may have morphed into sadness because you didn't feel safe enough to express rage. If sadness was viewed as weakness, you may have replaced tears with a punching bag. Consider the following possibilities:

> Fear can express itself as anxiety or anger.
>
> Sadness can express itself as rage.
>
> Rage can express itself as sadness.
>
> Depression may be rage turned inward.
>
> Every repressed feeling, including regret, harms the body and may become illness or disease.

In an ideal world, fear expresses itself as fear, anger expresses itself as anger, sadness expresses itself as sadness, and anxiety expresses itself as anxiety. But what if, as a child, you felt your only option was to cry when what you really wanted to do was yell? Or what if you wanted to cry but felt that it was only acceptable to yell? What if you wanted to make any sound whatsoever—any noise to prove that you were alive and mattered and had a voice—but you remained silent to keep from upsetting, triggering, or burdening others? What if you trained yourself to rapidly assess every interaction and instantly understand what others required from you? What if you tucked away crucial parts of your being so as not to inconvenience, overshadow, or upset a caregiver? What if large portions of your personality were shaped by an investment in not altering a culture or dynamic dictated by those with all the power? What if, by attempting to save others, you suffocated the most honest and essential parts of yourself? Perhaps the most essential work of our lives is to stop apologizing for the truth.

When someone stops feeling altogether, this is called disassociation. If feelings are so overwhelming or forbidden that access to them threatens a person's fundamental sense of safety, they may detach from them completely. For me, disassociation feels like a splitting of my mind and body, whereby I'm cognitively aware of what I'm experiencing without my feelings landing in my body. It's almost as if I'm hovering outside of my body and observing myself from the outside versus fully experiencing my internal world. Although the very nature of depression is cumbersome, heavy, and dark, it too may be a reaction to feelings being so overwhelming that a person is compelled to depress or numb them.

PLAYING A NEW ROLE

Young children spend a vast portion of their childhood pretending to be different people in far-off lands having magical experiences. As we grow into adults, reality overrides imagination at every turn. If you are curious about what lies beneath the surface for you emotionally, consciously try to enter an unfamiliar frame of mind, or imagine yourself as a character in a scene the way an actor would. Just for a moment, see if you can adopt a set of values, perceptions, and attitudes that stretch you outside of your comfort zone and challenge you to feel things you might not normally feel. Put yourself in a theoretical position that may cause you to think thoughts outside of your usual repertoire. Adopt the characteristics, mannerisms, language, and voice of someone whose personality intrigues or intimidates you. This exercise could occur exclusively in your imagination, or you could play-act in a private space where you feel comfortable speaking out loud and moving freely. You also could invite a friend, family member, or lover to improvise a scene with you.

Our personalities and ways of being do not always accurately or completely reflect who we are at our core, so playing a new role, even in our imaginations, may help us recognize parts of ourselves that we want permission to unleash. By flirting with alternate versions of reality, we disqualify the assumption that anything we could possibly feel or think is off-limits. We make it not only okay but essential to know all of ourselves.

The funny thing about acting is that the fictionalized version of you may bring to life very real hidden parts. Many of us have habituated to playing specific roles in our various relationships, and inherent to those roles are defining characteristics (perfect, compliant, brave, patient, and so on). Allow yourself to play a new role, even behind closed doors, and see which surprising characteristics you begin to associate yourself with on a less superficial level.

RELEASING JUDGMENT AND FEELING OUR FEELINGS

To experience our full range of feelings, we have no choice but to stop judging them. Various meditation practices have taught me to become aware of and narrate my inner world the way I would narrate the action of a bird flying by: *Here comes frustration. Yep, feeling pretty angry right about now…* At any given moment, you can pause and ask yourself, "What is my core feeling right now?" It may be sadness, anger, anxiety, disappointment, or mortification. It may be happiness, relief, elation, or gratitude. But judgment is the killer of freedom and will disempower you from accessing your full truth. It will always, without fail, shame you out of experiencing your real feelings and sometimes even prevent them from surfacing. It will demand that you thwart your core emotions and twist them into those that reinforce the roles that others rely on you to play. In my experience, the chronic suffocation and repression of feelings leads to mental as well as physical illness, the only remedy for which is truth. You do not need to act on everything you feel. You do not even need to believe everything you feel. But you do need to allow yourself to feel all of your feelings.

Turn to "Five Steps to Releasing Self-Judgment" in the workbook.

If I were on an important work call and my kids interrupted me repeatedly, I wouldn't calm myself with an internal voice that says, *I'm fine. I'm not upset. Everything is alright. I am in control. Nothing is bothering me.* Denial sabotages self-trust. I would give myself permission to react honestly, even if only internally, without editing myself: *I am annoyed. I want to scream. Everything feels out of control. Everyone is bothering me.* Then I would ask myself what I require in real time to feel safe accessing the full scope of my feelings. I also would ask myself what I need more of or less of to create an experience of calm. Sometimes, all we require is the permission to observe and marinate in our raw feelings. Other times, we require positive self-talk that reassures us that we're okay, or a strategic plan that accounts for our needs in more practical ways.

In the case of my children interrupting me, what I would probably require is the ability to self-soothe in conjunction with the creation of some concrete ground rules for future calls. By creating clear boundaries, I would lay the groundwork for success moving forward. If you master a comforting internal dialogue but don't take steps to support a more productive future, you may end up spinning your wheels. The ability to self-soothe is not intended to lock us indefinitely in uncomfortable situations; it is intended to ground us so that we can make healthier choices moving forward. We can organize a protest, confront our boss, or end a relationship as a result of understanding our core feelings and embracing them all as valuable and acceptable.

BEING FULLY HUMAN

In Marie Kondo's book *The Life-Changing Magic of Tidying Up*, she suggests that people thank the tangible things that once served them before giving them away or discarding them. I often do this with thoughts and feelings that are no longer useful. For example, the other day I was thinking about my life

---

>»•«

Tip: What's Real Versus What's True

In the case of severe depression, anxiety, or self-loathing, it is wise to question our internal narrative. Thoughts such as *I don't deserve to be on this planet*, *I hate myself*, or *I'm so messed up that nobody will ever love me* may lead to feelings of unworthiness, sadness, or shame. Our thoughts are always real, but they may not be true. Judgment of any kind is a good indicator that you should be questioning your thoughts, since self-love is defined by compassion, not judgment. Instead of shaming yourself for having judgmental thoughts that lead to negative feelings, leave room for the possibility that any thought that leads to harmful feelings is most likely untrue.

If you become aware of negative thought patterns that create disheartening feelings, work on transforming your thoughts instead of denying your feelings. Your feelings will naturally change once you hold yourself accountable for your thoughts. This process of transforming negative thought patterns falls under the category of cognitive behavioral therapy.

>»•«

and thought, *You haven't done anything truly significant*, which immediately incurred a sense of shame. Instead of denying my shame, I spoke to it. "Thank you, shame, for once being the thing that made me try to act perfect, so that I could keep myself safe. But I don't need you anymore, and the thought that I haven't done anything truly significant is simply not true. I am going to say goodbye to this thought and the feelings that follow because they no longer serve me."

We can only be as transparent with others as we are with ourselves. By allowing ourselves to be fully human, we increase the potential for intimacy with others. When you are authentic, you give your children permission to be authentic. You inspire your coworkers, family members, neighbors, clients, and friends to express who they really are. Instead of pushing uncomfortable feelings away, embrace them and ask what your feelings are trying to communicate to you. Your feelings exist for a reason. They are friendly guides to help you navigate both your internal world and how you relate to others. Thank them. Use them. They give you courage and make you brave. They may help redirect your life and reshape your perceptions. They are powerful tools to help you understand yourself and make sense of the world around you.

Turn to "Marie Kondo's Work Applied to Cognitive Behavioral Therapy" in the workbook.

ACKNOWLEDGING CORE FEELINGS

The reality of feeling deeply can be so scary for some of us that we go to great lengths to avoid it. Listed below are a few of the many possible ways we can block ourselves from core feelings. Start to notice your patterns. Do you recognize any of these strategies in your own life?

- Identifying with the secondary feeling instead of the core feeling (for instance, claiming rage, but denying sadness, or denying sadness, but claiming rage)

- Overcrowding your schedule with work, exercise, hobbies, relationships, and so on

- Drowning your feelings with an addiction (such as drugs, food, alcohol, TV, social media, sex, relationships, high-adrenaline sports, or excessive exercise)

- Talking incessantly about your feelings instead of actually feeling them

- Creating new drama to distract from old drama or unresolved issues

- Engaging in compulsive overthinking or looping thought patterns that block emotion

- Engaging in obsessive behaviors, such as perfectionism or OCD

- Using depression as a means to avoid other uncomfortable feelings

- Avoiding relationships that invite intimacy and favoring superficial friendships with people who don't really know you and whom you could easily say goodbye to without any emotional impact

Once you have acknowledged your core feelings, you can create a game plan that includes the support of loved ones and professionals, meditation, therapeutic music, medication, natural supplements, or whatever you believe will help ground you and give you wings. If you bark at a coworker instead of experiencing sadness, reactivity may be your coping mechanism. If you scream at your partner instead of sitting with the aloneness of your depression, you may be using explosive fights as an escape. Again, there is no need to judge the ways you've managed your feelings up until now. You have done the very best you could with the resources available to you. But starting now, you have a new way forward—and that way starts with allowing yourself to be fully human.

Turn to "Dimming the Drama," "Sitting with Uncomfortable Feelings," "Thought Reversal within the Framework of Cognitive Behavioral Therapy," "Stream-of-Consciousness Journaling," "Identifying Core Emotions," and "Reinforcing Positive Feelings" in the workbook.

— CHAPTER SUMMARY —

>»•«<

Tip: What's Real Versus What's True

Practice: Supplementation

To mellow inflammation and consequently help elevate and regulate your mood, try incorporating the following into your diet: organic saffron;[39] an organic turmeric supplement, along with organic coconut oil and synergistic spices such as black pepper;[40] and omega-3 fatty acids.[41] Eating certain foods and taking certain supplements are potentially a powerful way to transform your mood and bring balance to your body.

>»•«<

As tempting as it is to lead with our rational minds, we are all emotional beings at our core. Sadly, many of us did not feel safe expressing our full range of experiences as children, so we grew into adults who continue to suffocate, deny, and prematurely transmute our feelings in order to remain in the good graces of those we love or believe we rely on. But part of becoming an integrated and empowered adult is believing that it is okay to access, embrace, and express all of who we are and how we feel. To nurture and honor your authentic self, it is essential to release any potential judgment associated with your humanity. To feel is to be human.

CHAPTER 8

CREATING YOUR RHYTHM

For much of my life, I've felt like I'm behind. Regardless of where I am, I tend to harbor a chronic elusive sense that I should be somewhere else—namely, further along. But "further along" implies that there's a predictable trajectory, a straight path from A to Z. And as safe and comforting as the concept of a definitive Z sounds, my destination evolves and shifts as I do.

At one point, my goal was to be a teacher. Then it became recording an album. After that, it was starting a family and a wellness company. And now my focal point is to make a difference in the lives of people who want to heal. But even when I establish my Z, and maybe in some cases miraculously arrive at some version of it, I am satisfied for roughly half a second before leaping into the pursuit of my next mission. That hunger—the quest to create and become something new—keeps me growing and stretching. Maybe I'm in pursuit of evidence that life is meaningful and has purpose, and that *I* am meaningful and have purpose. Maybe a default setting of not feeling good enough motivates me to construct arbitrary standards of where I think I should be relative to where other people are. Whatever the reason, I have a habit of driving my life forward with specific visions for my future so as not to feel behind, and I must remind myself day after day that I am exactly where I should be, simply because I am there.

I'll never forget listening to an interview with record executive and *American Idol* judge Simon Cowell back when I was infatuated with the show. He talked about his experience as an intern in the entertainment industry, and how he brilliantly negotiated and finagled his way to success. At the end of the interview, he revealed that however much money, fame, and power he had acquired over the years, the most prized period of his life was when he was on the journey to the top. I've heard versions of this story again and again from some of the most famous and noteworthy people in the world, who all seem to agree that the process of *becoming* is as genuinely thrilling (and possibly even more so) as the experience of being what they hoped to become.

What you crave (such as a sense of security, emotional or financial freedom, pride, adoration, respect, power, or a feeling of aliveness) when you are working to achieve something may point to fundamental desires that have nothing at all to do with where you land, what you create, or whose attention you receive once you achieve your goals. Whatever qualifiers, accolades, or tangible evidence you theoretically may conceive of when considering success may not actually guarantee the sense of ease and contentment you are seeking. In the end, you may design your life to be a series of cat-and-mouse games that render you unworthy or convince you that you need to do better or more, unless you truly believe that your core value is completely distinct from status and accomplishments.

Regardless of what motivates and excites you, your journey of being alive is embedded with your unique rhythm. Since I have come to believe that every moment is equally valuable and that "the top" is at best elusive and most likely fictitious, I am less inclined to rush to get there. And yet the concept of rhythm is one that I've spent a lifetime negotiating. The demands of our culture, of our workplaces and homes, along with the expectations we create as to what our lives should *look* like, are often to the exclusion of what our lives should *feel* like. Why this doesn't work for many of us is that when we are out of sync with the natural rhythm of our bodies, they revolt.

TUNING IN TO YOUR BODY

Communications from our bodies about our emotions and thoughts occur in a variety of ways: headaches, indigestion, irritability, back pain, brain fog, apathy, anxiety, and depression. Ulcers, insomnia, and rashes all communicate a level of imbalance and the underlying need for some part of us to be seen or heard. A sense of lightness in the body, freedom from tension, a giddy flutter in one's chest, a sense of openness versus restriction, the propensity to smile and laugh easily, and conscious connection with gratitude also are indicators of what is going on in our inner worlds. As you begin to pay attention, notice the signs and signals of your body that let you know that you are off course or on the right track. To be clear, "the right track" is what feels right for you and is in alignment with your desires and intentions. There is no empirical, objective right track that can be measured and understood apart from your inner compass. Making choices or acting in a way that contradicts your true nature, core value, and genuine feelings is a good indicator that you may be off course.

Chronic anxiety, depression, and hypervigilance reveal that an unsettling feeling or set of feelings has become generalized or inspired the creation of protective armor. When we experience any of these three states, we may lose access to a broad range of potential feelings, whether positive or uncomfortable. If our brains have habituated to filtering all external stimuli through a specific and narrow set of criteria in order for us to feel safe, the first order of business is to determine why we don't feel safe experiencing the full range of our feelings. Once we process our trauma and shift the beliefs and mindset that create a myopic experience, we can let our guard down. When this happens, more feelings will become accessible, and we can begin to play more deeply with recognizing the physiological reactions of our bodies.

To hear the messages of our bodies, we can't rush past our experiences. Physical, mental, and emotional communications are occurring all the time, and the more we overlook or ignore warning signals, the louder and more extreme the messages are likely to become. A light headache may morph into a migraine. An aching back could lead to immobilization. In the emotional realm, you may find that a slight grudge snowballs into massive resentment, or occasional blues slide into a dark depression. Our minds flash images and words into our consciousness almost every moment of the day, and many of them are repetitive. What stories do you narrate about yourself, others, your job status, and the world? How does what you choose to think about shine a light on your deeper belief systems and values? What feelings do you tend to default to?

Many of us have accepted a frantic life pace as something that is inescapable, or that is even required for us to exist within a culture that values productivity and materialism along with an extreme work ethic. The juggling act involving family, friends, career, hobbies, and even self-care often drowns any opportunity for stillness and recovery. We may even find ourselves trying to keep up with events and obligations that don't sincerely interest or feed us, but which actually drain us instead.

There are countless variables that affect our mood, energy level, pace, and threshold for stress. A few of them include hormones, what we have or haven't consumed (physically or mentally), how much we've slept, the cycle of the moon, our level of physical activity, what we're choosing to think about, who and what we feel responsible for, the conversations we're processing, what we're working on or toward, and the people we associate with. Then there is the role of genetics. Hilarious and heartbreaking bestselling author Jenny Lawson has been very vocal about the challenging brain chemistry of so many of her family members, which she inherited, and which no gluten-free or dairy-free diet can balance. With so many variables in the mix, doesn't it make sense that from day to day, the needs of our bodies and minds would differ?

There is nothing inherently more valuable about moving slowly or quickly, or alternating between the two. What matters is that your pace reflects the real-time preferences of your body, mind, and heart. When you believe that you are running out of time or are behind, you are far more likely to rush past the communications of your body and make choices that don't serve you in the long run. How close do you feel you are to achieving specific goals? How does the tangibility or elusiveness of your deepest dreams affect your ability to enjoy the process of making them a reality?

If you are fixated on a goal, you may miss the signals of your beautiful, essential body as you work toward that goal. If all you can think about is your destination, you may sprint, stagger, or crawl there without even realizing how your approach affects your well-being. If you find yourself skipping sleep, glossing over restorative healing time, neglecting important relationships, or mowing over your body's messages, you may miss cues that something is awry or requires tending to. Slowing down long enough to hear your internal dialogue, feel your feelings, and detect what is really happening in your body is the only way to guarantee that your pursuit of anything—even nourishing things—is sustainable.

You may be moving very quickly, but be in a state of total bliss. You may be moving slowly and meticulously, but be depressed. Again, your technical pace is not the barometer for how you are feeling or what you are experiencing. The messages of your body, along with your thoughts and emotional landscape, are far more reliable indicators of whether your pace is reflecting your actual needs. Just as you receive nonverbal communication from others (such as an eye roll, a yawn, scowl, grin, or smile), you ultimately are communicating the same way within yourself to yourself all day long.

To establish your own authentic rhythm, it is useful to temporarily slow down. You can speed up again, if you choose to, the moment you become aware of how you are experiencing yourself emotionally, mentally, and physically, and how you are processing your external world. But it's challenging to develop a synergy of mind and body without first learning the unique ways in which they communicate.

Practice paying attention to how you move through life, and ask yourself if it's depleting you or giving you more energy.

Turn to "A Practice of Awareness: What
Feeds You?" in the workbook.

ESTABLISHING AN ORGANIC RHYTHM

Our needs shift from day to day and moment to moment, so establishing an organic rhythm isn't a one-time deal, it's a daily practice that is based on your current reality and is constantly evolving. As I said previously, it also is influenced by numerous factors. If you just found out that your dog has cancer, you may not want to attend your exercise class. If you were sleepless the night before a big presentation at your office, you may not want to go out and celebrate afterward as planned. If you were trapped on your computer all day, you may choose to ride your bike or take a walk after dinner instead of watching your favorite TV show.

It's not just okay to reconsider and revise previously established plans, it's appropriate and healthy. The willingness to shift course means that you are not only recognizing what your body is asking for but also responding to it. And responding to what is really happening—not to what we wish were happening or had imagined would happen—is how we create self-trust. Many of us have habituated to overriding the signs of our bodies, ignoring the thoughts that come to mind, and suppressing feelings that spontaneously well up inside of us, because they are not convenient, they interfere with our agenda, they contradict our hopes and dreams, or we fear some type of repercussion. Wherever it is you want to go, you will get there or somewhere better.

Actor, filmmaker, and podcast host Dax Shepard speaks very candidly on his show about the experience of arriving at his version of financial success. Previously, he believed that if he could secure a specific amount of money in his bank account, he would feel safe, at ease, and at peace. The reality of his experience was quite different, however. Every time he hit the number he had hoped to—the one he equated with safety—he would move the mark. When he reached the new mark, he still would feel unsettled. This is an example of why it's essential not to hinge our emotional security or experience of the world on external factors. More often than not, the things we believe will bring us peace do not. What brings us emotional freedom is emotional freedom; that is all. All of our other criteria and goals are our mind's way of trying to make sense of what we need, so that we feel more in control of our emotional trajectory.

This same experience has been described by authors, musicians, and performers of every kind. While receiving an award or some extraordinary level of recognition may feel thrilling in the moment, they are left only with themselves soon after. The next day, they are brushing their teeth, making coffee, and checking their email. People who have been validated and celebrated externally in such profound ways have two choices: they can spend the rest of their life trying to replicate or trump that level of validation, or they can value each and every moment as equally thrilling.

Every time we make our experience of the world and the quality of our emotional wellness dependent on achievement, recognition, validation, or fame, or tie it to material value, we lose all the moments between the present one and the one where we feel worthy. In my opinion, all the contingencies, qualifications, and stipulations for happiness that we create are an attempt to feel undeniably worthy. But our worth is undeniable, simply because we are human beings. And since that is true, we have access to feelings of worthiness in every moment of our lives. All we have to do is claim them.

THE NITTY-GRITTY OF RHYTHM

Each one of us is wired uniquely. Long ago, I stopped internalizing the guidance and mandates of those around me in regard to scheduling and rhythm, because those people are not in my body, and what works for them may not work for me. Back when I was songwriting and singing on a regular basis, a well-intentioned friend said that in order to be prolific and achieve mastery over my songwriting and voice, I had to practice four to six hours a day. I've watched master classes taught by bestselling authors who say that it's imperative to sit down each and every day and attempt to write, even if nothing or very little comes of it. Many of these authors suggest that the discipline of sitting down to write daily is what defines an author and creates the potential for success, especially if the practice occurs at the same time every day and in a tranquil environment with minimal disruptions and distractions. And to all of this, I say, "Wonderful that this approach or that way of doing things works for you. It doesn't work for me."

I believe that each and every individual can and should establish a rhythm that is sustainable, inspiring, and nourishing. I may go five days without even thinking about writing, then sit down and spill out four thousand words in a number of hours. I may write for an hour, get a snack, write some more, clean out a drawer, and write some more. Usually, I find that my writing is far more fluid and eventful when I take breaks as soon as my body and mind nudge me to do so. If there's a day when I really want to talk to a friend instead of write, I do. If I'm aching to lighten my mood by watching a sitcom, I do.

There is no right way to go about creating. Even scheduling breaks doesn't work for me. I take a break when I feel my body and brain need a rest. That may be just twenty minutes into writing or singing, or it may be three hours. The point is, I decide. My body determines these parameters, and my job is to check in with my body and respond to its demands. If my back is in pain from sitting for too long or being hunched over my computer, respecting my body looks like getting up and stretching. If I'm in a dark mood and it's making me feel cray-cray to create from that space, I stop. I listen. I lean into the truth of what is happening.

Preestablished rhythms simply don't work for everyone. They may be exactly what your body and mind need to accomplish what you set out to do, or they may not. Only you can determine what works or doesn't work for you. This past summer, I established a bit of a hybrid approach. There was a window during which my kids were at camp, and my intention every day was to sit down and write for a good portion of that window. But if my workload, mood, body, or priorities shifted, I pivoted and made a different plan. I am aware of deadlines and expectations, but within the framework of these more definitive parameters, I am flexible.

Time management is a completely different topic, and I understand that many people struggle with organizing their lives in a way that prioritizes their passions and dreams. Lots of wonderful books have been written about time management, but what I can offer you is the idea that creativity is not linear (just as healing is not linear), and that it doesn't always require giant blocks of time or perfectly curated environments. I've written a large percentage of my books at the very plain desk in my bedroom, without any view whatsoever. Sure, it would be completely wonderful if I had a writing room, a full-time nanny for my kids, and a personal chef to help support me, along with long stretches of time during which I could stop and start on a whim without losing my uninterruptable writing window. But I don't. So, I've learned to create in all kinds of ways, no matter where I am or what's going on around me. Right now, I am making eggs for my daughter while crafting this sentence. My computer travels with me around the house, as does my iPhone, which I often dictate sentences into when I'm cooking, breaking down boxes, or washing my face.

Very rarely will we experience the perfect conditions, sense of freedom, gorgeous view, and insatiable desire to create all at once for sustained periods of time. If that is your experience, bravo! But even if it is, the flexibility of knowing that you *could* create in less ideal conditions may empower and liberate you to experiment with rhythms that generate resiliency surrounding your process of creating. You may be creating a book, a spreadsheet, or a report, or doing laundry! It doesn't matter. All work is creative work.

Turn to "Hand on Body" in the workbook.

>> • <<

Tip: What Do You Need?

If you find yourself mindlessly going through the motions of the day, pause and take four deep breaths through your nose to reset. Then ask yourself what your body needs right now. Maybe it's a glass of water. Maybe it's to laugh or to lie down. Honor the truth of what your body is presenting by taking action and responding to its communication. By doing this, you will reinforce the core belief that you are worthy of respect, self-care, and love.

The same practice applies to feelings. If you're feeling sad or angry or any other heated emotion, pause, breathe, and ask yourself what you require in this very moment. Then, to the best of your ability, meet that need. If you cannot physically do the thing you want to do, imagine doing it. Imagination yields powerful results and can transition our nervous systems back to a parasympathetic state if we are dysregulated or have been triggered. Even if you find yourself living more in your imagination than in the reality of your life, this is beautiful information. Escapism is a sign that something may be missing or overwhelming. Ask yourself what you want more or less of in your life, and jot down at least three ways you can work to acquire or eliminate those things.

>> • <<

Turn to "Sing Your Body" in the workbook.

»•«

Practice: Conscious Awareness of Sound, and Clench and Release

One of the simplest ways you can reset is to pause an activity and take note of the sounds around you. If you're in a position to close your eyes and block out visuals, do so, as this will enhance your ability to tune in. What sounds do you hear in your environment? A bird chirping? A child laughing? A lawn mower? An airplane flying overhead? You can drift from one sound to the next, or commit to one sound to the exclusion of all others and track it for a minute or two.

Next, scan your body from head to toe in your mind's eye and see if you can detect any thick, sticky parts or areas that feel stuck or tight. Now take a deep belly breath, and on your exhalation, send oxygen to the parts of your body that feel tight or restricted. Imagine them expanding and releasing. If you become aware that a certain part of your body is "crunchier" than others (your shoulders, for example), bring full awareness to that body part, consciously tighten it, hold for a few seconds, and then relax completely. Simply tense your muscles with as much focus as you can for just a few seconds, then release and feel your body soften. I learned this clench-and-release exercise years ago from a yoga instructor, and it's a swift and simple way to let go of tension.

»•«

BREATHWORK

For pretty much my entire life, I've minimized the importance of breath. As a singer, I know that understanding how to use my breath determines how long I can hold a note, how choppy or smooth my delivery of lyrics is, and even the quality of my tone. There is no doubt that my voice is richer and fuller when I use my breath properly, and still my tendency is to gloss over my focus on breath in favor of sound.

Now more than ever, our awareness of breath impacts our well-being. With stressors such as viruses, a tense political climate, threats to the environment, and ongoing social unrest, our tendency is to hold our breath or to breathe shallowly. Unfortunately, low oxygen levels send a message to our brains that we are in danger, which triggers our sympathetic nervous systems and reinforces stress and anxiety.

Turn to "Using Breath to Manage Anxiety" in the workbook.

When you breathe slowly and deeply, you send your brain the message that you are okay. It believes that you are safe. It knows that you are alive. When your breath is shallow, your body remains in fight, flight, freeze, or fawn mode. Unfortunately, disturbing world events and personal struggles mingle in the psyche to facilitate a chronic sense of anxiety in many people, resulting in depression, exhaustion, and burnout. Modern life, as privileged as we are to be a part of it, possesses its own unique set of stressors. Breathing slowly and deeply helps us cope with stress as well as distinguish between real and perceived threats, by getting us out of our sympathetic nervous systems (which respond to danger and stress) and into our parasympathetic nervous systems (which promote a feeling of ease and calm).

MEDITATION

Meditation may feel daunting for people who have never practiced any form of it or who don't have a lot of time. I assure you, there is no right way to meditate, and shifting brain waves into a more relaxed state doesn't require a giant chunk of time. A little goes a long way, and your practice may be as simple as observing your thoughts, imagining a flower in bloom, or watching an ant carry a crumb from the edge of your patio to a blade of grass. Many of my friends find apps to be helpful for both breathing and guided meditations. There are many ways to approach meditation, and it is a beautiful and effective way to restore and nourish the nervous system.

The form of meditation I practice most consistently is called Vedic meditation. Ideally, practitioners do it twice daily for twenty minutes each time. A teacher generally provides a mantra, but we all have the power to create mantras for ourselves in regard to all areas of our lives. In the case of Vedic meditation, the origin of the mantra lies in Hinduism and Buddhism and is a word or sound that has no meaning attached to it. The magic of the mantra is not the word or sound itself, but rather the way in which it serves as guidance to steer us away from unhelpful distractions as we repeat it in our minds.

Here is an abbreviated overview of Vedic meditation. Find a relatively quiet space where you are alone. Sit comfortably, close your eyes, and whisper your mantra silently in your mind. Repeat the mantra for twenty minutes. (Note: This period of time may feel like an eternity at first, so feel free to practice more briefly to start, then gradually work your way up to twenty minutes.) If you notice a running monologue in your head, gently let it go. If you find yourself making a grocery list a minute into the meditation, notice it, then calmly and without judgment bring yourself back to the mantra.

In addition to nonmeaningful mantras, we can create ones that quickly and succinctly reinforce positive thoughts or lead us in the direction of emotional freedom. One of my briefest and most effective mantras in my twenties was the words a girlfriend spoke to me when I was obsessing over a boy. "You are enough," she told me. Those three words changed my life and helped rein in the part of me that was spiraling out of control. Every time I began to imagine my ex with someone else or create hurtful stories in my mind, I told myself, "I am enough." Another, even simpler, mantra that I sometimes chant silently to myself in my bed is "Surrender." I say it over and over again when thoughts enter my mind.

Turn to "Creating Your Own Mantra" in the workbook.

Some days, focus comes more easily than others. For most of us, it's almost always a struggle. Accept every meditation as equally valuable, regardless of how many thoughts enter your mind. It is all part of the process of learning how to let go, and it can be restorative without having to be perfect. Just as our brain waves shift in and out of different states while we sleep, we have the ability to shift into deeper states of relaxation during waking hours through meditation.

— CHAPTER SUMMARY —

Creating a unique rhythm that reflects the needs and desires of your body, soul, and mind is a key step in supporting every aspect of your well-being. By frequently tuning in to your body and responding to its messages, you will not only cultivate self-trust but establish productive and meaningful ways of being. Your efficiency, sense of ease, and overall wellness are deeply impacted by how you move through the world. There is no one-size-fits-all approach to establishing your rhythm, and your requirements and preferences may shift from day to day and minute to minute. Listen to your body, and you will be sure to experience the nourishing rewards of self-care.

CHAPTER 9

ADVOCATING FOR YOURSELF

A friend of mine recently went to a doctor after having lost almost twenty pounds in less than two weeks. She was too lethargic to jog and barely had enough energy to pick her kids up from school.

"It's probably just stress," the doctor told her.

"No, this is something different," my friend insisted.

"I've been at this for a long time," the doctor responded. "I know stress when I see it."

My friend called me in tears after her appointment. "I don't know what's wrong with me," she said. "My health feels entirely out of my control, and my doctor is telling me it's just stress!"

"Do you think it's stress?" I asked her.

My friend said no.

"Then march back into that office and tell your doctor that you want him to order you some panels. Have him check you for Lyme disease and viruses like Epstein-Barr, and do a full hormone panel, get your thyroid levels checked, test for parasites, and see if you're deficient in vitamin D. All the things."

"Parasites?" My friend sounded confused. "I haven't traveled internationally since 2019."

"You eat sushi at least twice a week," I reminded her. "Check for parasites."

"What if my doctor insists that it's stress or depression?"

"Then find a new doctor," I said. "This is your body. Take control."

My friend called her doctor after we hung up the phone and told him that she wanted to explore alternative explanations for her abrupt weight loss. Within a week, the doctor confirmed that she had parasites.

All too often, when we feel like another person (or people) in the room have all the power, we relinquish ours. This can occur with medical professionals, family members, professional colleagues, lovers, and friends. It can occur in the workplace, in a meeting with a potential client, or during an audition. But the perception that another person is more powerful, confident, or qualified to assert their will is simply that: a perception. The fear of something being taken away (such as a relationship, a job, an opportunity, respect, or love) compounds this false perception that we are in some way inferior or unqualified to state our needs, or to ask for what we want and deserve. When we feel that we don't measure up, we lose our voice. In essence, we surrender our willingness to advocate for ourselves.

Being a self-advocate doesn't mean being pushy, defensive, overprotective, or controlling. It involves recognizing your worth and creating boundaries and expectations accordingly. To effectively advocate for yourself, you must be willing to take responsibility for your attitude and actions, and potentially modify your beliefs and choices as you receive new information. Many of us tend to have very high expectations for ourselves and low expectations for others, or extremely high expectations for others and low expectations for ourselves. Reciprocity is based on the mutual desire for each party's needs to be met. Ideally, while we are busy advocating for ourselves, others simultaneously will be considering our preferences. However, because we cannot control how others think and behave or what they believe, it is ultimately our responsibility to account for our desires and requirements.

Turn to "Self-Advocacy" in the workbook.

Advocating for yourself doesn't always have to involve other people. You advocate for yourself when you tell your doctor that more information is required to solve a health puzzle, but you also advocate for yourself when you turn off social media that's preventing you from being present. You advocate for yourself when you pause to drink a glass of water or stretch. You advocate for yourself when you take a walk around the block, or gaze at the sunset instead of doing the dishes. You advocate for yourself when you say no to a dinner that doesn't truly interest you and yes to one that does. You advocate for yourself when you hijack the warm bubble bath you ran for your child because you realize that you too deserve a bubble bath.

WHAT PREVENTS US FROM ADVOCATING FOR OURSELVES?

There are many reasons why we might choose not to advocate for ourselves. Here are a few possibilities.

Negative responses from caregivers. Some of us may have grown up with caregivers who had all the control, or who in some way led us to believe that we were stupid, naïve, or powerless. Maybe your caregiver had a loud voice and commanded or shouted things to assert their authority. Perhaps they were soft and meek, but used silence, lack of accessibility, or withholding to con you into compliance. Any child who is physically or verbally abused or isolated, or whose caretaker withholds or punishes, learns very quickly to stop advocating for themselves. If speaking up leads to an undesirable outcome, including the loss of attention or affection, or even physical danger, the result may be habituated silence.

Fear of loss. The fear of losing something often is at the heart of why we don't advocate for ourselves. We may be afraid of losing respect, a relationship, a job, or any number of other things. When the fear of losing something outweighs the impulse to create a boundary or communicate honestly, we surrender our right to self-advocate.

The requirement of flawlessness. Many of us falsely assume that we need to be flawless and beyond reproach before we assert ourselves. Many of us feel we don't have the right to ask for what we want, demand what we deserve, or hold other people accountable for unthoughtful behavior, because we too make mistakes and aren't perfect. But our worth is not based on our being perfect humans. It's based on our being human, period. Stop waiting until you feel worthy of creating a healthy framework for yourself, your life, and the players in your life to take action. When you are willing to hold yourself accountable for your thoughts and decisions, shift and modify your beliefs and behaviors as needed, and change course when something doesn't feel right, you will inspire others to do the same.

Third-party deferral. You may postpone lovingly confronting someone who has disrespected or disappointed you because you have habituated to involving a third party. By venting with a person who has nothing to do with the issue you are struggling with, you relieve some of your tension and irritation. But by letting just enough air out of the bag for it to not burst, you may never end up communicating with the person who is directly contributing to your discomfort or frustration. It can be very productive to hash out ideas and possibly even role-play with trusted friends and loved ones before communicating honestly with the person with whom you are actually disgruntled. But consider whether your intention in doing so is to prepare for the harder conversation or to avoid it.

Surprisingly often, when I have confronted another person with my grievances, I have come to realize that there has been a misunderstanding of some kind. More often than not, people don't mean to offend or harm us, and our interpretation of their words and actions doesn't always reflect their intentions. Our takeaway sometimes is a product of our own fears or insecurities. Incidents from the past also may color how we perceive current events. By committing to direct conversations that are respectful and transparent, you will create space for clarification and mutual understanding that may even deepen the relationship.

Here are some very concrete ideas about how to be your own best advocate, based on the trial and error of my own life experiences.

GET VERY CLEAR ABOUT YOUR SELF-WORTH

Your worth isn't dependent on anything you do or say. You don't even have to understand it, believe it, or claim it for it to be yours. You are worthy of love, attention, and support simply because you exist. You do not have to earn or prove your worth for it to be real and true.

IDENTIFY YOUR PREFERENCES AND WHAT'S NONNEGOTIABLE

It's hard to advocate for yourself when you're not really sure what you want or expect, or you haven't identified what's imperative to you. Over the course of any given day, you have numerous opportunities to advocate for yourself. The majority of the time, you may find yourself apathetic about outcomes or unconcerned about details that feel superfluous. This is because if we were to scrutinize, analyze, or obsess over every aspect of our lives, we would drive ourselves (and others) crazy. We necessarily pick and choose our battles to conserve energy, allow for flow, and create a culture of compassion and flexibility, and so that we can identify the areas of our lives that really do require an advocate.

But in situations where something matters to you, or variables exist that will significantly impact an end result, ask yourself what you are willing to sacrifice and what is worth fighting for. Distinguish between what you prefer and what is nonnegotiable, and you will have a better sense of what is required of you in every situation. For instance, you may prefer to be seated next to a window at a café, but it's nonnegotiable for your food to not contain stray hairs. You may prefer your date to wear shoes that match the rest of their outfit, but that person treating you with kindness is nonnegotiable.

TRUST YOUR INNER GUIDANCE

From birth, we are guided in various ways away from our inner knowing and toward the expectations and norms of our caregivers and culture. But every single human being possesses an internal compass, an innate sense of truth that ushers us away from true danger and toward safety. Our inner guidance protects us from potential harm and also signals to us when opportunities and miracles are in our midst.

How does our inner guidance communicate with us? It may be through sensations in our body: a shiver up our spine, tenseness in our shoulders, a fluttery sensation in our chest. It may be through an undeniable instinct or urge to run from or toward something or someone. We may visualize images that play out like a scene from a movie. Some people experience chronic fantasies about something or someone (positive or negative), or imagine events unfolding in an almost tangible way. Sometimes ideas pop into our minds, seemingly out of nowhere, that feel meaningful or purposeful. Some of us have an elusive but unrelenting feeling when our inner guidance is communicating with us, as if we just know where to go or who to speak with or which job post to respond to without concrete evidence or reasons. That mystical, undefinable conviction may also alert us when we are on a date with somebody we shouldn't be with, or are about to drive down a street that some part of our deep inner knowing doesn't want us to drive down.

Conversations about inner guidance can include quantum physics, parallel realities, the timelessness of spirit, the sliding doors phenomenon, and countless other metaphysical topics. For the purpose of understanding how inner guidance relates to advocating for ourselves, what matters most is that if we trust the many ways our body, psyche, and spirit seek to communicate with us on a deeper level, we are more likely to communicate with confidence and take action when necessary. If we qualify, dismiss, minimize, or suppress our inner guidance, we may miss vital opportunities to be our own advocate.

RELEASE YOURSELF FROM SHAME

I believe that the number-one deterrent to believing and following our inner guidance is shame. If we shame ourselves out of unexplainable feelings, we rob ourselves of the opportunity to follow the unique path that is meant for only us to follow. If we convince ourselves that our experience is silly, or that we can't trust our inner guidance because we may not at all times in every moment know with 100 percent certainty that it is accurate, we put ourselves in an extremely precarious position. Just as with everything else in our lives, interpreting and understanding the language of our inner guidance require practice, and we may not always get it right.

I often hear friends talk themselves out of very real feelings because they deem themselves to be unreliable, based on prior mistakes. But our history has nothing to do with this present moment. If you feel that you can't trust yourself now because in the past you've made misguided choices, this brand of judgment will only further muddle your ability to navigate clearly moving forward. The shame that comes with judgment is never clarifying, enlightening, or helpful. On the contrary, it shrinks our capacity to assess all of a situation's variables accurately and openly and make the wisest choice. The way to overcome the paralysis of fear is not to abandon the power to make choices; it is to continue to make choices from a place of trust—not in the outcome but in yourself. It is not the result of your choices that you ultimately are reliant on, it is your resilience. If you engage in patterns that consistently yield negative or unfulfilling results, you may have blind spots worth investigating. But questioning why or how you make choices is different from judging your process. All of our approaches require fine-tuning and modifications as we grow and learn. If you have lost faith in your ability to choose wisely, breathe deeply and ask your inner guidance for support and direction.

EMBRACE YOUR INNER KNOWING

It is possible to confuse guidance with fear. It is also possible that what you perceive to be guidance may be an attempt to piece together a desirable narrative. That's okay. Nothing is more valuable than trusting yourself, and by desiring perfection or certainty in regard to your inner guidance, you are demanding that a somewhat magical aspect of being human should be quantifiable. Let math be quantifiable. Count the number of apples remaining in your fridge before going to the grocery store. Have an accountant nail down your taxes to the penny. What your soul requires is not quantifiable; there is no way to measure or assess its relationship to the tangible world. Above all else, what your soul requires is that you allow yourself to be guided by the immeasurable, undefinable, mystical forces that conspire to lead you to the deepest, most magical parts of yourself, which you may have abandoned when caregivers and culture told you who and how to be.

If we allow ourselves to linger in the possibility that we are guided by unseen forces within and possibly even outside ourselves, we become curious about those forces. What does your guidance sound like? Look like? Feel like? Is the sound of your guidance your own voice or a secondary voice? Does your guidance appear as symbols in your mind's eye or play out like scenes from a movie? Is your guidance a collection of physical sensations? How does your body react when you are afraid or curious or in the presence of someone who might change your life? When does your guidance appear most actively and forcefully? What does aggressive versus subtle guidance feel like? Does your guidance pipe up when you don't validate or act on it, or does it dim?

Trusting your inner guidance is a practice the way yoga is a practice. It requires experimentation and adjustments. You do not need to do or understand anything flawlessly. Take small and gentle steps toward believing your internal cues as often as you can. Every single time you pay attention to the part of you that feels led, you make progress. As with anything, the more you familiarize yourself with the language of your inner knowing and how it speaks to you, the easier it will be to recognize and respond to it.

The same process applies to understanding the language and nature of your personal experience and expression of fear. People often ask how they can know the difference between unhelpful fear and guidance. My own process of learning to differentiate between the two was to study my experience of fear in more objective cases. By learning what fear looks, sounds, and feels like in situations where you *know* that it is a projection of former trauma, or the result of questions surrounding the unknown, and so on, you establish a fear profile that serves as a point of reference. To build this profile, also note what fear looks, sounds, and feels like in cases where you can confirm that there is a substantial reason to be cautious, suspicious, or concerned. As you develop your fear profile, you will be more and more equipped to discern between appropriate, wise hesitation and fear that drains your energy or that is intended to (unnecessarily) protect you from experiences that aren't truly dangerous or undesirable.

If I'm having trouble distinguishing between fear and guidance, I speak to my fear—which may manifest as a strong reservation, a mysterious pause, an unwillingness to take action, or a bodily sensation—and ask it what it wants me to know. If I ascertain that my fear is not actually useful, I gently ask it to step aside. My dialogue with fear goes something like this: "Fear, thank you for trying to protect me. Please dissolve if you are not helpful in this situation, so that I am able to access accurate and clear inner guidance."

If I'm still unsure why a reaction is laced with fear, I imagine different scenarios playing out. Before envisioning each scenario, I take a deep breath and clear my head. Then I imagine whatever it is I am contemplating and tune in to what I feel in my body. Once I've worked my way through all of the imagined scenarios, I compare and contrast the various feelings and physiological experiences associated with each one. By skipping between fantasies and tuning in to my reactions to them, I begin to sense what feels like the ideal path.

There are several ways to sabotage the connection you have to your inner wisdom. One is to assume that if you are having difficulty distinguishing between guidance and fear, you should lead with your rational brain and dismiss the signs and cues of your body. Another is to claim that you can't trust yourself based on a history of conflating guidance and fear. You also may dismiss the whole notion of inner guidance if, in the past, you have followed what you believed was just that and it led to unhappy or unfulfilling conclusions.

Some of us may be so consistently afraid to act on our inner guidance that eventually it seems to vanish altogether. But if we stop judging ourselves and our process, we experience the freedom to simply do the best we can at any given moment. We learn to trust the spontaneous knowing that springs up within us and act accordingly. When we do this, we connect more and more deeply with our inner guidance over time, regardless of the outcomes of a few isolated events. When we live from the heart, trusting in our deepest knowing, life might not look the way we expected it to. But it should *feel* deeply connected, transparent, and full of peace, even in the midst of imperfections and unknowns.

In an ideal world, what others think of us would have no bearing on what we choose to believe or do. We would act in accordance with our intuition without feeling the need to justify or explain it to anyone. But because parts of us are fragile and may still identify with the helplessness of a child who doesn't want to be abandoned or unloved, we often do care. And telling ourselves we don't care doesn't help; it's just another form of denial. When I fear the judgment of others, I might say something to myself like, "You really care what that person thinks and are deeply afraid of their judgment and disapproval. That's okay. I've got you. Whatever happens, I'm here for you."

Many of us betray ourselves regularly by denying our inner knowing to avoid potential judgment. But our inner knowing often contains wisdom that the rational parts of our brains do not. It wants to help and support us. It connects us with inexplicable realities and truths. So, when we are tempted to ignore it, we might instead consciously connect with how it feels every time we betray ourselves: the pit that forms in our stomach when things backfire, the fatiguing devastation of regret that arises, the *Why didn't I just listen to my gut?* monologue that runs. An example of denying inner knowing is when a person signs a contract that looks good on paper but doesn't feel right, only to later discover they were scammed. A more common example is when a person is on a date and has a "gut feeling" that something is off but ignores it because their date is saying all the right things. Quite often, that unexplainable sixth sense is picking up on something the rational mind is not. And the longer we wait to act on our intuition (versus our practical analysis), the more detrimental the consequences tend to be.

Punishing yourself is never helpful under any circumstances whatsoever. When you deny your intuition and then things go wrong, take a deep breath and thank your inner guidance for continuing to show up, instead of stewing, brewing, and kicking yourself. Welcome compassion to comfort the parts of you that are still scared to act on your truth for fear of losing something or edging outside of your comfort zone. Then, from a place of feeling held, let go and move on.

BE AS TRANSPARENT AND HONEST AS POSSIBLE

Being honest is one of the hardest things to do, because it makes us feel vulnerable. Since many of us are still learning to self-soothe, being vulnerable can feel like a threat to our security. Many of us are consciously and subconsciously attempting at all times to protect and defend our identity, and transparency creates room for potential judgment. But the reality is that dishonesty, half-truths, qualifications, and excessive explanations can be really confusing.

People can't know what we truly need and desire if we aren't fully honest with them. And if we shield others from the truth, we can't expect them to help provide whatever it is we are hoping for. Honesty coupled with clear and kind communication makes advocating for ourselves possible.

DON'T LIVE IN REGRET

Regret may be helpful in helping us reflect on and modify our beliefs, behaviors, and choices. But dwelling on and obsessing over what we could have done differently is not only unnecessary but counterproductive. I have loads of experience with the R-word and have experienced firsthand its ability to steal joy, productivity, forward movement, and energy. Of course, contemplating things that we wish we had said or done differently may dissuade us from making similar choices in the future, but chronic regret stalls growth and momentum; we can neither nurture ourselves nor evolve when we are overwhelmed by it.

If you did not follow your inner guidance and the result was emotional or physical harm to yourself or others, learn from this. If you hushed your deepest knowing and now have FOMO (fear of missing out) about a missed opportunity, learn from this. If you followed your inner compass and dodged a bullet, learn from this. If you said yes to the inexplicable direction of your soul and collided with a missing link relating to your dreams, learn from this. All of life is a learning experience; try to minimize classifying choices as mistakes. Instead, compassionately take note of what happens when you deny your inner guidance, and applaud the moments when you do slow down, draw upon your courage, and follow your truest knowing.

ADVOCATING FOR YOURSELF: CASE STUDIES

Being your own advocate may take practice and feel unnerving. But ultimately, advocating for yourself is a way to reaffirm your worth and sharpen your awareness of what you truly value, desire, and require. The benefits of advocating for yourself may at times get crowded out by fear, so I'd like to share some success stories in the hope of encouraging you to use your powerful, important voice.

Case Study #1

After I weaned myself off sleeping pills, I developed a particular rhythm and routine surrounding sleep in an effort to foster a consistent level of trust that I didn't require meds. Part of this routine involved going to sleep at approximately the same time every night, which sometimes conflicted with opportunities to be out having fun with family and friends. At a certain point, a few people I adore began to make fun of me, and while their jokes were in no way malicious, they both embarrassed and hurt me. They also undermined my efforts to prioritize my sleep. Here is what I said to these people:

"I know that you love me and don't mean any harm by making what in your mind are frivolous jokes. I also imagine that it's hard for you that I'm not as available as I was when I was taking sleeping pills. But what I'm trying to do here for my health and future is harder than anything I've ever done, and I'm sensitive about it. I'd really appreciate you not commenting on the fact that I've given myself a bedtime, even if you say it in a joking way. Believe it or not, it still hurts. It also triggers the part of me that feels embarrassed and sad that I can't be more flexible right now. Thank you for understanding. It means a lot to me that I have your support."

In response to my declaration of truth, my friends became deeply sensitive to the challenges I was navigating and made a special effort to connect with me during the day. We ended up taking beautiful hikes, having picnics, and grilling outdoors, and funnily enough, we all realized that our quality of time together was enhanced by meeting earlier in the day. It was a win-win for everyone!

Case Study #2

One of my dear friends—let's call her Clara—works at a company that claims to encourage free thinking and outside-the-box ideas. But in her first position there, every time she generated a new angle or approached projects with a certain level of innovation, a colleague she reported to shut her down. After months of feeling defeated, she decided to give up and just produce the kind of work that she knew her colleague would approve and not question.

"Why don't you talk to your boss about it?" I asked Clara.

"I shouldn't need to," she replied. "She sees my work and is passing on it. That's my answer."

I urged Clara to confront her boss. This is the monologue we came up with:

"I agreed to this job because the culture of the office seemed to value ingenuity and thinking outside the box. But every time I come to you with a concept that I believe is unique and valuable, you pass. Can we discuss what your expectations are, so that I can determine how to best do my job while staying inspired? Are there any opportunities for me to go off-road a bit, or could we consider creating those opportunities?"

Clara's workplace promised the freedom to create with passion, but her superior's feedback was reinforcing a more predictable approach that wasn't satisfying Clara's cravings or allowing her to explore her talent. My friend's fear of losing her job kept her silent for many months, but the final result of the conversation with her boss was a promotion that involved more responsibility, extensive room for innovation, and creative control. Clara ended up having colleagues under her whom she encouraged to think radically, and the company ended up making a considerable profit because of this.

More important, Clara and her colleagues were thrilled to show up to work and use their gifts.

The conversation Clara had with her boss could very well have resulted in my friend losing her job at the company. But because she has an impeccable work ethic, is deeply inspired, and happens to be a joy to work with, I have no doubt that had she been let go, she would have found another, more flexible company to work for. Had she not found a new job, she might have made even more money and had more creative freedom doing freelance work. At any point, Clara can decide to start her own business and grow it slowly, even if this requires a little lead time to save money. In other words, the flip side to losing something is gaining something else—something that may be exponentially better. Clara did in fact "lose her job" as she knew it—and she gained one that was far more valuable to her.

Case Study #3

Another friend of mine—let's call her Sienna—wants to write a book. She has an amazing story, remarkable resources, and a desire to be of service to the world. I've been encouraging Sienna to write, but she keeps generating excuses as to why she can't: she doesn't have any time, her husband's job is very demanding, her kids need her, and on and on.

Recently, Sienna brought up her desire to write again. Instead of delving into my usual spiel about why she should get going, I tried a different approach. I echoed her sentiments and said, "Bummer that you don't have any time, your husband's job is so demanding, and your kids need you." She looked at me and said, "But *you* don't have any time, your husband is running a company, and you're an extremely present parent. How do you make it all work?"

"I don't allow fear to interfere with my passions," I told her. "I'm afraid of everything. But I talk to my fear instead of allowing it to take over my life. And I come up with very practical solutions to the more challenging parts of trying to create something that is in service to the world, while continuing to show up for myself and my family."

Later that week, Sienna began to work on her book. She had less time than usual to decompress with her husband, and he came across as snarky and resentful when she was fully immersed in her writing.

"He's acting super weird," Sienna told me over the phone. "It's like he wants me all to himself. Can't he just be supportive? I've put this off for so long!"

"Of course he wants you all to himself," I said. "That's what he's used to. But he can't have all of you all of the time, and he will gradually adapt to you prioritizing your dreams for this particular chapter of your life."

"I also feel like I want him to help out more with the kids, but I'm afraid to ask since he's already so swamped with work," Sienna said.

"Maybe he and the kids will both benefit from this extra time together," I said. "You're so used to putting everyone else first that you haven't made room for the possibility that everyone might win when you consider your own needs."

This is what we came up with for Sienna to say to her husband:

"Honey, I know that we really value our downtime together, and that you're missing it. I'm missing it too. But in order to feel like the best version of myself, I need to pursue things outside of home life that make me feel alive. And right now, writing is that thing. You aren't competing with my book. There's no competition; no one and nothing can replace you. I would really appreciate your support as I attempt to do something that's really difficult and scary for me."

I also encouraged Sienna to ask her husband if there was anything he felt was missing or wanted more of in his own life. When we see other people pursuing their dreams and passions, we may get jealous if we are not pursuing ours. And jealousy leads to resentment, which can result in dismissive, grumpy, or snarky behavior.

Sienna's husband revealed that he felt that all he did was work and that he didn't get enough time to be with their kids. His response not only explained his grumpiness but also provided a solution to Sienna's problem of needing more time to write. After their conversation, Sienna and her husband rearranged their schedules to allow for her husband to spend more of his downtime playing with their kids. This happened to be both therapeutic for him and something the kids had always longed for.

— CHAPTER SUMMARY —

Advocating for yourself benefits not only you but those around you. As uncomfortable as it may be to assert yourself and claim your value, it is an undeniable component of ensuring that your needs are met and that relationships with others are sustainable and mutually respectful. By getting clear about your self-worth, identifying your preferences and what's nonnegotiable, trusting your inner guidance, releasing yourself from shame, being as transparent as possible, and learning from the past, you will equip yourself to be your own best advocate. Every so-called mistake is simply another opportunity to grow, and it may very well direct you to a brighter future.

CHAPTER 10

BUILDING YOUR FUTURE

I am so intrigued by dreams that I wrote and recorded an entire album called *Dreamer's Dream*. Waking dreams, nighttime dreams—all dreams fascinate me. Friends and family have always referred to me as a dreamer, perhaps because I dip so often into the wilds of my imagination, or maybe because throughout most of my life, I have created a magical vision for my future.

The emphasis on living in the now that many brilliant philosophers, thought leaders, and some religions value has not evaded me. When I'm worrying about future unknowns or obsessing over a decision I made in the past, my most potent tool is to reel myself back into the present moment. Here is what my internal dialogue might sound like as I do:

> *Is the thing I'm worrying about happening now? What is happening now? Right now, the event I am anticipating and worrying about is not happening. At this moment in time, what is happening is that I'm taking a shower. I am capable of dealing with everything as it comes up. I do not need to anticipate or obsess over anything in order to secure my desired outcome. I trust myself to be present and handle everything that comes my way by fully accepting what is. I am resourceful and resilient. I am safe.*

In addition to a comforting internal dialogue, engaging your senses and tuning in to your body may help reel you back into the current moment. If you are in bed, how do the sheets feel against your skin? Are they silky or grainy? Are your toes intertwined with a blanket? If you are sitting down, what aromas are in your midst? Are you smelling cherry Chapstick or perfume? Is there a cool breeze against your face? Wiggle your toes and stretch your arms. Which parts of you feel activated and which parts feel sleepy?

There were periods of my life when I compulsively imagined my future in order to escape my present reality. I was either in a place I didn't want to be, doing something I didn't want to do, or feeling something I didn't want to feel. Maybe you've experienced this too. Perhaps the weight of your reality has been supported by fantasies that have carried you elsewhere.

I am extremely grateful to my imagination for its power to lift me out of impossibly heavy mental spaces and deliver me to some version of emotional freedom. During certain phases of my life, I felt my whole body lighten and my vibration shift when I imagined a safer place, a better way, or a more grounding or exhilarating experience. To this day, I love that I can travel back in time and recall moments when I felt my most inspired, cherished, ignited, or calm. But if your mind travels backward or forward more often than it engages with the now, or if you strongly prefer to call upon your past or envision your future rather than be where you are in the present, these are clues that something about your current life may not feel quite right. If you avoid true presence, you might feel dissatisfied or as if something is missing.

Maybe you feel overwhelmed, anxious, sad, or bored at any given time. Instead of immediately bringing yourself back to the present moment when your imagination starts to wander, or just allowing your thoughts to pass, you can try two things. First, notice that you are traveling. If you return again and again to the same memories from the past or visions for the future, this is particularly noteworthy. Something about the place, person, or feeling that you travel to may be haunting you for a reason. Second, talk to your memories and visions for the future:

What are you trying to tell me? What are you trying to show me? Who or what do I want more of? What do I want less of? What are you trying to teach me about how I want to feel or the kind of place where I'd like to be? Why am I thinking about you? What am I running from? What am I running toward?

Usually, when I find myself drifting from my present-moment reality, either it isn't satiating me or I'm feeling agitated, anxious, restless, or bored. It's as if deep down inside, I know there's a more satisfying, more thrilling, or more peaceful version of reality. Notice the moments when you metaphorically go away. Where are you going? Why are you going there? How do you feel when you get there? How do you feel when you return to the reality of where you truly are?

Imagination, as an escape, holds the potential to illuminate both our desires and fears. There is also, in my experience, a dream-making component to imagination whereby it can help us understand and possibly even generate what we want more of. If you frequently visualize yourself on a stage talking to audiences, what does this scene represent to you? If you envision yourself with a romantic partner, is it possible you're seeking more intimate connection? Imagination can help clarify what you want more of and how you want your life to look and feel.

Regardless of where you are today in your journey, how you are feeling, and what you want more or less of, I know in the deepest part of me that anything and everything is possible for you. You may not believe it right now, and that's okay. I believe it for you. If you are reading this book, you already are on a path to healing that will invite every kind of abundance into your life. So, just for now, if you are feeling skeptical about your future, use my belief in you to welcome the idea that there is more for you to create and enjoy than you could possibly even imagine. Breathe and relax as we explore together how I generate whatever it is I dream of.

CULTIVATING YOUR DREAMS

Most of us cultivate multiple dreams simultaneously. We have dreams for our love lives and our careers, for what it is we want to experience in the world, and for how we want to feel. I've never met a person whose sole dream was to become a pilot to the exclusion of experiencing love or contentment or being able to pay their bills without worrying. Your dream may be to help care for elderly people, or to use your voice to advocate for an environmental policy change, or to write books. Maybe your dream is to start a nonprofit, create an eco-friendly clothing line, use your artistic vision to design web pages, or be a good parent. Maybe your dream is to be at peace with yourself and the world and to experience unencumbered joy. Your dream could be to learn to survive in the wild with limited resources. Your dream could be to have a united family that communicates lovingly and with respect. Your dream could be to earn enough money to help your parents buy a house, or it could be to have a baby or fall in love. Or it could be many or all of the above!

There is no right dream, and you are the only person on the planet who can know truly what it is you dream of. Others can help guide you there, but you are the parent of your own dreams and will ultimately birth them. If you're not clear on what it is you truly desire, that's more than okay. In fact, that level of openness may allow you to open doors that many of us with more static versions of our dreams would ignore or pass by.

If you are not really sure what you want to do or where you want to go with your life, know that there is plenty of time to explore and experiment. There is no rush, and you are not behind. As a starting point, notice what you find yourself thinking and daydreaming about. As I've said before, every time you revisit your past or imagine your future, you receive clues about what you want more or less of. If you are in an office filing reports day after day and imagine yourself being outdoors in the fresh air, that's a great starting point! Your body is telling you what it needs. Little by little, steal moments

>> • <<

Practice: Cultivate Self-Trust

Sometimes we think of a dream as some big, grandiose future accomplishment or experience that we will one day arrive at. In my experience, we grow into and continuously create and re-create our dreams. And how we create our dreams is by following the clues of our bodies, minds, and hearts. So, here's where presence comes in. If you are dizzy, your back hurts, and your mind keeps wandering to the outdoor patio, see if you can slip away from your desk to stretch. By listening to your body and responding to the scenes painted by your imagination, you begin to cultivate self-trust. And self-trust is a huge part of taking chances and creating the future of your dreams.

>> • <<

away from your desk and enjoy the sense of aliveness you crave.

I am going to say it again, because this point is pivotal: you create dreams; you don't arrive at them. Every step along the way matters, and not because you may be thrown off course, sabotage your success, or miss your brightest and most promising path if you don't notice the steps. Every step matters because each time you choose to honor your body or respond to the yearnings and cravings of your heart, you build self-trust. Every time you commit to what you require *in the present moment*, you inch closer to your version of fulfillment.

Fulfillment is not a destination you arrive at either; it's a moment-by-moment choice to follow your inner guidance and do what feels best for you. It's also the result of claiming a perspective in your life that brings peace and joy, not condemnation and judgment. If you envision a goal but do not honor yourself along the way, how can you trust that you will feel secure, content, and joyful in having realized your dream?

The creation of dreams is an ever-morphing, ever-shifting experience that evolves with every decision you make on behalf of your real-time needs and desires. Visualizing your potential future in detail can be extremely powerful. But your future is no doubt shaped, influenced, and ultimately determined by your willingness to respond to what you want and need in each moment. If you dwell exclusively on your goal, you may miss or discount conversations, experiences, and revelations that could redirect you in powerful and important ways. It may feel helpful to have a loose blueprint of where you are headed, but the vision you have crafted of your future will shift and evolve for the better as you respond to the prompts of your body, mind, and heart each day.

As you go about your day, ask yourself the following questions:

"What would freedom choose right now?"

"What would love choose right now?"

"What would integrity choose right now?"

"What would inspiration choose right now?"

"What would passion choose right now?"

"What does my heart want?"

"What does my soul require?"

"What makes my body feel most alive?"

"What puts my mind, heart, and body at ease?"

"Where do I want to go?"

By checking in with yourself periodically, you will begin to recognize your present-moment needs and desires. Now, let's explore the nitty-gritty of your dream life.

THE SOUL OF YOUR DREAM

If you can identify one of your dreams and have crafted even a vague vision for it, start by writing it down on paper. Here's an example of an action-oriented, goal-based dream of mine: my dream is to publish my memoir. Once I am aware of what my dream is, I try to identify what I call the soul of my dream. For you, this will include identifying:

- The *why* of what it is you want to do
- The *who* and *what* the dream is in service of
- How you hope to feel as you create and work toward your dream
- The ways in which you hope the end result will influence your self-concept
- What you hope to gain or receive as a consequence of realizing your dream
- What you imagine you will feel after your dream is realized

If your dream is to become a millionaire, what is the soul of your dream? Is it that you want the resources to support disempowered and underprivileged people or endangered species? Would you like to help rebuild homes or entire towns that have been demolished or obliterated by war or natural disaster? Is it that you want freedom of some kind? (Freedom could mean the absence of worry and anxiety surrounding finances; the privilege of deciding where you want to be and when; the absence of having to be physically, energetically, or creatively accountable to others in a rigid way; and so on.) Is it that you value travel and experiences that you believe are contingent on having financial resources?

Do you anticipate feeling respected, admired, or loved as a consequence of achieving this goal? Are you hoping to gain social status or a secure position in your workplace, or receive love from a romantic partner or family member? Are you conflating secure attachment with achievement and hoping that by achieving something lofty, someone you love or who you believe you require won't abandon you?

It's valuable to establish the soul of your dream, because whatever you are pursuing (such as a job, tangible item, or relationship) may represent something deeper. Our souls desire peace, freedom, joy, and a sense of purpose, and we may assume that by doing or accomplishing certain things, we can guarantee fundamental aspects of our experience and identity. In reality, there are many ways to achieve emotional security and meaning and to reaffirm our self-concepts. And since that is the case, we may be more open to a variety of possible outcomes if we are clear on what we are hoping to gain or secure as a consequence of pursuing a particular goal, versus fixating on the goal itself. I consistently dream of being and doing certain things, but I am open to becoming, creating, and receiving so much more than I could ever even imagine. By meditating on the soul of my dream as much or more than on the dream itself, I become available to manifest realities that exceed my wildest expectations.

As human beings, we tend to conflate accomplishments with identity. As challenging as it is, try not to make your sense of well-being, the verification of your purpose, or the validation of your value and worth contingent upon what you accomplish or create. If you assume that once you do X, Y, or Z, you suddenly will feel liberated from the emotional tyranny of the human experience, you most likely will be disappointed. If you believe that the fruition of your dreams will bring lasting peace or joy, you may be setting yourself up for a chronic sense of failure or confusion. There are at least two reasons for this.

In my experience, we humans are very crafty at rapidly producing new goals, loftier standards, and more impressive visions for our futures than ones we have previously held. I've experienced this in relation to recording songs, writing books, and growing my wellness company. This may in part relate to the way dopamine works. When we cross the finish line of a goal, our dopamine levels spike; afterward, they drop below the baseline level in direct proportion to the magnitude of the spike at the time of completion or success. Eventually, dopamine makes its way back to baseline. But if we habituate to plunging directly from one achievement to the next, we are constantly forced to up the ante in an unconscious effort to regulate our dopamine levels.

For me, working toward a goal has less to do with the goal itself and more to do with who I am becoming as a consequence of pursuing it. When I record a song, the song is ultimately less interesting to me than the version of myself I am evolving into during the creation process. When I write, the parts of me that get excavated and challenged are the real gems, more valuable than the words that make their way onto the page. As I've learned to parent my children, it is the experience of my own patience, warmth, insecurities, and imperfections that has brought texture and depth to my role as mother. We cannot know who or what we truly are or grasp the scope of our potential if we don't actively engage in our lives.

But if history has proven anything, it is that some of the most materially wealthy and professionally successful people on the planet have struggled the most. Perfectionism, depression, anxiety, burnout, and the absence of a definable purpose have plagued many of the public figures the world worships and adores. People such as Marilyn Monroe and Elvis Presley mirror the plight of modern-day pop stars like Britney Spears. I personally know a number of highly successful people who are not public figures, but who, as their success skyrocketed, had an even harder time grounding themselves in a lasting sense of purpose and value. It's natural to believe that being adored or classically successful will lead to lasting feelings of peace, satisfaction, and exhilaration. But in reality, extraordinary titles and noteworthy levels of success, as defined by society, often make celebrities feel more alone. Some of my own friends express the belief that if they get a raise or a promotion, or earn some type of tangible or honorary award, the value they assign to themselves will increase. Not believing that we are 100 percent valuable and lovable regardless of what we do or do not create and achieve creates a cycle of constantly wanting to prove ourselves worthy of existence.

So, what is the difference between a life that *looks* successful versus one that *feels* successful? These are what I believe to be the ingredients of a life that *feels* successful:

- An unshakable awareness of your inherent and unchanging value
- Meaningful connections with people who truly know, love, and respect you for who you are—not for who they want you to be or for who you are becoming
- The use of your talents and gifts
- A self-defined sense of purpose
- The inclusion of rest and pleasure alongside the pursuit of your dreams
- A consistent practice of giving back or caring for others

You may technically *be* successful, as success is defined by the world, your colleagues, or even yourself, but if any of the above ingredients are missing, you actually may not benefit emotionally from the beauty of your accomplishments.

CREATE SPACE TO DREAM

Many of us are so action-oriented that we forget how much creation occurs in the pause. In my own life, ideas are generated, dreams spontaneously spring up, and visions are etched into my mind's eye because I have created the space for inspiration. If you are constantly looking down at your cell phone, scrolling through social media, chatting with friends, or stimulating and distracting yourself in other ways, you may lack the space to hear the whispers of the universe or your own heart.

While connection and stimulation are meaningful and essential, take note of how quickly you turn on music in moments of silence, or immediately call a friend when you hit traffic. Challenge yourself every now and then to breathe through the stillness and just see what comes up. Dreams aren't born exclusively of action. Sometimes, there's not just restoration but progress in the pause.

Turn to "Honoring the Pause" in the workbook.

DREAMS EVOLVE

For years, every time one of my mentors would ask me how I was doing, I would say something along the lines of "I'm going through another transition." My life felt like an unrelenting series of transitions, and the moment things would appear to be organized, understandable, and grounded, I would enter another transitional phase.

Then, when I was in my mid-twenties, I asked her when she thought I might feel settled. "I feel as if for twenty-five years, I've been on a plane headed toward a very beautiful destination, and I'm just really ready to touch down," I told her. "Please just tell me when I'm going to land this plane."

My mentor laughed and said, "You're not going to like what I'm about to say."

I sighed. "What is it?"

"As long as you're growing, the plane never lands."

The nature of life is constant transition. When we're desperate to touch down and to have everything figured out, what we might really be yearning for is the experience of peace. I didn't crave peace to the exclusion of exhilaration or discovery, but I was desperate to engage with the unknown without anxiety and believe that I would have everything I needed and desired. I wanted to be sure that everything would work out. I was eager to feel okay in my own skin and with the trajectory of my life. I wanted to trust myself through the ever-constant change that is one of life's guarantees, and to be sure that wherever I ended up was where I was meant to be. Looking back at the twenty-five-year-old me, I realize that I didn't want to land the plane; I wanted to feel safe soaring through the open expanse of the sky.

As we evolve, our dreams most likely will evolve. We may intentionally change course, or life might gently or forcefully redirect us. Saying goodbye to an old dream may feel like saying goodbye to an old friend. But some friendships run their course, and certain dreams do as well. Other times, friendships and dreams and even our self-concept may just require an upgrade. What might appear to be the end may in reality be a transitional phase during which growth leads to a more meaningful version of our reality. We can move toward our dreams while making room for the possibility that whatever materializes may be different but even more fulfilling than what we originally had hoped for.

If you allow for fluidity as you travel your chosen path, you'll never interpret a closed door as a rejection. If you receive a no of any kind, or the door you are knocking on refuses to open, one of three things may happen: a better door may open, the door that is now closed will open at a more opportune time, or you may be redirected to explore alternative paths. My dear friend Devonne always says, "Rejection is God's protection," and I truly believe in the spirit of that sentiment. You *live* the dream not when you arrive at a specific destination but when you feel free to improvise because you trust that your life is imbued with purpose and energized by joy.

Since we cannot always control our life circumstances or direct our path in tangible ways, it's important to keep in mind that what we can always control is our frame of mind and attitude about our life circumstances. We can strive to experience emotional peace and freedom even in the midst of distress and struggle. And we can do our best to preserve the hope that our lives will feel meaningful and full of ease regardless of what challenges we face.

Please know that those around you will feel the confidence you possess in your life. Without you being consciously aware of why, people will be drawn to the magnetism of your confidence and the grace and ease with which you move through the world. If you believe in the full spectrum of possibilities for your life, and that everything around you will conspire on your behalf, you cannot help but radiate an energy and light that ignites those around you and piques their curiosity.

Confidence is contingent on—and quite possibly the result of—two foundational commitments that all of us can make to ourselves. Commitment number one is to be who we truly are in the world, regardless of our audience or the consequences of being fully and unapologetically authentic. Commitment number two is to believe that we are irreplaceable. When we marry authenticity with the awareness that there is no one exactly like us, we lay the foundation for unimaginable success as we define it.

Our planet *requires* a diversity of ideas, perspectives, and contributions. When all individuals offer their unique spin on life, the world evolves. Stagnancy is impermissible; the confluence of many perspectives, purposes, and dreams is what keeps the planet moving forward. No one can do you but you. You are the only person who possesses your talents, insights, and voice.

The symbiosis of expecting to receive the miraculous and being aware that opportunities are almost always in your midst leads to mind-blowing outcomes. If you exude confidence but don't actively recognize the potential that exists all around you at all times, you may miss pivotal conversations or information. If you are searching for opportunities to connect and advance but lack confidence and self-trust, others may be less likely to take a chance on you or spontaneously engage with you. It is the dance of what you imagine, what you exude, what you search for, and what you feel worthy of receiving that creates miracles. I try to remain as open as possible to potential connections and relationships that may advance my established dreams or redirect them. And because I believe that I am irreplaceable and most valuable in a state of total authenticity, I feel free to pursue these opportunities with a sense of deep trust and excitement.

SEIZE THE MOMENT

An incident occurred when I was seven years old that forever influenced my perspective on taking chances and seizing the moment. I was on the subway in Manhattan with my mother when we spied an actress who, at the time, was the star of my favorite television show. I very much wanted her autograph but was unspeakably nervous about approaching her. My mother pulled a cocktail napkin and a pen from her purse and nudged me in the direction of my idol.

"Go for it," my mom whispered.

My heart drummed frantically in anticipation of asking for what I wanted. I took a single step forward and stopped. A moment later, the subway stopped. My chest clenched as I imagined the actress walking off. But to my relief, she continued to lean against a metal pole as the subway regained momentum.

"Now's your chance," my mother said.

She touched my shoulder, but I was paralyzed. I didn't know what would happen if I were to ask the celebrity for her autograph. I wasn't sure how she would respond. It was one thing for me to dance at a drum circle in Central Park in front of strangers, but it was another to step into the light of someone I perceived to be more powerful and important than me without any idea of what the outcome would be.

I froze and silently practiced asking for the autograph as the subway stopped and its doors opened and closed once again. The actress was reading a newspaper and didn't budge. Three stops later, crinkled cocktail napkin in my small hand, I was finally ready. I had memorized the speech. I could do this. I took a deep breath, and as I made my way toward my idol...she walked off the train.

I'll never forget the look on my mother's face when I glanced back at her with wet eyes. At seven years of age, I instantly understood why my mother hadn't just grabbed my hand and marched me over to Sandy Duncan. She had wanted me to own my dream. She had expected me to use my voice. She had hoped that I was confident enough to take a chance, regardless of the outcome.

This one incident is why, twenty years later, when I was in Manhattan on my own and passed by a handsome young man seated on the patio of a café, I plopped myself down at the table next to him. That man is now my husband and the father of my children. I could have passed by him and let the metaphorical subway doors close. But I marched right over and claimed my future instead.

THE FIVE STEPS TO CREATING DYNAMIC AND INSPIRED POSSIBILITIES

The following are my top strategies for living your most inspired life.

Secret #1: Don't Play It Safe, and Don't Play It Small

Taking chances and trusting in your mental and emotional resilience to buffer potential disappointment or pain is part of living a bold life. If you desire and expect the extraordinary, you may have to step far outside your comfort zone. Confidence and the willingness to take chances are essential components of moving forward, regardless of what you are pursuing.

When we talk about confidence, we tend to envision fearless individuals with swagger who storm around declaring their worth and expecting the best. In truth, confidence doesn't look or sound any particular way. It doesn't require a specific volume, appearance, vibration, or tone. Confidence can be a quiet self-knowing or the grounded awareness of being special enough to receive and create beauty, joy, and meaning in life, despite any hesitations or fears. You may happen to be loud, or an extrovert, or soft, or someone who favors alone time. Approaching a stranger on the street or reaching out to someone you admire on social media may feel exhilarating, terrifying, or both. It doesn't matter. Again, confidence is authenticity plus the belief of being irreplaceable. It is up to you to define your authentic self-concept and learn to believe that no one can ever replace you. Being authentic also means expressing yourself authentically, and that can look however you want it to. If you aren't taking action because you don't sincerely believe in the value of what you alone offer the world, consider the chicken-and-egg phenomenon. To feel authentic, you may first have to practice authenticity.

No one can ever do what you would do in exactly the way you would do it. That is why the world requires each and every one of us: the introverts and extroverts, those who sing and those who paint, those who march and those who crawl. The world needs your blueprint, your hands, your mind, and your heart. If ten people were to sing the same song, we would hear ten different voices. No one has sung the song the way you would sing it, written a book the way you would write it, painted a painting the way you would paint it, or danced a dance the way you would dance it.

It may be tempting to make yourself small, because you fear that someone else is more accomplished or more worthy of attention and love. Perhaps you fear that if you do the thing you dream of doing, you will fail. Or maybe you fear that you are so damn big that if you were to explode all of your potential into the world, you might obliterate the people around you. In other words, if you take the plunge, you might succeed, and the people you love might wind up feeling small. Fear of taking up space and shining light on our full potential can be every bit as paralyzing as suspecting that we're not enough.

The whole notion of success versus failure is built on the faulty premise that those are real things. If we are authentic and genuine and feel that we deserve love, what else is there? If we move toward our vision and goals with the sense that we are irreplaceable, isn't everything we create valuable? If there is no singular destination and the plane never really lands, isn't it all just about growth anyway? Isn't the real healing accepting who we truly are, doing the things we love, and reveling in the joy that follows? Let's celebrate for a moment that whatever your dreams may be, what matters most is that you live your way into them with delight and freedom from fear. You may find in the end that emotional freedom and healing are the most fulfilling dreams anyway.

Secret #2: Listen to Your Inner Guidance and Intuition

I talked extensively about inner guidance and intuition in chapter 9, so I won't belabor the topic here. But you know how I took a chance and seated myself next to the man who is now my husband? The reason I was in a position to plop down next to him at the café was because I had moved up my flight from Los Angeles to New York by two days. At the time, it did not make any logical sense to me, but instead of flying out on June 23, some inner guidance urged me to head to Manhattan on June 21. And I listened.

At first, the guidance was subtle and came as a thought that spontaneously entered my mind (in my own voice). But because I disregarded the thought on account of its being illogical, it morphed into a relentless demand of sorts, interrupting mundane tasks and keeping me awake at night. At one point, I saw *June 21* spelled out in my mind's eye in a kind of golden light. While the rational part of my brain was trying to convince me that because there was no known reason to change my flight and rearrange my plans in order to fly out earlier, I shouldn't do it, some deeper knowing was relaying a message. That knowing may have come from within me entirely, or perhaps unseen forces were at play. All I know is that I changed my flight, flew out on June 21, and met my future husband that evening. He left New York City on June 23, and had I continued to shove aside the urgent voice instructing me to be in Manhattan two days earlier, I would have missed him entirely.

Do not overthink your guidance. If you believe that your guidance is instructing you to engage in behavior that is destructive or harmful to yourself or others, this is not your guidance. The one exception to this would be an extreme act of self-defense or the requirement to protect another from danger. Otherwise, our true guidance acts exclusively from a place of love and in support of our well-being and the well-being of others. If you are not clear on what is guidance and what is not, ask out loud. In my experience, guidance generally does not feel like overwhelming anxiety. It may include the awareness of potential danger that is experienced as stress, but this is different from incapacitating fear and worry.

In my twenties, I was driving to a birthday party, and some part of me felt compelled to take a different, less scenic route than the one I was accustomed to. It didn't make sense, especially because I was running behind, but I kept envisioning alternative streets. Everything in my body had the impulse to pivot from my usual course. I followed that impulse and later learned that there had been a fatal three-car crash in exactly the neighborhood and at exactly the time I would have driven through it had I not changed course. When it comes to materializing the vision you have for your life, listen actively to your deeper knowing. It will provide clues and connections, some subtle and some loud, and continue to shepherd you onto the path that will most gracefully support your highest evolution.

Secret #3: Follow the "Sacred Crumbs"

Until my thirties, my life felt like a puzzle that destiny had assigned me to perfectly piece together. This paradigm of viewing my life as a sort of riddle that I was responsible for decoding caused great amounts of stress and massive anxiety, because I didn't want to get it wrong.

I now believe that it is impossible to get life wrong. If you are doing your best to make choices that support your well-being, they are right simply because you made them. On the other hand, if you are actively and consistently ignoring your inner guidance or sabotaging your dreams because deep down inside you don't feel worthy of them, you may be denying yourself the ability to prosper and flourish. But even that isn't wrong. There can be nothing wrong about your life, with the exception of inflicting harm on others, but there are always opportunities to grow. And every experience you choose—

or that chooses you—is meaningful and valuable if you decide it is. You create your destiny moment by moment, and while you always have the power of choice, you need not ever fear that your dreams are too big or unattainable.

Through my current lens, I view life as a series of choices. None of them is "right," and none of them is "wrong," but they may lead to different outcomes. I believe the urge within me to pursue certain talents and dreams or create things is my body's way of guiding me toward a version of my life that will bring relief, joy, satisfaction, and healing to myself and others. Because I believe that I am guided, I try as often as possible to follow that guidance. And when I don't, I have compassion for the scared parts of myself that have chosen to stay small or play it safe. My disappointment then fuels a commitment to new opportunities to be guided.

You cannot miss what it is you are meant to do and be, because you are co-creating your reality on a moment-to-moment basis. I say "co-creating" and not "creating" because I believe that unseen forces are supporting us as we navigate our lives. Regardless of whether or not the concept of unseen forces resonates with you, we all exist in a perpetual state of creation, and there are countless ways to express and experience yourself and the world around you. I refer to my guidance as "sacred crumbs." My guidance may be that I burst into tears, or that I get grumpy every time I think about something that I believe I have to do. It may be words that pop into my brain, such as *Keep Max home today.* Guidance can come to us in the form of everyday conversations, or as something we witness or read.

When a strong feeling about or reaction to someone or something is present, ask this feeling if it is fear or guidance. Then ask yourself if this feeling is current and relevant, or if you are being triggered. It is important to differentiate between our bodies' current guidance and the cellular presence of past experiences in our bodies that may cause emotional reactions. Our past can distract us from receiving or interpreting our guidance clearly, simply because we are projecting historical events onto our current realities. Because our bodies store memories, it is important to honor and heal those memories so that they do not possess the power to dictate our futures.

Magic isn't always passive. Quite often, we create magic by showing up, doing the work, and following the sacred crumbs. Show up for the magic, and it will show up for you.

Secret #4: Be Open to Receiving and Giving

Every single person on this planet possesses the same amount of value—no more, no less. Some of the most valuable advice, insights, and direction I have ever received were from unsuspecting strangers or passing acquaintances who may never have known the impact of their words on me. In my twenties, I was emotionally reactive to the extreme. And while my entire existence sometimes felt to me like a fire hazard, something about my openness and vulnerability seemed to ignite miraculous wisdom from the victims of my spontaneous outbursts. I don't even know the names of many of the people who guided my soul or reshaped the way I thought about things. I cannot recall their faces. But they showed up at the exact moment I needed them to, and for this, I will forever be grateful.

Shortly before meeting my husband, I broke up with someone who lived in New York because we couldn't agree on where to start a family. Right after leaving his apartment, I hopped into the cab of an elderly man from the Middle East and broke down in hysterics.

"Miss, are you okay?" the man asked in a concerned voice.

"No," I said. "I just broke up with a guy I really love, and I'm not sure I'll ever get over it."

What the man said next changed everything. "Congratulations on your *liberation*!"

My liberation? But I was devastated!

"If this man let you go, he is not your man. Your man would not let you go. You have been liberated!"

>•<<

Practice: Being of Service to Others

Being of service is just as important as receiving. Not only is it good for your emotional health to support and contribute positively to the lives of other human beings, it can help lift you out of the ruts that keep you from living your best life. It also may help ease compulsive worry and depression. As essential as it is to honor your own struggles and seek to resolve them, part of that resolve might involve transferring some of your attention to others. Being of service does not involve distracting ourselves from our own lives; it is a parallel journey. Giving to others ultimately is a way of giving to ourselves, as it chemically alters our brains for the better, creates a sense of purpose, helps us reflect back to ourselves the beauty of our own humanity, and provides opportunities to practice compassion and kindness.

Your contribution might not involve working hands-on with others; you might channel your energy to oceans or rainforests or animals. You might pick up trash from the sidewalk or smile at a stranger passing by. Whatever your offering is, know that it is valuable and important. Every molecule of your breath that is devoted to elevating the planet matters, and it is not your place to judge, criticize, or quantify your contribution.

>•<<

The way this man reframed my breakup is the reason why, despite loving my ex, I could move on from him. Six weeks later, I met my husband. You never know which people and circumstances will help usher the most growth into your life. Strangers from all parts of the world have guided and inspired me, because the threads of our humanity have been the same, even if our experiences have differed. Get curious about people. Ask them about their stories. You never know where the insights or direction you require will come from. Be open to receiving guidance in unsuspecting moments.

Secret #5: Ask for Help

Do not hesitate to ask for help. Asking for what you want and need is a wonderful way to reaffirm to yourself (and others) the immense value you bring to the world. If you believe that you are valuable and irreplaceable, it is almost incumbent on you to approach those who may support you in expressing your authenticity. You might want to ask for a job, a mentorship, or an introduction to a third party. You might want to ask for coaching, help acquiring new skills, or support in honing and refining your talent. You might want to ask for advice, emotional support, friendship, a date, or material resources. And while you can never control the reactions of others or manipulate their responses to your requests, you can continue to believe that the right door will open at the right time if you persist.

If you are open to asking for help from the universe or unseen forces, you might try saying the following prayer: *Today, please help me to go where I need to go, meet who I need to meet, see what I need to see, hear what I need to hear, feel what I need to feel, and know what I need to know. Please heighten my inner guidance and direct me on a path that will lead to my highest good and the most profound evolution of others.*

THE PRACTICAL SIDE OF CREATION

Based on the many logistical steps often required to manifest our dreams, some people might assume the process is exclusively action-based. Alternatively, I've spoken with people who spend all of their time visualizing their future without pursuing any of the more practical avenues to guide their vision to fruition. I believe that the most effective way to support our dreams is to lean into imagination *and* action, and also to create space for spontaneous inspiration.

Even if someone appears seemingly out of the blue and offers you an opportunity or a job or asks you out on a date, it is still on you to say yes. You have to agree to what shows up for you. In some cases, you may need to prepare in advance, so that when the magic shows up, you are ready for it. And it's imperative to trust that moment by moment, you possess the talent, confidence, resilience, and faith to navigate uncharted territory.

There is no mandate to be unafraid as you show up for the life you are co-creating. If there were, most of us would be a no-show the majority of the time. Showing up for your life may look like saying, "No, thank you," or "Not right now." Saying no may in some cases be just as essential as saying yes when it comes to manifesting your dreams. As a dear friend reminds me often, saying no to one person or opportunity creates the space to say yes to someone or something else. There are many potential paths to leading a fulfilling, breathtaking life. Simply saying yes or saying no will influence which path you travel down at any given moment in time.

Sometimes what a moment requires is for you to do nothing at all. Or the directive may be to find a serene space and veg out. There are not enough exclamation marks in the world to emphasize this point: all of my best ideas have sprung from quiet, ordinary moments. I will be taking a shower, washing the dishes, or walking around the block, when all of a sudden, *bam!* A melody enters my mind, I know what I want to write about, it's clear what I need to say to my husband, or the next product for my wellness company is obvious.

All of my ideas that required strategy began as a tiny seed that got mysteriously and quietly planted in my heart while I was in my pajamas. I love a good game plan, but plans are made once ideas have fueled imagination and imagination has fueled ideas. For me, over-scheduling does not leave space for either. I work hard, but I also take time to stretch. I love to create, but sometimes I need to lie on my back and zone out. The balance of expending energy and conserving it is what creates sustainability for my body and mind, and periods of conservation often give birth to my most profound ideas.

If you are completely paralyzed to the point of never taking action, either because you don't know what you want to do or you are scared to try, there may be a point when you just need to leap in. It's wonderful to consciously grow a seed that's been planted in your heart, but I know people who do nothing at all because they're waiting for crystal-clear direction or want to feel compelled by an undeniable idea. If this is you, tease your curiosity by exposing yourself to different possibilities and trying things out. Take the job, but know that you can quit. Travel to the place where you might want to live. Join a club and tinker with a new hobby. Trust that you will know if something doesn't feel right and will be able to redirect accordingly. I tend to act based on a seed of curiosity or desire, but it's every bit as possible to create that seed or desire by trying new things and seeing how they feel and where they lead you.

Turn to "Planting the Seeds of Curiosity" in the workbook.

ALL WORK IS MEANINGFUL WORK

One of the most influential life strategies I've employed to maintain my sense of sanity is to stop categorizing and defining what qualifies as "meaningful" work. I tend to get cranky when I have to do redundant tasks that are just part of being in a human body on planet Earth. I used to practically go mad thinking about the number of hours I spent washing my face, brushing my teeth, doing the dishes, filling my car with gas, and on and on. *Life is so brief and so valuable, and I'm spending it bathing!*

In order to not resent large portions of my life, I required a mental shift. I needed to establish a paradigm that made me feel that *no* time was *ever* being wasted. But how could driving in circles looking for a parking spot compare to recording a song in the studio? Until my paradigm shift, I rushed through what I considered to be menial, everyday tasks. But rushing gave me anxiety, so that didn't work for me. After that, I tried going about tasks I deemed boring in an ordinary, blasé kind of way—neutral and unattached, so to speak. But that made me feel dead inside. Then I just complained and moaned to myself about being in a human body in a physical world. But resenting reality doesn't change reality, so holding a grudge became fatiguing and depressing.

Enter the shift. I decided that instead of rushing through tasks that felt superfluous or tangential to my "real" creative life, I would slow them all down. I would take back control by assigning purpose to *everything*, not just the things that I had once thought of as productive, special, or meaningful. So, I redefined menial daily tasks as play and began to create opportunities for the rinse-and-repeat to be a kind of meditation, an opportunity to call a friend, or time to reflect on something that was bothering me. I began to watch webinars while doing the dishes, to create song melodies while making my bed, to breathe more deeply while washing my face.

Every moment is an opportunity to feel something that we would benefit from feeling. It's not so much what we do that defines our experience, but rather how we feel when we're doing it. And that is always in our control, because how we're feeling often is a product of what we're thinking—the story we're telling ourselves about what we're doing and why. Why shouldn't all work feel playful *and* be creative? Why can't wiping up the spilled orange juice be a kind of meditation, even when it's your child's fourth spill of the day? You get to choose how you experience and perceive each and every moment of your life. So, why wouldn't you choose to make all moments equally meaningful?

This approach is why I rarely, if ever, fear missing out these days. If I decide that wherever I am and whatever I am doing are the absolute best choices for me simply because of the way I *feel* about them, I am always in the right place doing the most ideal thing. As I said, our perception of events is what influences our experience, not the events themselves. So, by being at peace with the reality of wiping up OJ, you may have a more positive and fulfilling experience than you would sailing on a yacht. It's all a matter of perspective.

WHERE DO WE BEGIN?

I have several amazing friends who are trying to determine what to do next with their lives. One of them was fired from her job. Another is going through a divorce. A very savvy friend retired at fifty after selling a company and now wants a second act.

"What do you *feel* like doing?" I ask them. It's such a simple question that it's almost confusing. I see my friends scratch their heads and start to overcomplicate things. They launch into all kinds of backstories about their lives and tangential monologues about their relationships to lovers and family and on and on, until they run out of things to say and still haven't answered the question. So, I ask it again. "Right now, at this stage of your life, what do you *feel* like doing?"

Often, people do know what they want to do, but are afraid to exit their comfort zone and enter an unknown landscape. Or they believe that what they want to do isn't practical or definable enough, or that it isn't as valuable as previous jobs or dreams. Sometimes people can identify the *kinds* of things they want to do, but get stuck trying to assign job titles to their interests. And of course, there are times when people genuinely may not know what they want to pursue next. If that's the case, they usually need to do one of two things, or both sequentially: pause and rest, or pursue what they feel the most passionate about. It's really hard to dream up next steps for your life if you are burned out and your nervous system is fried. So, if you are tired, then hydrate, grab a blanket, and watch a movie. Nap, meditate, spend time with friends, or eat nourishing food.

If you are ready to follow the sacred crumbs, consider what you would do if money were not an issue, and eliminate the need for a job title. The title will come. Your starting point is what it is you actually want to do. Would you like to spend your days talking to people about their struggles? Coding on the computer? Hiking? Designing clothes? If you were going to be paid an equal amount for various possible pursuits, where would that lead you? If you're not entirely clear on where you would go and what you would do, is anyone you personally know or know of doing something that you are curious about? Anyone whose life you admire or fantasize about? What is it about their life that makes you curious, or even envious? Your curiosity and envy may provide clues about what it is you want more of.

In my own life, I write the words I want to read and sing the songs I want to hear. Most of us do not have the luxury of abandoning our current jobs overnight to pursue our heart's desires; the purpose of this line of questioning is to create the framework for that beautiful possibility.

Turn to "What Does Your Heart Want
More Of?" in the workbook.

Once you consciously connect with what you desire to create or do, pinpoint the perceived emotional and physical benefits you associate with that experience. Is an adrenaline or dopamine rush involved? A sense of meaning and purpose? A feeling of ease? The magnification of beauty? Does your vision for the future bring you to a place in nature? Does it allow you to access parts of yourself you otherwise feel forbidden to experience or express? Does it highlight your gifts? Does it create a sense of emotional freedom? Does it make you feel powerful? Does it generate a sense of fun or facilitate a feeling of ease, buoyancy, or excitement?

When it comes to filling out the body of your dreams, you can start with the skeleton (the idea of what it is you want to do), and then pad this skeleton by engaging with potential sources of joy, inspiration, and intrigue. As you experiment, you naturally will be inclined to pivot and adjust according to what brings music to your life (metaphorically speaking). If the result is more joy, excitement, and curiosity, you probably are on a track that will create a more fulfilling version of your life. Accompanying these experiences may be a sense of ease, peace, and openness, and a physical body that feels lighter. But fear of change and the unknown can sometimes block our access to joy in relation to the pursuit of our dreams. If you think you are feeling this, gently thank the fear for trying to protect you and ask it to step aside. In the absence of fear, you are free to determine what feels right to you and what changes, if any, you need to make.

SEPARATING DREAM MANIFESTATION FROM HAPPINESS

At many points throughout my life, I have fallen prey to the belief that once I achieve certain things or acquire something I desire (a relationship, a body type, financial stability, an accolade, and so on), I will experience fulfillment and happiness. It's tempting to convince ourselves that once we buy the fancy car, land the dream job, or marry our ideal partner, we will suddenly feel fulfilled and content. Presumably, by expecting happiness, we are hoping for the guarantee that at some point we will no longer experience feelings of meaninglessness, discontent, confusion, disappointment, anxiety, and so on. But according to Laurie Santos, cognitive scientist and professor of psychology at Yale University, what determines true happiness often has little to do with our circumstances and almost nothing to do with what we achieve or acquire. Santos has determined that the following variables create sustained positivity:

- Social connection (prioritizing time with friends and family)
- An outward focus (contributing thoughtfully to the lives of others, volunteering, donating money to charity, and the like)
- A mindset of gratitude and presence

Note that none of the above have anything to do with achievement. So, while whatever you are working on or toward may feel meaningful and important, take comfort in knowing that your happiness is ultimately in your own hands and not contingent on results of any kind.

Turn to "Avoiding Creative Burnout through Journaling" in the workbook.

THE ELEMENTS OF MATTER AND MANIFESTATION, BY MILSEY MONTEAGUDO

A dear friend and mentor Milsey Monteagudo recently shared with me a paradigm of manifestation unlike any other I'd ever heard. It came to her on a monthlong solo trip to Sedona, Arizona, where she received a message from what she refers to as her higher self. This beautiful series of metaphors may be helpful in visualizing and internalizing the concept of manifestation, and it reminds us of our profound connection to nature. Milsey believes that manifesting occurs in stages, and that we can call upon the elements within ourselves and in nature to help bring our dreams to fruition.

> *Stage 1: Intention and Thought (Air).* Manifestation begins with a thought. The thought is concrete, but we allow the air to carry and transmit it into the universe.
>
> *Stage 2: Desire and Will (Fire).* Our desire and will kindle the fire within us that incentivizes action. When we burn with what we want, we viscerally experience that burning in our bodies. How does your body burn with desire? Is it with goose bumps, a racing heart, or a chest that feels as if it may explode with excitement?
>
> *Stage 3: Realization (Water).* Once we manifest what we desire, we enter a state of flow. This flow is like water that runs through us and around us. There is a sense of ease and fluidity when everything is as it should be. How does your body experience fluidity? Imagine your body feeling at ease, and imprint that feeling.

What about the element of earth? We are the earth. We are grounded and balanced. We are our own foundations.

When you visualize yourself as all four elements and marry them with tenacity, earnestness, persistence, and belief, you will know that what you are manifesting is meant to be yours.

— CHAPTER SUMMARY —

Your dreams hold the potential to be as powerful as you are. By establishing the soul of your dreams, you will become more aware of your core desires and better equipped to direct your future accordingly. By following the previously outlined Five Steps to Creating Dynamic and Inspired Possibilities, you will set the stage to manifest all that you imagine, and even more. By understanding what your heart wants more of, pursuing your curiosity, and being willing to ask for help, you will support your intangible desires in becoming a reality. No one knows what you dream of as specifically and meaningfully as you do. Become the captain of your own ship by believing that all things are possible, and watch the magic unfold.

CONCLUSION

R egardless of where you have come from and where you are going, being human is, in a word, hard. We desire to be unapologetically who we are, and yet we are faced with the pressures of external influences that challenge our core identity and lead us away from our inner knowing. But you were born to be your authentic self, not the person you believe you should be or the version of yourself others want you to be. And I have incredible faith that the tools and insights you have received from this book will provide you with a new sense of hope for your future. Your identity, dreams, and experience on this planet are yours to claim, and you are doing the very hard work of dissolving assumptions, questioning indoctrination, and creating infinite possibilities for your life.

By creating and softening boundaries, you will empower yourself to commit to all that you truly align with and divorce yourself from negativity and toxicity. By learning to self-soothe, you will reparent yourself with stunning vulnerability and compassion. By softening perfectionism and hypervigilance, you will embrace your humanity and wash away unrealistic expectations of who you should be. By redefining your self-concept, you will question the identity you unconsciously assumed, and with great awareness and care begin to establish who you truly are. By assessing your relationship with sleep and reaffirming its value, you will establish a pivotal foundation for your emotional and mental health. By beginning to examine potential trauma, you will take the very brave step of supporting your healing. By giving yourself permission to feel fully and extensively, you will celebrate what it is to be fully human. By consciously creating your rhythm, you will create flow in your life and heighten your productivity. By advocating for yourself, you will honor your deepest knowing and lay the groundwork for all that you imagine to come to fruition. By nurturing your vision for the future, you will take steps toward manifesting the life of your dreams—one that is even more profound and joyful than you can imagine.

Just as there is no one way to create an identity or build a future, there is no right or linear path to healing. Ultimately, you are the boss of you. You will discover or create the tools you require to experience emotional freedom and thrive. My hope in writing this book is not to suggest that my ideas and exercises are the ticket to your liberation but to inspire you to liberate yourself. If any of what I have shared resonates with you, I encourage you to use it as a prompt for further exploration and self-discovery. You know all that you need to know and possess all of your own answers. Please, at all times, in every area of your life, circle back around to the most empowered part of you that believes you are your wisest sage and most intelligent guide.

Thank you for sharing this journey with me. Please know that I am holding you in my heart as you seek answers to your questions and clarity surrounding your dreams. I am wishing you confidence, self-compassion, and resilience as you work toward emotional freedom and relief. You are brave and inspired and guided. All that is meant to be yours will be yours, and your life will be informed by peace, laughter, love, and joy. I know this to be true, and I believe in you fully. You've got this.

ENDNOTES

1. Tara Parker-Pope, Christina Caron, and Mónica Cordero Sancho, "Why 1,320 Therapists Are Worried about Mental Health in America Right Now," *New York Times*, December 16, 2021, https://www.nytimes.com/interactive/2021/12/16/well/mental-health-crisis-america-covid.html.

2. See the following two articles:

   J. Jaffe, B. Beebe, S. Feldstein, C. L. Crown, and M. D. Jasnow, "Rhythms of dialogue in infancy: coordinated timing in development," PubMed (NIH National Library of Medicine), 2001, https://pubmed.ncbi.nlm.nih.gov/11428150/.

   Beatrice Beebe, Joseph Jaffe, Sara Markese, Karen Buck, Henian Chen, Patricia Cohen, Lorraine Bahrick, Howard Andrews, Stanley Feldstein, "The origins of 12-month attachment: a microanalysis of 4-month mother-infant interaction," January 12, 2010, https://pubmed.ncbi.nlm.nih.gov/20390524/.

3. Saul McLeod, "John Bowlby's Attachment Theory," Simply Psychology, updated June 16, 2023, https://www.simplypsychology.org/bowlby.html#:~:text=Bowlby's%20evolutionary%20theory%20of%20attachment,This%20is%20called%20monotropy.

4. Saul Mcleod, "Freud's Theory of Personality: Id, Ego, and Superego," Simply Psychology, updated June 6, 2023, accessed January 17, 2023, https://www.simplypsychology.org/psyche.html.

5. Merriam-Webster online dictionary, s.v. "ego," accessed January 17, 2023, https://www.merriam-webster.com/dictionary/ego.

6. Wikipedia, s.v. "hypervigilance," https://en.wikipedia.org/wiki/hypervigilance.

7. Hope Bundrant, "NLP – What's Neuro-Linguistic Programming and Why You Should Learn It," iNLP Center, May 9, 2022, https://inlpcenter.org/what-is-neuro-linguistic-programming-nlp/.

8. For pattern interrupt, see the following three articles:

    "Pattern Interrupt (Definition + Examples)," Practical Psychology, February 16, 2022, https://practicalpie.com/pattern-interrupt/.

    Patricia Duchene, "The Science behind Pattern Interrupt," *Forbes*, July 17, 2020, https://www.forbes.com/sites/patricia duchene/2020/07/17/the-science-behind-pattern-inter rupt/?sh=35f096a42075.

    Max Trance, "What Is a Pattern Interrupt? (Hypnosis and NLP)," *Max Trance* (blog), June 14, 2021, accessed November 23, 2022, https://maxtrance.com/pattern-interrupts/.

9. The following four articles discuss ways to release trauma and tension:

    "What Is TRE®," TRE for All, accessed January 19, 2023, https://traumaprevention.com/what-is-tre/.

    David Berceli, "TRE: Tension and Trauma Releasing Exercises," accessed January 19, 2023, https://www.david-berceli.com/.

    Jay Tang, "How Does Vibration Therapy Work?" Vibration Care, February 4, 2023, https://www.vibrationcare.com/vibration-the rapy-mechanism.html.

    Edward R. Laskowski, "Is Whole-Body Vibration a Good Way to Lose Weight and Improve Fitness?" Mayo Clinic, accessed April

12, 2022, https://www.mayoclinic.org/healthy-lifestyle/fitness/expert-answers/whole-body-vibration/faq-20057958.

10. The following two articles discuss Rapid Transformational Therapy (RTT):

Bonnie Gifford, "Rapid Transformational Therapy'," Hypnotherapy Directory, October 2022, accessed January 19, 2023, https://www.hypnotherapy-directory.org.uk/approach/rapid-transformational-therapy.html.

"What Is Rapid Transformational Therapy'? (RTT')," Rapid Transformational Therapy, accessed October 27, 2022, https://rtt.com/about/.

11. M. R. Lepper, D. Greene, and R. E. Nisbett, "Undermining Children's Intrinsic Interest with Extrinsic Reward: A Test of the 'Overjustification' Hypothesis," APA PsycNet, https://psycnet.apa.org/doiLanding?doi=10.1037%2Fh0035519.

12. Carol S. Dweck, *Mindset: The New Psychology of Success* (New York: Random House, 2016).

13. Eric Suni and Kimberly Truong, "100+ Sleep Statistics," Sleep Foundation, updated May, 2023, https://www.sleepfoundation.org/how-sleep-works/sleep-facts-statistics#statistics-about-insufficient-sleep-2.

14. Laura Smith, "45 Insomnia Statistics: How Many People Suffer from Insomnia?" The Good Body, updated May 13, 2022, accessed November 11, 2022, https://www.thegoodbody.com/insomnia-statistics/.

15. "Global Insomnia Statistics in 2022 & 2023," Helsestart, https://www.helsestart.no/news/global-insomnia-statistics.

16. Eric Suni and Kimberly Truong, "100+ Sleep Statistics," Sleep Foundation, updated May 2023, https://www.sleep foundation.org/how-sleep-works/sleep-facts-statistics# statistics-about-insufficient-sleep-2.

17. Hermina Drah, "30 Astonishing Insomnia Statistics & Facts for 2023," MedAlertHelp, May 7, 2021, https://medalerthelp.org/blog/insomnia-statistics/.

18. "Insomnia," Mount Sinai, accessed January 19, 2023, https://www.mountsinai.org/health-library/report/insomnia#:~:text= Insomnia%20is%20often%20categorized%20by,for%20a%20 month%20or%20longer.

19. The following two articles discuss insomnia:

    Jelena Kabić, "2023 Insomnia Statistics that Will Keep You Up at Night," Review42, updated May 20, 2023, https://review42. com/resources/insomnia-statistics/.

    Daniel P. Windred, Angus C. Burns, Jacqueline M. Lane, Richa Saxena, Martin K. Rutter, Sean W. Cain, Andrew J. K. Phillips, "Sleep regularity is a stronger predictor of mortality risk than sleep duration: A prospective cohort study," Oxford University Press, September 21, 2023, https://academic.oup.com/sleep/article/47/1/zsad253/7280269.

20. "Exercising for Better Sleep," Johns Hopkins Medicine, accessed August 8, 2021, https://www.hopkinsmedicine.org/health/well ness-and-prevention/exercising-for-better-sleep.

21. Laura Smith, "45 Insomnia Statistics: How Many People Suffer from Insomnia?" The Good Body, updated May 13, 2022, accessed November 11, 2022, https://www.thegoodbody.com/insomnia-statistics/.

22. The following four articles discuss grounding:

Stephen T. Sinatra, "What Is Earthing or Grounding?" HeartMD Institute, updated April 13, 2023, https://heartmdinstitute.com/alternative-medicine/what-is-earthing-or-grounding/.

Eleesha Lockett, "Grounding: Exploring Earthing Science and the Benefits Behind It," Healthline, updated March 27, 2023, https://www.healthline.com/health/grounding.

Grounded.com (a website devoted to grounding/earthing resources), accessed January 19, 2023, https://grounded.com/.

Gaetan Chevalier, Sheila Patel, Lizabeth Weiss, Deepak Chopra, and Paul J. Mills, "The Effects of Grounding (Earthing) on Bodyworkers' Pain and Overall Quality of Life: A Randomized Controlled Trial," PubMed (NIH National Library of Medicine), accessed January 19, 2023, https://pubmed.ncbi.nlm.nih.gov/30448083/.

23. Timothy Roehrs and Thomas Roth, "Insomnia as a Path to Alcoholism: Tolerance Development and Dose Escalation," PubMed Central (NIH National Library of Medicine), https://www.ncbi.nlm.nih.gov/pmc/articles/PMC6093330/.

24. Syama Allard, "5 Things to Know about Om," Hindu American Foundation, July 16, 2020, https://www.hinduamerican.org/blog/5-things-to-know-about-om.

25. The following three articles discuss EMDR:

"Eye Movement Desensitization and Reprocessing (EMDR) Therapy," American Psychological Association, accessed January 19, 2023, https://www.apa.org/ptsd-guideline/treatments/eye-movement-reprocessing.

Michael Hase, Ute M. Balmaceda, Luca Ostacoli, Peter Liebermann, and Arne Hofmann, "The AIP Model of EMDR Therapy and Pathogenic Memories," Frontiers, September 21, 2017, https://www.frontiersin.org/articles/10.3389/fpsyg.2017.01578/full.

"The Adaptive Information Processing Model (AIP)," EMDR Europe, accessed January 19, 2023, https://emdr-europe.org/about/the-aip-model/.

26. Richard C. Schwartz, *No Bad Parts: Healing Trauma and Restoring Wholeness with the Internal Family Systems Model* (Boulder, CO: Sounds True, 2021).

27. The following two articles discuss Internal Family Systems (IFS) therapy:

"What Is Internal Family Systems?" IFS Institute, accessed April 26, 2022, https://ifs-institute.com/.

"What Is Internal Family Systems Therapy?" Welldoing.org, updated May 15, 2020, accessed January 18, 2023, https://welldoing.org/types/internal-family-systems.

28. The following four sources discuss cognitive behavioral therapy (CBT):

Aaron Beck, *The Blueprint of Cognitive Behavior Therapy*, Beck Institute for Cognitive Behavior Therapy, December 4, 2013, YouTube video, https://www.youtube.com/watch?v=07JqktJGyyA.

Suma P. Chand, Daniel P. Kuckel, and Martin R. Huecker, "Cognitive Behavior Therapy," NIH National Library of Medicine, updated May 23, 2023, https://www.ncbi.nlm.nih.gov/books/NBK470241/.

Kathleen Davis, "How Does Cognitive Behavioral Therapy Work?" MedicalNewsToday, updated January 6, 2023, accessed January 19, 2023, https://www.medicalnewstoday.com/articles/296579#how-does-it-work.

Lisa Tams, "ABC's of Changing Your Thoughts and Feelings in Order to Change Your Behavior," Michigan State University Extension, July 9, 2013, https://www.canr.msu.edu/news/abcs_of_changing_your_thoughts_and_feelings_in_order_to_change_your_behavio.

29. The following two sources discuss Emotional Freedom Techniques (EFT):

Kiara Anthony, "EFT Tapping in 5 Steps," Healthline, April 6, 2023, https://www.healthline.com/health/eft-tapping#treatment.

Betty Moore-Hafter, Jade Barbee, Carna Zacharias-Miller, and Lynne Shaner, PhD, *Free Tapping Manual: A Comprehensive Introductory Guide to EFT (Emotional Freedom Techniques)*, EFT International, accessed January 19, 2023, https://eftinternational.org/wp-content/uploads/EFT-International-Free-Tapping-Manual.pdf.

30. "Trauma," American Psychological Association, accessed January 18, 2023, https://www.apa.org/topics/trauma/.

31. Martha Eddy, "A Brief History of Somatic Practices and Dance: Historical Development of the Field of Somatic Education and Its Relationship to Dance," *Journal of Dance and Somatic Practices*, vol. 1, no. 1, accessed January 18, 2023, http://www.wellnesscke.net/downloadables/AbriefhistoryofSomaticanddance.pdf.

32. Bessel van der Kolk, *The Body Keeps the Score: Mind, Brain, and Body in the Transformation of Trauma* (New York: Penguin Books, 2015).

33. The following four sources discuss somatic therapy:

"Somatic Therapy," *Psychology Today*, accessed January 19, 2023, https://www.psychologytoday.com/us/therapy-types/somatic-therapy.

Ariane Resnick, CNC, "What Is Somatic Therapy?" Verywell Mind, updated October 22, 2022, https://www.verywellmind.com/what-is-somatic-therapy-5190064.

Crystal Raypole, "A Brief Intro to the World of Somatics," Healthline, April 17, 2020, https://www.healthline.com/health/somatics.

Crystal Raypole, "How Somatic Experiencing Can Help You Process Trauma," Healthline, February 28, 2020, https://www.healthline.com/health/somatic-experiencing#the-freeze-response.

34. The following two sources discuss neurofeedback:

"What Is Neurofeedback?" Center For Brain Training, accessed January 19, 2023, https://www.centerforbrain.com/neurofeedback/what-is-neurofeedback/.

"Neurofeedback," *Psychology Today*, accessed January 19, 2023, https://www.psychologytoday.com/us/therapy-types/neurofeedback.

35. Jon Cooper, "Stress and Depression," WebMD, September 26, 2023, https://www.webmd.com/depression/features/stress-depression.

36. "Gwyneth Paltrow x Becky Kennedy: Finding the Good in Us," *Goop* (podcast), September 6, 2022, https://goop.com/the-goop-podcast/gwyneth-paltrow-x-becky-kennedy-finding-the-good-in-us/.

37. "How Family Secrets Shape Us: Emotional Inheritance with Dr. Galit Atlas," *We Can Do Hard Things* (podcast), Apple Podcasts, May 19, 2022, https://podcasts.apple.com/si/podcast/how-family-secrets-shape-us-emotional-inheritance-with/id15 64530722?i=1000562428933.

38. The following three articles discuss Reiki:

"What Is Reiki, and Does It Really Work?" Cleveland Clinic, August 29, 2021, https://health.clevelandclinic.org/reiki/.

Tim Newman, "Everything You Need to Know about Reiki," MedicalNewsToday, updated June 14, 2023, https://www.medicalnewstoday.com/articles/308772.

Evan Starkman and Kristin Mitchell, "What Is Reiki Therapy?" WebMD, accessed January 19, 2023, https://www.webmd.com/pain-management/reiki-overview.

39. Mohammad J. Siddiqui, Mohammed S. M. Saleh, Siti N. B. Binti Basharuddin, Siti H. Binti Zamri, Mohd H. bin Mohd Najib, Muhammad Z bin Che Ibrahim, Nur A Binti Mohd Noor, Hanin N. Binti Mazha, Norazian Mohd Hassan, and Alfi Khatib, "Saffron (*Crocus sativus* L.): As an Antidepressant," PubMed Central (NIH National Library of Medicine), October–December 2018, https://www.ncbi.nlm.nih.gov/pmc/articles/PMC6266642/.

40. Jayesh Sanmukhani, Vimal Satodia, Jaladhi Trivedi, Deepak Tiwari, Bharat Panchal, Ajay Goel, and Chandra Bhanu Tripathi, "Efficacy and Safety of Curcumin in Major Depressive Disorder: A Randomized Controlled Trial," PubMed (NIH National Library of Medicine), January 1, 2014, https://pubmed.ncbi.nlm.nih.gov/23832433/.

41. Shima Jazayeri, Mehdi Tehrani-Doost, Seyed A. Keshavarz, Mostafa Hosseini, Abolghassem Djazayery, Homayoun Amini, Mahmoud Jalali, and Malcolm Peet, "Comparison of Therapeutic Effects of Omega-3 Fatty Acid Eicosapentaenoic Acid and Fluoxetine, Separately and in Combination, in Major Depressive Disorder," PubMed (NIH National Library of Medicine), March 2008, https://pubmed.ncbi.nlm.nih.gov/18247193/.

ACKNOWLEDGMENTS

Without these folks this book would exist as a mere idea.

Avi: You allow me to live in my imagination and don't fear my darkest parts. Partner extraordinaire and best friend, thank you for allowing me to be exactly who I am.

Mom: Thank you for making me, supporting my research, and indulging all of my rants.

Dad: You have always loved me unconditionally with your impossibly huge heart. Thank you for celebrating everything I do and for laughing after everybody else stops.

Max and Maya: You are the joy that feeds all of my creative pursuits and my very favorite creations.

Stephanie Hansen: You have believed in and championed every word I have written from the beginning. I worship your loyalty and steadfastness in an unsteady world.

Adriana Senior: You claimed this book and gave it wings. I am forever grateful that you took a chance on me.

Gretchen Young: You are evidence that a woman should be President. Thank you for your commitment to my work and to my being.

Aleigha Koss: You gave the bones of this book a body. Your patience is magic.

Elena Vega: Your invisible work allows creatives to not understand punctuation whatsoever. I appreciate your quiet genius.